The Cross

PEARLS

OF

BY

REV. H. HASTINGS WELD.

New York:

ALLEN BROTHERS.

PEARLS

OF

SACRED POETRY.

BY

REV. H. HASTINGS WELD.

ILLUSTRATED.

PUBLISHED BY
ALLEN BROTHERS,
NEW YORK.

TO THE

RT. REV. ALONZO POTTER, D.D. LL.D.,

BISHOP OF THE PROTESTANT EPISCOPAL CHURCH

IN THE

STATE OF PENNSYLVANIA,

This Work

IS RESPECTFULLY INSCRIBED.

PREFACE.

All readers have observed that many of the finest moral and religious lines in the poets are paraphrases of Holy Scripture. Some years ago, the compiler of this book purposed to arrange some of the most striking passages from Shakspeare, in parallel columns with their Bible originals. These would have formed a thin pocket volume—a neat little addition to "The Curiosities of Literature."

The subject was casually mentioned to the publishers, without any definite thought of completing the design. But the plan found favour with the gentlemen, (may the public endorse their sagacity,) and the projector was desired to finish the work. There was some difference, however, between the author's shadowy conception and the publishers' practical embodiment. He thought of a pocket-manual—they stipulated for a larger volume. Here it is.

The expansion of the work required a wider range. Instead of draughts on one poet alone, there are extracts in this volume from over three hundred; and the number of quotations is about two thousand. The character of the book has been changed from the original critical and circumscribed design, to a more general, and we trust more profitable purpose. The extracts do not present that close resemblance, in all cases, to the very words of Scripture, which might have been preserved in the smaller volume

If the reader will turn to the department of "Poetry," he will find there, in the language of Cowper, the reason why the number of authors quoted is not thrice as large as we have made it.

There are thousands of moral epigrams scattered through the poets, which fall short of the Scriptural point at which this volume aims. Many quotations have been admitted, excellent in themselves, though liable to the above exception. Paucity of material made this departure necessary; and the advantage of variety atones for the breach of strict rule.

Some good things have been discarded, because of their mythological allusions. The age in which the SAVIOUR could be celebrated under the name of PAN has passed. Other quotations have been left out, notwithstanding their appositeness, as too generally familiar. But when a man has pursued a long research in a particular direction, his own mind is no longer a safe guide as to what is trite, and what is less common. We may therefore have grasped some pebbles, and rejected many gems. The names of works quoted have not been given, because not a few of the quotations are "pearls from Ethiop ears." The alternative was presented to omit such extracts altogether, or to retain them, and suppress the strange, odd titles; sometimes ludicrous, and often offensive. The latter course was taken, and all names of works are omitted, to maintain uniformity.

The classification of subjects has presented many perplexities to the compiler; but the full index will obviate all difficulty to the reader. If he do not find at the head of any department the particular verse of Scripture which he expects, it is usually because it has been cited upon some kindred subject; for the same text is not repeated except in one or two necessary instances.

The volume, the product of much pleasant labour, is now dismissed from the compiler's hands with the hope that it may prove as agreeable to the student of English Sacred Literature, for the purposes of reference and comparison, as it has been to him in the process of collection.

CONTENTS.

INVOCATION.

O, WHEN wilt thou come unto me! I will walk within my house with a perfect heart. PSALM ci, 2.

It is time to seek the Lord, till He come and rain righteousness upon you. HOSEA, x, 12.

Let the words of my mouth, and the meditation of my heart, be alway acceptable in Thy sight, O Lord, my strength and my Redeemer. PSALM xix, 14.

Hear Thou in Heaven Thy dwelling place, and forgive, and do, and give to every man according to his ways, whose heart Thou knowest; for Thou, even Thou only knowest the hearts of all the children of men. I. KINGS, viii, 39.

Lead me in Thy truth and teach me: for Thou art the God of my salvation; on Thee do I wait all the day. PSALM xxv, 5.

Awake up, my glory, awake psaltery and harp: I myself will awake early. PSALM lvii, 8.

O Lord, open Thou my lips, and my mouth shall show forth Thy praise. PSALM li, 15.

There is a spirit in man, and the inspiration of the Almighty giveth them understanding. JOB xxxii, 8.

COME to my aid, Celestial Wisdom, come;
From my dark mind dispel the doubtful gloom:
My passions still, my purer breast inflame,
To sing that God from whom existence came!

BOYSE.

O, BLEST Redeemer, from thy sacred throne
Where saints and angels sing thy triumphs won,
From that exalted height of bliss supreme
Look down on those who bear thy Sacred Name;
Restore their ways, inspire them by thy grace,
Thy laws to follow, and thy steps to trace;
Thy bright example to thy doctrine join,
And by their morals prove their faith divine! BOYSE.

O, God of times, and yet, in time a man!
  Before all times thy time of being was;
And yet in time thy human birth began,
  Lest we should fade, untimely, like the grass,—
  Thou that hast said thy word shall never pass,
And thou that dost all times begin and end,—
Vouchsafe thy comfort to my sad soul send.

G. Ellis.

In ardent adoration joined,
  Obedient to Thy holy will
Let all my faculties combined
  Thy just desires, O God, fulfil!
From thee derived, Eternal King,
To thee our noblest powers we bring:
O, may thy hand direct our wandering way!
O, bid thy light arise, and chase the clouds away!

Lorenzo de Medici.

O King supreme,
Infinite Being, Thou who didst of old
To Thy anointed delegates reveal
The secret volume of mysterious fate,
O, All-sufficient Power, do thou direct
The aspiring lay! 'Tis Thine, and Thine alone,
To animate the muse to Heavenly themes.

Samuel Hayes.

O All-Sufficient, All-Beneficent!
Thou God of goodness and of glory, hear!
Thou who to lowest minds dost condescend,
Assuming passions to enforce thy laws,
Adopting jealousy to prove thy love!
Thou who resigned humility upholdest,
E'en as the florist props the drooping rose;
But quellest tyrannic pride with peerless power,

E'en as the tempest rives the stubborn oak!
O All-sufficient, All-beneficent!
Thou God of goodness and of glory, hear!
Bless all mankind, and bring them in the end
To heaven, to immortality, and Thee! SMART.

ALL-POWERFUL Grace, exert thy gentle sway,
And teach my rebel passions to obey;
Lest lurking folly, with insidious art,
Regain my volatile, inconstant heart!
MRS. CARTER.

SAVIOUR of mankind, Man, Emanuel!
Who, sinless, died for sin: who vanquished Hell;
The first fruits of the grave; whose light did give
Light to our darkness; in whose death we live;
O strengthen thou my faith, convert my will,
That mine may thine obey; protect me still,
So that the latter death may not devour,
My soul sealed with thy seal! SANDYS.

ETERNAL Spirit! Thou who think'st not scorn
To make thyself a lowly habitant
In the mean cottage of the human breast,
When purity has been thy harbinger:
Come then, and lead the virtues in Thy train;
Allot to each her office; ceaseless guard
Still let them hold around this earth-born heart,
And watch, with closest glance, its languid pulse.
JOHN HEY.

AND chiefly Thou, O Spirit that dost prefer
Before all temples, the upright heart and pure,
Instruct me, for Thou knowest: Thou from the first
Wast present, and with mighty wings outspread
Dove-like sat'st brooding on the vast abyss,

And mad'st it pregnant. What in me is dark,
Illumine; what is low raise and support;
That to the height of this great argument
I may assert eternal Providence,
And justify the ways of God to men. MILTON.

O, UNEXAMPLED Love!
Love no where to be found less than Divine!
Hail, Son of God, Saviour of men, Thy Name
Shall be the copious matter of my song
Henceforth, and never shall my harp Thy praise
Forget, nor from Thy Father's praise disjoin.
MILTON.

O THOU bless'd Spirit: whether the Supreme,
Great ante-mundane Father; in whose breast,
Embryo creation, unborn being, dwelt,
And all its various revolutions rolled,
Present, though future; prior to themselves;
Whose breath can blow it into naught again;
Or, from His throne some delegated power,
Who, studious of our peace, dost turn the thought
From vain and vile, to solid and sublime!
Unseen Thou lead'st me to delicious draughts
Of Inspiration, from a purer stream,
And fuller of the God, than that which burst
From famed Castalia. YOUNG.

DICTIONARY

OF

SACRED QUOTATIONS.

AARON.

BEHOLD how good and how pleasant it is for brethren to dwell together in unity! It is like the precious ointment upon the head, that ran down upon the beard, even Aaron's beard: that went down to the skirts of his garments. PSALM cxxxiii, 1, 2.

And Moses stripped Aaron of his garments, and put them upon Eleazar his son; and Aaron died there in the top of the mount: and Moses and Eleazar came down from the mount. NUMBERS, xx, 28.

E'EN as the ointment whose sweet odours blended,
From Aaron's head upon his beard descended,
And, falling thence, with rich perfume ran o'er
The holy garb the prophet wore:
So doth the unity that lives with brothers
Share its best blessings and its joy with others.

KAMPHUYZEN.

So, with trembling hand,
He hasted to unclasp the priestly robe,
And cast it o'er his son, and on his head
The mitre place; while, with a feeble voice,
He blessed, and bade him keep his garments pure
From blood of souls. But then, as Moses raised
The mystic breastplate, and that dying eye
Caught the last radiance of those precious stones,
By whose oracular and fearful light

2*

Jehovah had so oft His will revealed,
Unto the chosen tribes whom Aaron loved
In all their wanderings—but whose promised land
He might not look upon—he sadly laid
His head upon the mountain's turfy breast,
And with one prayer, half wrapped in stifled groans,
Gave up the ghost.

MRS. SIGOURNEY.

ABRAHAM.

By faith Abraham, when he was called to go out into a place which he should after receive for an inheritance, obeyed; and he went out, not knowing whither he went.

By faith he sojourned in the land of promise, as in a strange country, dwelling in tabernacles with Isaac and Jacob, the heirs with him of the same promise:

For he looked for a city which hath foundations, whose builder and maker is God. HEBREWS, xi, 8, 9, 10.

Abraham believed God, and it was counted unto him for righteousness. ROMANS, iv, 3.

HIM God the Most High, vouchsafed
To call by vision, from his father's house,
His kindred, and false gods, into a land
Which He did show him, and from him did raise
A mighty nation; and upon him shower
His benedictions so, that in his seed
All nations shall be blest; he straight obeyed,
Not knowing to what land, yet firm believed:
He left his gods, his friends, and native soil,
Ur of Chaldea, passing now the ford
To Haran; after him a cumbrous train
Of herds and flocks, and numerous servitude,
Not wandering poor, but trusting all his wealth
To God, who called him, in a land unknown.

MILTON.

Like Abraham ascending up the hill
To sacrifice, his servants left below,
That he might act the great Commander's will
Without impeach to his obedient blow;
Even so the soul, remote from earthly things,
Should mount salvation's shelter,—mercy's wings.

Robert Southwell.

Though round him numerous tribes,
Sworn foes to Heaven's dread Ruler, pitch their tents,
No wayward doubts or coward fears appal
The Patriarch's soul. By the bright hope sustained,
That in his seed all nations should be blest,
Calm and unmoved the delegated seer
Submissive bends to the Eternal Will.

Samuel Hayes.

ADAM—EDEN—EVE—THE FALL.

So God created man in his own image, in the image of God created he him; male and female created he them. Genesis, i, 27.

By one man sin entered into the world, and death by sin; and so death passed upon all men, for that all have sinned. Romans, v, 12.

For since by man came death, by man came also the resurrection of the dead.

For as in Adam all die, even so in Christ shall all be made alive. I. Corinthians, xv, 21, 22.

The first man Adam was made a living soul; the last Adam was made a quickening spirit. I. Corinthians, xv, 45.

Thou man thy image mad'st, in dignity,
In knowledge and in beauty like to thee;
Placed in a heaven on earth: without his toil,
The ever flourishing and fruitful soil
Unpurchased food produced: all creatures were
His subjects, serving more for love than fear.

Sandys.

O, HAPPY pair,
Lords of fair Eden's blooming range, where earth,
Benignant parent, from her verdant lap
Spontaneous poured immortal sweets, and gave
Whate'er could minister delight! Too soon,
Alas, this scene was closed: behold them now,
So lately rich in happiness, and blessed
With converse of the Living God, o'erwhelmed
In misery, and tortured by the stings
Of conscious guilt! SAMUEL HAYES.

FOR contemplation he, and valour formed;
For softness she, and sweet attractive grace;
He for God only, she for God in him:
His fair large front and eye sublime, declared
Absolute rule; and hyacinthine locks
Round from his parted forelock manly hung
Clustering, but not beneath his shoulders broad:
She as a veil down to the slender waist,
Her unadorned golden tresses wore
Dishevelled, but in wanton ringlets waved
As the vine curls her tendrils: which implied
Subjection, but required with gentle sway,
And by her yielded, by him best received. MILTON.

POOR man! How happy once in thy first state!
When yet but warm from thy great Maker's hand,
He stamped thee with His image, and well pleased,
Smiled on his last fair work! BLAIR.

WHAT weaker breast,
Since Adam's armour failed, dares warrant his?
That, made by God of all His creatures best,
Straight made himself the worst of all the rest:

If any strength we have, it is to ill;
But all the good is God's, both power and will:
The dead man cannot rise, though he himself may kill.

GILES FLETCHER.

TROOPS of unknown diseases, sorrow, age,
And death assail him with successive rage.
Hell let forth all her furies: none so great
As man to man, ambition, pride, deceit;
Wrong armed with power, lust, rapine, slaughter reigned,
And flattered vice the name of virtue gained. SANDYS.

WHEN by his Word God had accomplished all,
Man to create He did a council call;
Employed His hand to give the dust He took
A graceful figure and majestic look;
With His own breath conveyed into his breast
Life and a soul fit to command the rest.

WALLER.

DIFFERENCE of good and ill for man to know
Was needless sure, while with the fearless eye
Of an obedient son, he might look up
To the Almighty Father of his race,
And claim his guidance. JOHN HEY.

LET us make now, Man in our image, Man
In our similitude, and let them rule
Over the fish and fowl of sea and air,
Beast of the field, and over all the earth,
And every creeping thing that creeps the ground.
This said, He formed thee, Adam, thee, O Man,
Dust of the ground, and in thy nostrils breathed
The breath of life: in His own image He
Created thee, in the image of God
Express. MILTON.

Her rash hand, in evil hour,
Forth reaching to the fruit, she plucked, she ate!
Earth felt the wound, and Nature from her seat,
Sighing, through all her works gave signs of woe,
That all was lost!
MILTON.

THE ADVENT—THE SECOND COMING.

LET the floods clap their hands, let the hills be joyful together before the Lord; for He cometh to judge the earth: with righteousness shall He judge the world, and the people with His truth. PSALM xcvi, 8, 9.

Prepare ye the way of the Lord, make straight in the desert a highway for our God.

Every valley shall be exalted, and every mountain and hill shall be made low: and the crooked shall be made straight, and the rough places plain.

And the glory of the Lord shall be revealed, and all flesh shall see it together, for the mouth of the Lord hath spoken it. ISAIAH, xl, 3, 4, 5.

The Spirit of the Lord God is upon me, because the Lord hath anointed me to preach good tidings unto the meek; He hath sent me to bind up the broken-hearted, to proclaim liberty to the captives, and the opening of the prison to them that are bound; to proclaim the acceptable year of the Lord. ISAIAH, lxi, 1, 2.

THE chariot! the chariot! its wheels roll on fire,
As the Lord cometh down in the pomp of his ire;
Self-moving it drives on its pathway of cloud,
And the heavens with the burthen of Godhead are bow'd!

The glory! the glory! by myriads are pour'd
The host of the angels to wait on their Lord,
And the glorified saints and the martyrs are there,
And all who the palm-wreath of victory wear.

H. H. MILMAN.

WELL then, my soul, joy in the midst of pain;
Thy Christ, that conquered hell, shall from above
With greater triumph yet return again,
And conquer His own justice with His love—
Commanding earth and seas to render those
Unto His bliss, for whom He paid His woes.

HENRY WOTTON.

WHEN Thou, attended gloriously from Heaven,
Shall in the sky appear, and from Thee send
The summoning archangels to proclaim
Thy dread tribunal, forthwith from all winds
The living, and forthwith the cited dead
Of all past ages, to the general doom
Shall hasten.

MILTON.

MESSIAH comes!—Let furious discord cease;
Be peace on earth before the Prince of Peace!
Disease and anguish feel His blest control,
And howling fiends release the tortured soul!
The beams of gladness Hell's dark caves illume,
And mercy broods above the distant gloom.

BISHOP HEBER.

MESSIAH comes! ye rugged paths, be plain;
The Shiloh comes, ye towering cedars bend;
Swell forth, ye valleys; and, ye rocks, descend;
The withered branch let balmy fruits adorn,
And clustering roses twine the leafless thorn;
Burst forth, ye vocal groves, your joy to tell—
The God of Peace redeems His Israel.

C. H. JOHNSON

HE comes not in the pride of martial pomp,
High in triumphal chariot, while around
The poor remains of vanquished kingdoms grace
The trophied car; not such as Judah's sons,
By empire's flattering dreams misled, conceived,
Vindictive monarch over prostrate Rome.
Beyond the confines of this nether world,
At the right hand of the Almighty Sire,
Enthroned he sits; no partial King, to all
Who unfeigned homage offer, He, benign,
The treasure of His boundless love vouchsafes.

SAMUEL HAYES.

For, in like manner as He went,—
My soul, hast thou forgot?—
Shall be His terrible descent,
When man expecteth not!
Strength, Son of Man, against that hour,
Be to our spirits given,
When thou shalt come again with power
Upon the clouds of heaven!

William Croswell.

Lift up your heads, ye everlasting gates,
The King of Glory comes! He comes to clothe
This mortal in the unperishable garb
Of immortality! Hear it, ye dead,
Hear the glad tidings! and with trembling hope
Expect that day, when at th' Archangel's trump,
From the long sleep of many thousand years
Ye shall awake—awake to sleep no more;
Hear it, O living man, ere greedy Death
Consigns thee to the prison of the tomb;
Hear and be wise, seek thy Redeemer's throne;
On bending knees implore His healing grace,
Chaunt forth His praise and venerate His name.

William Bolland.

Methinks I see from th' empyrean skies,
Preceded by His bright Angelic host,
The Judge descend: how changed from Him, who late
The thorny crown and reedy sceptre bore!
Glory arrays Him, from His countenance beams
Splendour ineffable: stars clustering weave
A rich tiara for His head, who gave
Their beauteous lamps to shine.

George Bally.

ADVERSITY—AFFLICTION.

Before I was afflicted, I went astray, but now have I kept thy word. Psalm cxix, 67.

It is good for me that I have been afflicted, that I might learn thy statutes. Psalm xxix, 71.

I know that the Lord will maintain the cause of the afflicted, and the right of the poor. Psalm cxl, 12.

He was oppressed and He was afflicted, yet He opened not His mouth: He is brought as a lamb to the slaughter, and as a sheep before his shearers is dumb, so opened He not His mouth. Isaiah, liii, 7.

In all their affliction He was afflicted, and the angel of His presence saved them: in His love and in His pity He redeemed them; and He bare them and carried them all the days of old. Isaiah, lxiii, 9.

Come, and let us return unto the Lord: for He hath torn, and He will heal us; He hath smitten, and He will bind us up. Hosea, vi, 1.

For our light affliction, which is but for a moment, worketh for us a far more exceeding and eternal weight of glory. II. Corinthians, iv, 17.

Behold, happy is the man whom God correcteth; therefore despise not thou the chastening of the Almighty: For He maketh sore, and bindeth up; He woundeth, and His hands make whole. He shall deliver thee in six troubles; yea, in seven there shall no evil touch thee. Job, v, 17, 18, 19.

For whom the Lord loveth He chasteneth, and scourgeth every son whom he receiveth. Hebrews, xii, 6.

When urged by strong temptation to the brink
Of guilt and ruin, stands the virtuous mind,
With scarce a step between; all-pitying Heaven,
Severe in mercy, chastening in its love,
Oft-times in dark and awful visitation,
Doth interpose, and leads the wanderer back
To the straight path, to be forever after
A firm, undaunted, onward-bearing traveller,
Strong in humility, who swerves no more.

Joanna Baillie.

Perfumes, the more they're chafed, the more they render
Their pleasant scents, and so affliction
Expresseth virtue fully. John Webster.

For God has marked each sorrowing day,
And numbered every secret tear,
And Heaven's long years of bliss shall pay
For all His children suffer here.

Wm. C. Bryant.

If misfortune comes, she brings along
The bravest virtues. Thomson

When grief, that well might humble, swells our pride,
And pride, increasing, aggravates our grief,
The tempest must prevail till we are lost. Lillo.

Though woe to joy! And though at morn thou weep,
And though the midnight find thee weeping still,
Good cheer! good cheer! The shepherd loves his sheep
Resign thee to the watchful Father's will.

Rosegarten.

Blaspheme not Heaven with rash, impatient speech,
Nor deem, at thine own hour, its rest to reach,
Unhappy child! The full-appointed time
Is His to choose; and when the sullen chime
And deep-toned striking of the funeral bell,
Thy fate to earthly ears shall sadly tell,
O! may the death thou talk'st of as a boon,
Find thee prepared, nor come, even then, too soon!

Mrs. Norton.

Heaven but tries our virtues by affliction,
And oft the cloud which wraps the present hour
Serves but to brighten all our future days.

Dr. Brown

Afflictions clarify the soul,
And, like hard masters, give more hard directions,
Tutoring the non-age of uncurbed affections.

Francis Quarles

COME then, Affliction, if my Father bids,
And be my frowning friend: a friend that frowns,
Is better than a smiling enemy.
We welcome clouds that bring the former rain,
Though they the present prospect blacken round,
And shade the beauties of the opening year,
That, by their stores enriched, the earth may yield
A fruitful summer and a plenteous crop. SWAINE

THEY who have rarest joy, know joy's true measure;
They who most suffer, value suffering's pause;
They who but taste the simplest pleasure,
Kneel oftenest to the Giver and the Cause.
MRS. NORTON.

WE overstate the ills of life, and take
Imagination, given us to bring down
The choirs of singing angels, overshone
By God's clear glory,—down our earth, to rake
The dismal snows instead; flake following flake,
To cover all the corn. We walk upon
The shadow of hills, across a level thrown,
And pant like climbers. Near the alder-brake
We sigh so loud, the nightingale within
Refuses to sing loud, as else she would.
O, brothers! let us leave the shame and sin
Of taking vainly, in a plaintive mood,
The holy name of Grief!—holy herein,
That by the grief of One, came all our good.
MISS BARRETT.

GOD hath created nights
As well as days to deck the varied globe;
Grace comes as oft clad in the dusky robe
Of desolation, as in white attire. JOHN BEAUMONT.

To bear affliction with a bended brow,
Or stubborn heart, is but to disallow
The speedy means to health. FRANCIS QUARLES.

A LIFE all ease is all abused;—
O, precious grace! that made thee wise
To know — affliction rightly used
Is mercy in disguise. G. B. CHEEVER

IF affliction grasps thee rudely
And presents the rack and cup,
Drink the draught and brave the torture—
Even in despair,—look up!
Still look up! For One there liveth
With the will and power to save—
One who knows each human sorrow,
From the cradle to the grave. J. L. CHESTER.

BESIDE one deed of guilt, how blest is guiltless woe!
SIR E. BULWER LYTTON.

CHRIST had his sorrows. When he shed
His tears, O, Palestine, for thee—
When all but weeping woman fled,
In His dark hour of agony.
Christ had his sorrows — so must thou,
If thou wilt tread the path He trod—
O then, like Him, submissive bow,
And own the sovereignty of God. ANONYMOUS.

THE good man suffers but to gain,
And every virtue springs from pain;
As aromatic plants bestow
No spicy fragrance while they grow;
But crushed or trodden to the ground
Diffuse their balmy sweets around. GOLDSMITH.

'Mid pleasure, plenty, and success.
  Freely we take from Him who lends;
We boast the blessings we possess,
  Yet scarcely thank the One who sends.
But let affliction pour its smart,
  How soon we quail beneath the rod!
With shattered pride, and prostrate heart,
  We seek the long-forgotten God.   Eliza Cook

Affliction has a taste as sweet
As any cordial comfort.   Shakspeare.

The man, perhaps,
Thou pitiest, draws his comfort from distress.
That mind so poised, and centred in the good
Supreme, so kindled with devotion's flame,
Might, with prosperity's enchanting cup
Inebriate, have forgot the All-giving hand;
Might on earth's vain and transitory joys
Have built its sole felicity, nor e'er
Winged a desire beyond.   George Bally.

Graces withered by too warm a beam,
May spread and flourish in the dreary shade:
And pleasure, to voluptuous guilt denied,
May bloom ambrosial from affliction's thorn.
George Bally.

(*See also* Consolation, Patience.)

AGE.

I SAID, Days should speak, and multitude of years should speak wisdom. JOB, xxxii, 7.

Thou shalt rise up before the hoary head, and shalt honor the face of the old man, and fear thy God. LEVITICUS, xix, 32.

Great men are not always wise, neither do the aged understand judgment. JOB, xxxii, 8.

The hoary head is a crown of glory, if it be found in the way of righteousness. PROVERBS, xvi, 31.

That the aged men be sober, grave, temperate, sound in faith, in charity, in patience. The aged women likewise, that they be in behaviour as becometh holiness. TITUS, ii, 2, 3.

The days of our years are three score years and ten; and if, by reason of strength, they be four score years, yet is their strength labour and sorrow; for it is soon cut off, and we fly away. PSALM xc, 10.

Now also, when I am old and grey-headed, O God, forsake me not; until I have showed thy strength unto this generation, and thy power to every one that is to come. PSALM lxxi, 18.

And even to your old age I am he: and even to hoar hairs will I carry you. ISAIAH, xlvi, 4.

Cast me not off in the time of old age; forsake me not when my strength faileth. PSALM lxxi, 9.

The righteous shall still bring forth fruit in old age; they shall be fat and flourishing. PSALM xcii, 14.

If a man live many years, and rejoice in them all; yet let him remember the days of darkness, for they shall be many. ECCLESIASTES, xi, 8.

How pure
The grace, the gentleness of virtuous age!
Though solemn, not austere; though wisely dead
To passion, and the wildering dreams of hope,
Not unalive to tenderness and truth,—
The good old man is honored and revered,
And breathes upon the young-limbed race around
A grey and venerable charm of years.

ROBERT MONTGOMERY.

YOUTH, with swift feet, walks onward in the way,
The land of joy lies all before his eyes;
Age, stumbling, lingers slower day by day,
Still looking back, for it behind him lies.

FRANCES ANN KEMBLE.

Reason's proud triumph, passion's wild control
No more dispute their mastery o'er his soul;
As rest the billows on the sea-beat shore,
The war of rivalry is heard no more;
Faith's steady light alone illumes his eye,
For Time is pointing to Eternity!

Katharine A. Ware.

Oh! Youth is firmly bound to earth,
  When hope beams on each comrade's glance;
His bosom-chords are tuned to mirth,
  Like harp-strings in the cheerful dance;
But Age has felt those ties unbound,
Which fixed him to that spot of ground
  Where all his household comforts lay;
He feels his freezing heart grow cold,
He thinks of kindred in the mould,
And cries, amid his grief untold,
  "I would not live alway."

William Knox.

On he moves to meet his latter end,
Angels around befriending virtue's friend;
Sinks to the grave with unperceived decay,
While resignation gently slopes the way;
And, all his prospects brightening to the last,
His heaven commences ere the world be past.

Goldsmith.

What folly can be ranker? Like our shadows,
Our wishes lengthen as our sun declines.

Young.

If thou well observe
The rule of not too much, by temperance taught,
In what thou eat'st and drink'st, seeking from thence
Due nourishment, not gluttonous delight,
Till many years over thy head return:

So mayest thou live till, like ripe fruit, thou drop
Into thy mother's lap, or be, with ease
Gathered, not harshly plucked, for death mature.
This is old age, but then thou must outlive
Thy youth, thy strength, thy beauty, which will change
To withered, weak, and grey. MILTON.

THE aged Christian stands upon the shore
  Of Time, a storehouse of experience,
Filled with the treasures of rich heavenly lore;
  I love to sit and hear him draw from thence
Sweet recollections of his journey past,
A journey crowned with blessings to the last.
MRS. ST. LEON LOUD.

As those we love decay, we die in part,
String after string is severed from the heart;
Till loosened life, at last, but breathing clay,
Without one pang is glad to fall away.
Unhappy he who latest feels the blow,
Whose eyes have wept o'er every friend, laid low,
Dragged lingering on, from partial death to death,
Till, dying, all he can resign is breath. THOMSON.

The seas are quiet, when the winds are o'er,
So calm are we, when passions are no more!
For then we know how vain it was to boast
Of fleeting things, so certain to be lost.
Clouds of affection from our youthful eyes
Conceal the emptiness which age descries:
The soul's dark cottage, battered and decayed,
Lets in new light through chinks that time has made.
Stronger by weakness, wiser men become
As they draw near to their eternal home;
Leaving the old, both worlds at once they view,
That stand upon the threshold of the new. WALLER

WHY should old age escape unnoticed here,
That sacred era to reflection dear?
That peaceful shore where passion dies away,
Like the last wave that ripples o'er the bay?
O, if old age were cancelled from our lot,
Full soon would man deplore the unhallowed blot!
Life's busy day would want its tranquil even,
And earth would lose her stepping-stone to Heaven.

CAROLINE GILMAN

WHEN trembling limbs refuse their weight,
And films slow gathering, dim the sight,
And clouds obscure the mental light
'Tis nature's precious boon to die.

MRS. BARBAULD.

O, I have seen, (nor hope perhaps in vain
Ere life go down, to see such sights again)
A veteran warrior in the Christian field,
Who never saw the sword he could not wield;
Grave without dulness, learned without pride,
Exact, yet not precise, though meek, keen-eyed;
A man that would have foiled, at their own play,
A dozen would-be's of the modern day;
Who, when occasion justified its use,
Had art as bright, as ready to produce;
Could fetch the records of an earlier age,
Or from philosophy's enlightened page
His rich materials, and regale your ear
With strains it was a privilege to hear:
Yet, above all, his luxury supreme,
And his chief glory was the gospel theme;
There he was copious as old Greece or Rome,
His happy eloquence seemed there at home,—
Ambitious not to shine, or to excel,
But, to treat justly what he loved so well. COWPER.

THE fruits of age, less fair, are yet more sound
Than those a brighter season pours around;
And, like the stores autumnal suns mature,
Through wintry rigours unimpaired endure.
COWPER.

BUT were death frightful, what has age to fear?
If prudent, age should meet the friendly foe,
And shelter in his hospitable gloom. YOUNG.

WEARINESS will follow those
Who touch upon their journey's close
But as the sun, though setting, burns
Still brightly, and to glory turns
The very clouds that round him roll;
So, even so, do thou my soul,
With in-born radiance, more and more,
Illume the shades of Sixty-four.

Nay, let a yet diviner power
Glorify thy latter hour:
Too long faithless and forlorn
Earthly image thou hast borne;
Now that heavenly impress seek,
Which, when flesh is frail and weak,
Gives the soul new power to soar
Eagle-winged, at Sixty-four. BERNARD BARTON.

AGE, by long experience well informed,
Well read, well tempered, with religion warmed,
That fire abated, which impels rash youth,
Proud of his speed, to overshoot the truth,
As time improves the grape's authentic juice,
Mellows and makes the speech more fit for use,
And claims a reverence, in his shortening day,
That t is an honour and a joy to pay. COWPER.

HE passeth calmly from that sunny morn,
Where all the buds of youth are newly born,
Through varying intervals of onward years,
Until the eve of his decline appears;
And while the shadows round his path descend,
And down the vale of age his footsteps tend,
Peace o'er his bosom sheds her soft control,
And throngs of gentlest memories charm the soul;
Then, weaned from earth, he turns his steadfast eye
Beyond the grave, whose verge he falters nigh,
Surveys the brightening regions of the blest,
And, like a wearied pilgrim, sinks to rest.

WILLIS G. CLARK.

O MY coevals! remnants of yourselves!
Poor human ruins, tottering o'er the grave!
Shall we, shall aged men, like aged trees,
Strike deeper their vile root, and closer cling,
Still more enamoured of this wretched soil?
Shall our pale, withered hands be still stretched out,
Trembling, at once, with eagerness and age?
With avarice and convulsions griping hard?
Grasping at air! For what has earth beside?
Man wants but little, nor that little long:
How soon must he resign his very dust,
Which frugal nature lent him for an hour!

YOUNG.

AGE should fly concourse, cover in retreat
Defects of judgment, and the will subdue;
Walk thoughtful on the silent solemn shore
Of that vast ocean it must sail so soon;
And put good works on board; and wait the wind
That shortly blows us into worlds unknown.

YOUNG.

SHE in her Saviour's ranks had done
A veteran's service, and with Polycarp
Might say to Death, "For more than fourscore years
He was my Lord—shall I deny him now?"
No! no! Thou could'st not turn away from Him
Who was thy hope from youth, and on whose arm
The feebleness of holy hoary hairs was staid.
Before His Father, and the Angel host,
He will adjudge thee faithful. So farewell,
Blessed and full of days! MRS. SIGOURNEY.

IT is not growing like a tree
In bulk doth make man better be;
Or standing long, an oak three hundred year,
To fall a log at last, dry, bald, and sere;
A lily of a day
Is fairer far in May;
Although it fall and die that night,
It was the plant and flower of light.
In small proportions we just beauties see,
And in short measures life may perfect be.
BEN JONSON.

AMBITION.

For men to search their own glory is not glory. Proverbs, xxv, 27.

A high look, and a proud heart, and the ploughing of the wicked is sin. Proverbs, xxi, 4.

Whosoever will be chief among you, let him be your servant. Matthew, xx, 27.

Though thou exalt thyself as the eagle, and though thou set thy nest among the tars, thence will I bring thee down, saith the Lord. Obadiah, 4.

Woe unto you, Pharisees, for ye love the uppermost seats in the synagogues, and greetings in the markets. Luke, xi, 43.

They loved the praise of men, more than the praise of God. John, xii, 43.

The sons of earth
Who, vexed with vain disquietude, pursue
Ambition's fatuous light through miry pools
That yawn for their destruction, stray, foredoomed,
Amid delusive shadows to their end.

William Herbert.

Ambition, when the pinnacle is gained
With many a toilsome step, the power it sought
Wants to support itself, and sighs to find
The envied height but aggravates the fall.

George Dally.

Give me the mind that, bent on highest aim,
Deems virtue's rugged path sole path to fame;
Great things with small compare, in scale sublime,
And life with death, eternity with time.

C. C. Colton.

O momentary grace of mortal men!
Which we more hunt for than the grace of God,
Who builds his hope in air of your fair looks,
Lives like a drunken sailor on a mast,
Ready with every nod to tumble down.

Shakspeare.

I CHARGE thee, fling away ambition;
By that sin fell the angels: how can man then,
The image of his Maker, hope to win by 't?
Love thyself last, cherish those hearts that hate thee,
Corruption wins not more than honesty.
Still in thy right hand carry gentle peace,
To silence envious tongues. Be just and fear not,
Let all the ends thou aim'st at, be thy country's,
Thy God's, and truth's. SHAKSPEARE.

THE vain wish
To float upon the memory of men
After his term of being, oft becomes
A master passion, and for that one aim,
He barters all that his Creator gave
Of joy or solace in the vale of life,
And that inheritance of perfect bliss
Which might be his forever. WILLIAM HERBERT.

TWICE told the period spent on stubborn Troy,
Court favor, yet untaken, I besiege;
Ambition's ill judged efforts to be rich.
Alas! Ambition makes my little, less;
Embittering the possessed: why wish for more?
Wishing, of all employments, is the worst. YOUNG.

WOE to thee, wild Ambition! I employ
  Despair's low notes thy dread effects to tell;
Born in high heaven, her peace thou could'st destroy
  And but for thee, there had not been a hell.

Through the celestial domes thy clarion pealed;
  Angels, entranced, beneath thy banners ranged,
And straight were fiends; hurled from the shrinking field,
  They waked in agony to wail the change.

Darting through all her veins the subtle fire,
The world's fair mistress first inhaled thy breath;
To lot of higher beings learned to aspire;
Dared to attempt, and doomed the world to death.
MARIA A. BROOKS.

ANGELS.

THE angel of the Lord encampeth round about them that fear Him, and delivereth them. PSALM xxxiv, 7.

There is joy in the presence of the angels of God, over one sinner that repenteth. LUKE, xv, 10.

I am Gabriel, that stand in the presence of God, and am sent to show thee these glad tidings. LUKE, i, 19.

Then the devil left Him, and behold angels came and ministered unto Him. MATTHEW, iv, 11.

Thinkest thou that I cannot ask of my Father, and that he will presently give me more than twelve legions of angels? MATTHEW, xxvi, 53.

And he dreamed, and behold a ladder set on the earth, and the top of it reached to Heaven: and behold the angels of God, ascending and descending upon it. GENESIS, xxviii, 12.

Verily, verily, I say unto you, hereafter ye shall see Heaven open, and the angels of God ascending and descending upon the Son of Man. JOHN, i, 51.

And I saw another angel fly in the midst of Heaven, having the everlasting gospel to preach unto them that dwell on the earth. REVELATIONS, xiv, 6.

And I beheld, and I heard the voice of many angels round about the throne, and the beasts, and the elders: and the number of them was ten thousand times ten thousand, and thousands of thousands; Saying with a loud voice, Worthy is the Lamb that was slain to receive power, and riches, and wisdom, and strength, and honour, and glory, and blessing. REVELATIONS, v, 11, 12.

For He shall give His angels charge over thee, to keep thee in all thy ways.

They shall bear thee up in their hands, lest thou dash thy foot against a stone. PSALM xci, 11, 12.

WHEN by a good man's grave I muse alone,
Methinks an angel sits upon the stone;
Like those of old, on that thrice-hallowed night,
Who sate and watched in heavenly raiment bright;
And with a voice inspiring joy, not fear,
Said, pointing upward, that he is not here,
That he is risen! SAMUEL ROGERS.

Elysian race! while o'er their slumbering flocks
The Galilean shepherd watched, ye came
To sing hosannas to the heaven-born Babe,
And shed the brightness of your beauty round:
Nor have ye left the world, but still, unseen,
Surround the earth, as guardians of the good,
Inspiring souls, and leading them to heaven!
And oh! when shadows of the state unknown
Advance, and life endures the grasp of death,
'T is yours to hallow and illume the mind,
The starry wreath to bring, by angels worn,
And crown the spirit for her native sphere.

Robert Montgomery.

Millions of spiritual creatures walk the earth,
Unseen, both when we sleep, and when we wake.

Milton.

And who is he, the vast, the awful form,
Girt with the whirlwind, sandalled with the storm?
A western cloud around his limbs is spread,
His crown a rainbow, and a sun his head,
To highest Heaven he lifts his kingly hand,
And treads at once the ocean and the land;
And hark! His voice amid the thunder's roar,
His dreadful voice — that time shall be no more!

Bishop Heber.

The multitude of angels, with a shout
Loud as from numbers without number, sweet
As from blest voices uttering joy, Heaven rung
With jubilee, and loud Hosannas filled
The eternal regions: lowly reverent
Towards either throne they bow, and to the ground,
With solemn adoration down they cast
Their crowns inwove with amarant and gold.

Milton.

How oft do they their silver bowers leave,
To come to succour us that succour want!
How oft do they with golden pinions cleave
The flitting skies, like flying pursuivant,
Against foul fiends to aid us militant.
They for us fight, they watch and duly ward,
And their bright squadrons round about us plant;
And all for love, and nothing for reward:
Oh! why should heavenly God to man have such regard!

SPENSER.

THESE are the haunts of meditation, these
The scenes where ancient bards the inspiring breath,
Ecstatic felt: and, from this world retired,
Conversed with Angels, and immortal forms,
On gracious errands bent: to save the fall
Of virtue, struggling on the brink of vice;
In waking whispers, and repeated dreams,
To hint pure thought, and warn the favoured soul,
For future trials fated, to prepare. THOMSON.

THEY are God's minist'ring spirits, and are sent,
His messengers of mercy to fulfil,
Good for salvation's heirs. For us they still
Grieve when we sin, rejoice when we repent;
And on the last dread day they shall present
The severed righteous at His holy hill,
With them God's face to see, to do His will,
And bear with them His likeness. Was it meant,
That we this knowledge should in secret seal,
Unthought of, unimproving? Rather say,
God deigned to man His angel hosts reveal,
That man might learn, like angels, to obey;
And those who long their bliss in Heaven to feel,
Might strive on earth to serve him ev'n as they.

BP. MANT.

ANGELS are men of a superior kind;
Angels are men in lighter habit clad,
High o'er celestial mountains winged in flight;
And men are angels loaded for an hour,
Who wade the miry vale, and climb with pain,
And slippery step, the bottom of the steep.
Angels their failings, mortals have their praise;
While here, of corps ethereal, such enrolled,
And summoned to the glorious standard soon,
Which flames eternal crimson through the skies.
Nor are our brothers thoughtless of their kin,
Yet absent, but not absent from their love.
Michael has fought our battles; Raphael sung
Our triumphs; Gabriel on our errands flown,
Sent by the Sovereign; and are these, O man!
Thy friends and warm allies, and thou (shame burn
Thy cheek to cinder!) rival to the brutes! YOUNG.

THE APOSTLES.

AND the wall of the city had twelve foundations, and in them the names of the twelve apostles of the Lamb. REVELATIONS, xxi, 14.

He called unto Him His disciples, and of them He chose Twelve, whom also He named Apostles. LUKE, vi, 13.

By the hands of the Apostles were many signs and wonders wrought among the people. Acts, v, 12.

And He said unto them, Go ye into all the world, and preach the gospel to every creature. He that believeth and is baptized shall be saved, and he that believeth not shall be damned. MARK, xvi, 15, 16.

As ye go, preach, saying, The kingdom of Heaven is at hand.

Heal the sick, cleanse the lepers, raise the dead, cast out devils: freely ye have received, freely give. MATTHEW, x, 7, 8.

It is enough for the disciple that he be as his master, and the servant as his Lord. If they have called the master of the house Beelzebub, how much more shall they call them of his household? MATTHEW, x, 25.

And he gave some, apostles; and some, prophets; and some, evangelists; and some pastors and teachers. EPHESIANS, iv, 11.

Ye shall be witnesses unto me both in Jerusalem, and in all Judea, and in Sama ria and unto the uppermost part of the earth. ACTS, i, 8.

THESE, O Lord,
Were all thy scanty followers; by Thee
First called, first rescued from a world of woe,
To spread salvation into distant climes;
And tell the meanest habitant of earth
"Glad tidings of great joy." MADAN.

YE hallowed martyrs, who with fervent zeal,
And more than mortal courage, greatly dared
To preach the name of Jesus; ye, who stood
The undaunted champions of eternal truth,
Though maddened priests conspired, though princes frowned,
And persecution, with ingenious rage,
Prepared ten thousand torments. WILLIAM BOLLAND.

A CÆSAR'S title less my envy moves,
Than to be styled the man whom Jesus loves;
What charms, what beauties in his face did shine,
Reflected ever from the face divine! WESLEY.

WITH sudden burst,
A rushing noise, through all the sacred band
Silence profound, and fixed attention claimed.
A chilling terror crept through every heart,
Mute was each tongue, and pale was every face.
The rough roar ceased; when, borne on fiery wings,
The dazzling emanation from above
In brightest vision round each sacred head
Diffused its vivid beams: mysterious light!
That rushed impetuous through th' awaking mind,
Whilst new ideas filled th' impassive soul,
Fast crowding in, with sweetest violence.
'T was then amazed, they caught the glorious flame;
Spontaneous flowed their all-persuasive words,
Warm from the heart, and to the heart addressed.
CHARLES JENNER.

Thy eloquence, O Paul, thy matchless tongue,
With strong persuasion, as with magic's voice,
From heathen darkness to the paths of light
Led the benighted wanderers, who, like thee,
Through superstition's gloomy mazes strayed,
Till, Heaven's effulgence bursting on the view,
To thy astonished and enraptured sight
Revealed the glories of unfading day.

William Bolland.

For them the fulness of His might is shown,
O'erleaping the strong bounds of Nature's law;
Grim death for them controls his hasty stride,
And checks his dart, ev'n in the act to strike;
His horrid messengers, disease and pain,
Loose their remorseless grasp unwillingly,
And leave their prey to ease and thankfulness;
For them bright wisdom opens all her stores,
Her golden treasures spreading to their view,
Whilst Inspiration's all-enlivening light
Hangs hovering o'er their heads in glittering blaze:
Warmed by the ray, they pour the sacred strain
In eloquence seraphic.

Charles Jenner.

'T is pitiful
To court a grin, when you should woo a soul;
To break a jest, when pity would inspire
Pathetic exhortation; and to address
The skittish fancy with facetious tales,
When sent with God's commission to the heart!
So did not Paul. Direct me to a quip
Or merry turn in all he ever wrote,
And I consent you take it for your text,
Your only one, till sides and benches fail.
No, he was serious in a serious cause,
And understood too well the mighty terms

That he had taken in charge. He would not stoop
To conquer those by jocular exploits,
Whom truth and soberness assailed in vain.

Cowper.

Whose is that sword—that voice and eye of flame,
That heart of unextinguishable ire?
Who bears the dungeon-keys; and bonds, and fire?
Along his dark and withering path he came—
Death in his looks, and terror in his name,
Tempting the might of heaven's Eternal Sire.
Lo, the Light shone! the sun's veiled beams expire—
A Saviour's self a Saviour's lips proclaim!
Whose is yon form stretched on the earth's cold bed,
With smitten soul, and tears of agony,
Mourning the past? Bowed is the lofty head—
Rayless the orbs that flushed with victory.
Over the raging waves of human will
The Saviour's spirit walked—and all was still!

Roscoe.

Rash was the tongue, and unadvisedly bold,
Which sought, Salome, for thy favoured twain
Above their fellows, in Messiah's reign
On right, on left, the foremost place to hold.
More rash, perhaps, and bolder, that which told
Of power the Saviour's bitter cup to drain,
And, passing stretch of human strength, sustain
His bath baptismal. Lord, by thee enrolled
Thy servant, grant me Thy Almighty grace,
My destined portion of Thy griefs to bear,
Ev'n what Thou wilt! But chiefly grant, Thy face
Within Thy glory's realm to see, whene'er
Most meet Thy wisdom deems; whate'er the place,
It must be blest, for Thou, my God, art there.

Bp. Mant.

THE gazing synagogue, in wonder wrapt,
Devour his pregnant speech. Th' instructive page
With simple style, deliberate address,
And nervous argument, now vindicates
The great Messiah. Now with words that live,
And thoughts that burn, the last tremendous day,
Expiring nature, and the doom of man
He thunders on the soul. Sin's ghastly front,
Her shape deformed, the poison of her touch,—
Behind her, vengeance, with eternal fire
He next describes. Affrighted conscience wakes;
The murderer starts aghast; the oppressor groans;
The adulterer trembles, and the harlot weeps.
What heart so pure, so innocent of vice,
But shuddered there!—Now with mellifluous tongue,
He soothes the scorpion sting of conscious guilt.
Behold, each faded countenance relumed
With hope and gladness, while the chosen saint
Unfolds the mysteries of redeeming love,
Of grace and mercy infinite, displays
The high rewards of penitence, and life
Reformed; the freedom of the Christian yoke
Avers, and testifies the eternal league
'Twixt happiness and virtue. Now, to crown
The preacher's task, with sweet persuasive phrase,
He wins the enchanted auditors to peace,
Long-suffering, gentleness, and social love,
The godlike spirit of his Master's laws.

JOHN LETTICE.

ASCENSION.

Lift up your heads, O ye gates, and be ye lift up, ye everlasting doors, and the King of glory shall come in.

Who is this King of glory? The Lord of Hosts, He is the King of glory. Psalm, xxiv, 9, 10.

While they beheld, He was taken up, and a cloud received Him out of their sight.

And while they looked steadfastly toward Heaven, as He went up, behold two men stood by them in white apparel;

Which also said, Ye men of Galilee, why stand ye gazing into Heaven? This same Jesus, which is taken up from you into Heaven, shall so come in like manner as ye have seen Him go into Heaven. Acts, i. 9, 10, 11.

Lift up your heads, ye everlasting gates,
And give the King of glory to come in;
Who is the King of glory? He who left
His throne of glory for the pang of death;
Lift up your heads, ye everlasting gates,
And give the King of glory to come in;
Who is the King of glory? He who slew
The ravenous foe that gorged all human race!
The King of glory, He whose glory filled
Heaven with amazement at His love to man,
And with divine complacency beheld
Powers most illumined wildered in the theme.

Young.

Lift up your heads, ye gates, and O prepare,
Ye living orbs, your everlasting doors,
The King of glory comes!
What King of glory? He, whose puissant might
Subdued Abaddon, and the infernal powers
Of darkness bound in adamantine chains:
Who, wrapt in glory, with the Father reigns,
Omnipotent, immortal, infinite! James Scott.

MAJESTICAL He rose
Upborne, and steered a flight of gentlest wing
His native Heaven to gain; whilst from their eye,
That to its centre fixed, in mute survey
Pursued the ascending glory, a bright cloud,
Of bidden access, his latest presence caught:
By angel forms supported, who in song,
Not unperceived, and choral symphony,
Though Heaven's wide empyrean loud rejoiced.

THOMAS HUGHES.

Now, O my soul,
On the blest summit light a holy flame!
From the last foot-print of the Prince of Peace,
The conqueror of death, let incense rise,
And enter Heaven with thine ascending Lord!
Shake off the chains, and all the dust of earth!
Go up and breathe in the sweet atmosphere
His presence purified, as He arose!

HANNAH F. GOULD.

CIRCLED round with angel powers,
Their triumphant Lord and ours,
Conqueror o'er death, hell and sin,
Take the King of glory in:
Him though highest Heaven receives,
Still He loves the earth He leaves;
Though returnéd to His throne,
Still He calls mankind His own.

MADAN.

ATHEISM.

The fool hath said in his heart, There is no God. PSALM xiv, 1.

Is not God in the height of Heaven? and behold the height of the stars, how high they are!

And thou sayest, How doth God know? can he judge through the dark cloud? JOB, xxii, 12, 13.

The wicked, through the pride of his countenance, will not seek after God: God is not in all his thoughts. PSALM x, 4.

And they say, How doth God know; and is there knowledge in the Most High? PSALM lxxiii, 11.

For this they willingly are ignorant of, that by the word of God the heavens were of old, and the earth standing out of the water, and in the water. II. PETER, iii, 5.

Having no hope, and without God in the world. EPHESIANS, ii, 12.

WHO can look on the earth,
And view the varied beauty, and the bloom
That lingers still, with Eden loveliness,
Upon the mountain top, and on the plain,
And say, "There is no God?" DAVID BATES.

"There is no God," the foolish saith—
But none, "there is no sorrow:"
And Nature oft the cry of Faith
In bitter need will borrow.
Eyes which the preacher could not school,
By way-side graves are raised;
And lips say "God be pitiful,"
That ne'er said "God be praised."
MISS BARRETT.

ATHEIST, use thine eyes,
And having viewed the order of the skies,
Think, if thou canst, that matter blindly hurl'd
Without a guide, should frame the wondrous world.
CREECH.

5

AN Atheist's laugh 's a poor exchange,
For Deity offended. BURNS.

THESE are they
That strove to pull Jehovah from His throne,
And in the place of Heaven's Eternal King,
Set up the phantom Chance. GLYNN.

"There is no God," the fool in secret said:
"There is no God that rules or earth or sky."
Tear off the band that binds the wretch's head,
That God may burst upon his faithless eye!
Is there no God? — The stars in myriads spread,
If he look up, the blasphemy deny;
While his own features, in the mirror read,
Reflect the image of Divinity.
Is there no God? — The stream that silver flows,
The air he breathes, the ground he treads, the trees,
The flowers, the grass, the sands, each wind that blows,
All speak of God; throughout, one voice agrees,
And, eloquent, His dread existence shows:
Blind to thyself, ah, see him, fool, in these!
GIOVANNI COTTA.

THEY eat
Their daily bread, and draw the breath of Heaven
Without or thought or thanks; Heaven's roof, to them,
Is but a painted ceiling hung with lamps,
No more, that lights them to their purposes.
They wander loose about; they nothing see,
Themselves except, and creatures like themselves,
Short-lived, short-sighted, impotent to save.
So on their dissolute spirits, soon or late,
Destruction cometh, like an armed man,
Or like a dream of murder in the night,
Withering their mortal faculties, and breaking
The bones of all their pride. CHARLES LAMB.

THE owlet Atheism,
Sailing on obscene wings across the noon,
Drops his blue-fringed lids, and shuts them close,
And, hooting at the glorious sun in Heaven,
Cries out, "Where is it?" COLERIDGE.

NO God! Who warms the heart to heave
With thousand feelings, soft and sweet,
And prompts the aspiring soul to leave
The earth we tread beneath our feet,
And soar away on pinions fleet,
Beyond the scene of mortal strife,
With fair ethereal forms to meet,
That tell us of an after life? WILLIAM KNOX.

HARDENING by degrees, till double steel'd,
Take leave of Nature's God, and God reveal'd—
Then laugh at all you trembled at before;
And, joining the freethinker's brutal war,
Swallow the two grand nostrums they dispense—
That Scripture lies, and blasphemy is sense;
If clemency, revolted by abuse
Be damnable, then damn'd without excuse.
COWPER.

And hath *Man* the power, with his pride and his skill,
To arouse all nature with storms at will?
Hath he power to colour the summer cloud,
To allay the tempest when hills are bowed?
Can he waken the Spring with her festal wreath?
Can the sun grow dim by his lightest breath?
Will he come again when death's vale is trod?
Who then shall dare murmur "There is no God!"
WILLIS G. CLARK.

(*See also* UNBELIEF.)

THE ATONEMENT.

WITHOUT shedding of blood, is no remission. HEBREWS, ix, 22.

God commendeth His love toward us, in that, while we were yet sinners, Christ died for us. ROMANS, v, 8.

We also joy in God through our Lord Jesus Christ, by whom we have now received the atonement. ROMANS, v, 11.

Whom God hath set forth to be a propitiation through faith in his blood, to declare his righteousness for the remission of sins that are past. ROMANS, iii, 25.

He is the propitiation for our sins; and not for ours only, but for the sins of the whole world. I. JOHN, ii, 2.

Wherefore Jesus also, that he might sanctify the people with His own blood, suffered without the gate. HEBREWS, xiii, 12.

Who His own self bare our sins in His own body on the tree, that we, being dead to sins, should live unto righteousness: by whose stripes ye were healed. I. PETER, ii, 84.

For Christ also hath once suffered for sins, the just for the unjust. I. PETER, iii, 18.

AND shall the sinful heart, alone,
 Behold, unmoved, the atoning hour,
When Nature trembles on her throne,
 And death resigns his iron power?
O, shall the heart,—whose sinfulness
Gave keenness to His sore distress,
And added to His tears of blood—
Refuse its trembling gratitude? WHITTIER.

WHAT needs my blood, since thine will do,
To pay the debt to justice due?
O, tender mercy's art divine!
Thy sorrow proves the cure of mine!
Thy dropping wounds, thy woeful smart,
Allay the bleedings of my heart:
Thy death, in death's extreme of pain,
Restores my soul to life again! PARNELL.

THOU, rather than thy justice should be stained,
Did stain the cross. YOUNG

O, WHAT a groan was there! a groan not His.
He seized our dreadful right; the load sustained,
And heaved the mountain from a guilty world.
YOUNG.

THUS Truth with Mercy met, and Righteousness,
Stooping from highest heaven, embraced fair Peace,
That walked the earth in fellowship with Love.
POLLOK.

GOD'S own son, unblemished victim, gave
Himself a sacrifice, and by His blood,
Upon the cross poured forth, washed out the stain
Of primal sin. SAMUEL HAYES.

So Man, as is most just,
Shall satisfy for man, be judged and die,
And dying, rise, and rising, with Him raise
His brethren, ransomed with His own dear life.
MILTON.

NOR can this be,
But by fulfilling that which Thou didst want,
Obedience to the law of God, imposed
On penalty of death, and suffering death,
The penalty to Thy transgression due:
So only can high justice rest appaid. MILTON.

'TIS nothing thou hast given; then add thy tears
For a long race of unrepenting years;
'Tis nothing yet, yet all thou hast to give;
Then add those may-be years thou hast to live;
Yet nothing still; then poor and naked come;
Thy Father will receive his unthrift home,
And thy blest Saviour's blood discharge the mighty sum.
DRYDEN.

THE Son of God
Only begotten, and well-beloved, between
Men and His Father's justice interposed;
Put human nature on, His wrath sustained,
And in their name suffered, obeyed, and died;
Making His soul an offering for sin,
Just for unjust, and innocence for guilt. POLLOK

ADVANCE, hopeless mortal, steeled in guilt,
Behold, and if thou canst, forbear to melt!
Shall Jesus die, thy freedom to regain,
And wilt thou drag the voluntary chain?
Wilt thou refuse thy kind assent to give,
When, dying, He looks down to bid thee live?
Perverse, wilt thou reject the proffered good,
Bought with His life, and streaming in His blood?
Whose virtue can thy deepest crimes efface,
Reheal thy nature, and confirm thy peace!
Can all the errors of thy life atone,
And raise thee from a rebel to a son. BOYSE.

LAMB of God! Our Priest and Pastor,
  Who canst bid all evil cease,
Ever dear and holy Master,
  Make our feeble love increase!
So that when we seek Thee, owning
  That Thy wrath is our deserts,
Thou, blest Lord, at whose atonement
  All iniquity departs,
Mayest speak forth from Thine enthronement,
  To our rent and wearied hearts,
    "Sinner, go in peace!" C. D. McLEOD.

LOOK humbly upward, see His will disclose
The forfeit first, and then the fine impose;
A mulct thy poverty could never pay,
Had not eternal wisdom found the way,

And with celestial wealth supplied thy store;
His justice makes the fine, His mercy quits the score.
See God descending in the human frame;
The offended suffering in the offender's name:
All thy misdeeds to Him imputed see,
And all His righteousness devolved on thee.

DRYDEN.

(*See also* REDEMPTION.)

AVARICE—COVETOUSNESS.

WE brought nothing into this world, and it is certain we can carry nothing out. I. TIMOTHY, vi, 7.

Some remove the landmarks; they violently take away the flocks, and feed thereof. JOB, xxiv, 2.

They drive away the ass of the fatherless, they take the widow's ox for a pledge. JOB, xxiv, 3.

They turn the needy out of the way; the poor of the earth hide themselves together. JOB, xxiv, 4.

Woe unto them that join house to house, that lay field to field, till there be no place, that they may be placed alone in the midst of the earth! ISAIAH, v, 9.

Your gold and silver is cankered; and the rust of them shall be a witness against you, and shall eat your flesh, as it were fire. Ye have heaped treasure together for the last days. JAMES, v, 3.

Behold, the hire of the labourers who have reaped down your fields, which is of you kept back by fraud, crieth: and the cries of them which have reaped, are entered into the ears of the Lord of Sabaoth. JAMES, v, 4.

The wages of him that is hired shall not abide with thee all night, until the morning LEVITICUS, xix, 13.

Thou shalt not covet. EXODUS, xx, 17.

HIS treasures fly to clog each fawning slave,
Yet grudge a stone to dignify his grave.
For this, low-thoughted craft his life employed;
For this, though wealthy, he no wealth enjoyed;
For this he griped the poor, and alms denied,
Unfriended lived, and unlamented died. SAVAGE.

WOE to the worldly men, whose covetous
Ambition labours to join house to house;
Lay field to field, till their enclosures edge
The plain, girdling a country with one hedge:
They leave no place unbought; no piece of earth
Which they will not engross; making a dearth
Of all inhabitants; until they stand
Unneighboured as unblest within the land.

BISHOP KING.

STARVE beside the chests, whose every corn
At the Last Day, shall in the Court of Heaven
Witness against thee. SIR E. B. LYTTON.

O CURSED lust of gold! when for thy sake
The fool throws up his interest in both worlds;
First starved in this, then damned in that to come!

BLAIR.

Gold! gold! in all ages the curse of mankind,
Thy fetters are forged for the soul and the mind:
The limbs may be free as the wings of a bird,
And the mind be the slave of a look or a word.
To gain thee, men barter eternity's crown,
Yield honour, affection, and lasting renown.

PARK BENJAMIN.

BUT should my destiny be quest of wealth,
Kind Heaven, oh! keep my tempted soul in health!
And should'st thou bless my toil with ample store,
Keep back the madness that would seek for more!

THOMAS WARD.

THE thirst for gold
Hath made men demons, till the heart that feels
The impulse of impartial love, nor kneels
In worship foul to Mammon, is contemned.

W. H. BURLEIGH.

AVARICE o'ershoots
Its destined mark; and with abundance cursed,
In wealth, the ills of poverty endures.

GEORGE BALLY.

Oh! life misspent — Oh! foulest waste of time!
No time has he his grovelling mind to store
With history's truths, or philosophic lore.
No charms for him has God's all-blooming earth —
His only question this — "What are they worth?"
Art, nature, wisdom, are no match for gain;
And even Religion bids him pause in vain.

THOMAS WARD.

IF thou art rich, thou art poor;
For, like an ass, whose back with ingots bows,
Thou bearest thy heavy riches but a journey,
And death unloads thee. SHAKSPEARE.

FOR of his wicked pelf his god he made,
And unto hell himself for money sold:
Accursed usury was all his trade,
And right and wrong alike in equal balance weighed.

SPENSER.

THE Miser comes, his heart to mammon sold —
His life, his hope, his god, his all is gold.
"To-morrow, and to-morrow," he will say;
"Soul, take thine ease, for thou hast many a day
Whose smiling dawns will make thee to rejoice."
Hush! Hark the echoes of that awful voice!
Thou fool! This night yield up thy earthly trust!"
Gaze once again, his treasures are but dust!

B. D. WINSLOW.

GOLD glitters most where virtue shines no more,
As stars from absent suns, have leave to shine.

YOUNG.

BAPTISM—JOHN BAPTIST.

Go ye therefore, and teach all nations, baptizing them in the name of the Father, and of the Son, and of the Holy Ghost. MATTHEW, xxviii, 19.

And it came to pass in those days, that Jesus came from Nazareth of Galilee, and was baptized by John in Jordan.

And straightway coming up out of the water, he saw the Heavens opened, and the Spirit, like a dove, descending upon Him:

And there came a voice from Heaven, saying, Thou art My Beloved Son, in whom I am well pleased. MARK, i. 4.

One Lord, one Faith, one Baptism. EPHESIANS, iv. 5.

Buried with Him in Baptism, wherein also ye are risen with Him, through the faith of the operation of God, who hath raised Him from the dead. COLOSSIANS, ii. 12.

The like figure whereunto, even Baptism doth now save us, (not the putting away of the filth of the flesh, but the answer of a good conscience toward God. I. PETER, iii, 21.

THE heir of Heaven, henceforth I dread not Death:
In Christ I live, in Christ I draw the breath
Of the true life. Let Sea and Earth and Sky
Wage war against me: on my front I show
The mighty Master's seal! In vain they try
To end my life, who can but end its woe.

COLERIDGE.

THEN who shall believe
Baptizing in the profluent stream, the sign
Of washing them from guilt of sin, to life
Pure, and in mind prepared, if so befal,
For death like that which the Redeemer died.

MILTON.

NOW had the great Proclaimer, with a voice
More awful than the sound of trumpet, cried
Repentance, and Heaven's kingdom nigh at hand
To all baptized: to his great baptism flocked
With awe, the regions round, and with them came

From Nazareth, the Son of Joseph deemed,
To the flood Jordan, came as then obscure;
Unmarked, unknown: but Him the Baptist soon
Descried, divinely warned; and witness bore
As to his worthier, and would have resigned
To Him this heavenly office, nor was long
His witness unconfirmed; on Him baptized
Heaven opened, and in likeness of a dove
The Spirit descended, while the Father's voice
From heaven pronounced Him His Beloved Son.

MILTON.

THE cross of Christ! The cross of Christ!
While yet my days were few,
'Twas traced upon my infant brow,
Fresh with life's morning dew;
In token that in after years,
Strong in its power and might,
I should beside Christ's followers stand,
Under His banners fight.

MATILDA F. DANA.

WELL mayest thou tremble, Baptist; well thy cheek,
Now flushed, now pale, thy labouring soul bespeak!
'Tis He, the Christ, by every bard foretold!
Hear Him, ye nations, and ye Heavens behold!
The Virgin-born, to bruise the Serpent's head,
The Paschal Lamb, to patient slaughter led,
The King of kings, to crush the gates of Hell,
Messiah, Shiloh, Jah, Emmanuel!
See, o'er His head, soft sinking from above,
With hovering radiance hangs the mystic Dove:
Dread from the cloud Jehovah's voice is known,
"This is my Son, my own, my well-loved Son!"

C. H. JOHNSON.

BAPTIZED as for the dead, He rose
  With prayer from Jordan's hallowed flood:
Ere long by persecuting foes,
  To be baptized in His own blood:
The Father's voice proclaimed the Son,
The Spirit witnessed;—these are one.

JAMES MONTGOMERY.

THUS, made partakers of Thy love,
  The Baptism of the Spirit ours,
Our grateful hearts shall rise above,
  Renewed in purposes and powers;
And songs of joy again shall ring
  Triumphant through the arch of heaven;—
The glorious song which angels sing,
  Exulting over souls forgiven!

W. H. BURLEIGH.

WHY crowd ye cities forth? some reed to find,
Some vain reed trembling to the careless wind?
Or throng ye here to view with doting eye,
Some chieftain stand in purple pageantry?
Such dwell in kingly domes—no silken form
Woos the stern wind and braves the mountain storm.
What rush ye there to seek? some Prophet-seer?
One mightier than the Prophets find ye here—
The loftiest bard that waked the sacred lyre,
To him in rapture poured his lips of fire;
Attuned to him the voice of Sion fell—
Thy name, Elias, closed the mystic shell.

C. H. JOHNSON.

SINCE, Lord, to Thee
  A narrow way and little gate
Is all the passage; on my infancy
  Thou didst lay hold, and antedate
    My faith in me,

O let me still
Write Thee, great God, and me, a child:
Let me soft and supple to Thy will,
Small to myself, to others mild,
Be-hither ill. GEORGE HERBERT.

THE BIBLE.

SEARCH the Scriptures; for in them ye think ye have eternal life; and they are they which testify of me. JOHN, v, 39.

The Holy Scriptures, which are able to make thee wise unto salvation, through faith which is in Christ Jesus.

All Scripture is given by inspiration of God, and is profitable for doctrine, for reproof, for correction, for instruction in righteousness. I. TIMOTHY, iii, 15, 16.

For whatsoever things were written aforetime, were written for our learning; that we, through patience and comfort of the Scriptures, might have hope. ROMANS, xv, 4.

The sword of the Spirit, which is the word of God. EPHESIANS, vi, 17.

And beginning at Moses and all the prophets, He expounded unto them in all the Scriptures, the things concerning Himself. LUKE, xxiv, 27.

FANCY, Hope, and Conscience could not prove,
A future state, without the Word of God.
This is Hope's charter, this gives Fancy power,
And this arms Conscience with authority.
This partly lifts the veil which else had hung
Before our eyes, concealing from our view
The Spirit Land. JOSEPH H. WYTHES.

FATHER! that book
With whose worn leaves the careless infant plays,
Must be the Bible. Therein thy dim eyes
Will meet a cheering light; and silent words
Of mercy breathed from Heaven, will be exhaled
From the blest page into thy withered heart.
JOHN WILSON.

THERE wilt thou learn what to thy ardent mind
Will make this world but as a thorny pass
To regions of delight; man's natural life,
With all its varied turmoil of ambition,
But as the training of a wayward child
To manly excellence; yea, death itself
But as a painful birth to life unending.

JOANNA BAILLIE.

THOU truest friend man ever knew,
  Thy constancy I've tried;
When all were false I found thee true,
  My counsellor and guide.
The mines of earth no treasures give
  That could this volume buy:
In teaching me the way to live,
  It taught me how to die.

GEO. P. MORRIS.

HAST thou ever heard
Of such a book? The author, God Himself;
The subject, God and man, salvation, life,
And death — eternal life — eternal death.

POLLOK.

THE priest-like father reads the sacred page,
  How Abram was the friend of God on high;
Or Moses bade eternal warfare wage
  With Amalek's ungracious progeny;
Or how the Royal Bard did groaning lie,
  Beneath the stroke of Heaven's avenging ire;
Or Job's pathetic plaint and wailing cry;
  Or wrapt Isaiah's wild, seraphic fire;
Or other holy seers that tune the sacred lyre.

Perhaps the Christian volume is the theme,
  How guiltless blood for guilty man was shed;
How He who bore in Heaven the Second Name,
  Had not, on earth, whereon to lay His head;

How His first followers and servants sped;
The precepts sage they wrote to many a land:
How he who, lone in Patmos banished,
Saw, in the sun, a mighty angel stand;
And heard great Bab'lon's doom pronounced by Heaven's command.
BURNS.

THE sacred page
With calm attention scan! If on thy soul,
As thou dost read, a ray of purer light
Break in, O check it not, give it full scope!
Admitted, it will break the clouds which long
Have dimmed thy sight, and lead thee, till at last,
Convictions like the sun's meridian beams,
Illuminate thy mind.
SAMUEL HAYES.

WHENCE, but from Heaven, could men unskilled in arts,
In several ages born, in several parts,
Weave such agreeing truths? or how, or why,
Should all conspire to cheat us with a lie?
Unasked their pains, ungrateful their advice,
Starving their gain, and martyrdom their price.
DRYDEN.

So has this Book entitled us to Heaven,
And rules to guide us to that mansion given;
Tells the conditions how our peace was made,
And is our pledge for the great Author's aid.
His power in nature's ample book we find,
But the less volume doth express his mind.
WALLER.

A CRITIC on the sacred book should be
Candid and learned, dispassionate and free:
Free from the wayward bias bigots feel,
From fancy's influence, and intemperate zeal.
COWPER.

WITHIN this ample volume lies
The mystery of mysteries;
Happiest they of human race
To whom their God has given grace,
To read, to fear, to hope, to pray,
To lift the latch, to force the way;
And better had they ne'er been born,
That read to doubt, or read to scorn.

SIR WALTER SCOTT.

(*See also* GOSPEL, REVELATION.)

BROTHERHOOD—FRIENDSHIP.

IF a house be divided against itself, that house cannot stand. MARK, iii, 25.

None of us liveth to himself. ROMANS, xiv, 7.

God hath made of one blood all the nations of men, for to dwell on all the face of t earth. ACTS, xvii, 26.

FOR God, who made this teeming earth so full,
And made the proud dependent on the dull—
The strong upon the weak, thereby would show
One common bond should link us all below.

MRS. NORTON.

CHRIST had His friends—His eye could trace
In the long train of coming years,
The chosen children of His grace,
The full reward of all his tears.
These are His friends, and these are thine,
If thou to Him hast bowed the knee;
And where these ransomed millions shine
Shall thy eternal mansion be.

ANONYMOUS

E'en as the dew, that, at the break of morning,
All nature with its beauty is adorning,
And flows from Heaven, calm and still,
And bathes the tender grass on Zion's hill,
And to the young and withering herb resigns
The drops for which it pines:
So are fraternal peace and concord ever
The cherishers without whose guidance, never
Would sainted quiet seek the breast,—
The life, the soul of unmolested rest,—
The antidote to sorrow and distress,
And prop of human happiness. Kamphuyzen.

How, in one house,
Should many people, under two commands
Hold amity? Shakspeare.

No man is lord of any thing,
Though in and of him there be much consisting,
Till he communicate his parts to others.
Shakspeare.

Strange is it that our bloods,
Of colour, weight, and heat, poured all together,
Would quite confound distinction, yet stand off
In difference so mighty. Shakspeare.

'Tis not enough to help the feeble up,
But to support him after. Shakspeare.

The amity that wisdom knits not, folly
May easily untie. Shakspeare.

O, sweet it is, through life's dark way
In Christian fellowship to move,
Illumed by one unclouded ray,
And one in faith, in hope, in love.
Charlotte Elizabeth.

THE BLIND—BLINDNESS.

THE Lord openeth the eyes of the blind. PSALM cxlvi, 8.

Then shall the eyes of the blind be opened. ISAIAH, xxv, 5.

He hath sent me to heal the broken-hearted, to preach deliverance to the captives and recovering of sight to the blind. LUKE, iv, 18.

BUT in God's temple the great lamp is out,
And he must worship glory in the dark!
Till death, in midnight mystery, hath brought
The veiled soul's re-illuminating spark—
The pillar of the cloud enfolds the Ark!
And, like a man that prayeth underground
In Bethlehem's rocky shrine, he can but mark
The lingering hours by circumstance and sound,
And break, with gentle hymns, the solemn silence round.

Yet still life's Better Light shines out above!
And in that village church, where first he learned
To bear his cheerless doom, for heaven's dear love,
He sits, with wistful face, for ever turned
To hear of those who Heavenly pity earned;
Blind Bartimeus, and him desolate,
Who for Bethesda's waters vainly yearned:
And only sighs, condemned so long to wait,
Baffled and helpless still, beyond the Temple gate!

MRS. NORTON.

FOR now in truth I find
My Father all his promises hath kept;
He comforts those who here in sadness wept.
Eyes to the blind
Thou art, O God! Earth I no longer see,
Yet trustfully my spirit looks to thee.

MRS. NEAL.

THESE eyes, though clear,
To outward view, of blemish or of spot,
Bereft of light, their seeing have forgot;
Nor to their idle orbs doth sight appear
Of sun, or moon, or star, throughout the year,
Or man, or woman. Yet I argue not
Against Heaven's hand or will, nor bate a jot
Of heart or hope; but still bear up and steer
Right onward. MILTON.

WHEN I consider how my light is spent
Ere half my days in this dark world and wide,
And that one talent which is death to hide,
Lodged with me useless, though my soul more bent
To serve therewith my maker, and present
My true account, lest he returning chide;
"Doth God exact day-labour, light denied?"
I fondly ask: but patience, to prevent
That murmur, soon replies, "God doth not need
Either man's works, or his own gifts; who best
Bear His mild yoke, they serve Him best: His state
Is kingly, thousands at his bidding speed,
And post o'er land and ocean without rest;
They also serve, who only stand and wait."
MILTON

CAPTIOUSNESS—CENSURE.

JUDGE not, that ye be not judged. MATTHEW, vii, 1.

And why beholdest thou the mote that is in thy brother's eye, and considerest not the beam that is in thine own eye? MATTHEW, vii, 3.

Let us not therefore judge one another any more, but judge this rather, that no man put a stumbling-block, or an occasion to fall, in his brother's way. ROMANS, xiv, 13.

HE that deals blame, and yet forgets to praise,
Who sets brief storms against long summer days,
Hath a sick judgment. MRS. NORTON.

AND shall we all condemn, and all distrust,
Because some men are false, and some unjust?
MRS. NORTON.

BE not too ready to condemn
The wrong thy brothers may have done;
Ere ye too harshly censure them
For human faults, ask, "Have I none?"
ELIZA COOK.

HE whom censure singles from the herd
To brand with infamy, whom envy loads
With blackening colours, to the Omniscient Judge,
Whom nought can bias, and whom nought deceives,
May otherwise appear. GEORGE BALLY.

HAST thou created man, or canst thou make
Allowance for infirmity? Canst thou
Against his reason weigh his passion's force,
And thence pronounce his doom? By what base crime
Can he, thy equal, lose a natural right,
That thou shouldst rise so high above his state,
And, as a judge, consign him to destruction?
C. P. LAYARD.

CHARITY.

CHARITY suffereth long and is kind; charity envieth not; charity vaunteth not itself, is not puffed up,

Doth not behave itself unseemly, seeketh not her own, is not easily provoked, thinketh no evil;

Rejoiceth not in iniquity, but rejoiceth in the truth;

Beareth all things, believeth all things, hopeth all things, endureth all things. I CORINTHIANS, xiii, 4, 5, 6, 7.

And now abideth faith, hope, charity, these three; but the greatest of these is charity 1. CORINTHIANS, xiii, 13.

LOVE never fails: though knowledge cease,
Though Prophecies decay,
Love, Christian Love, shall still increase,
Shall still extend her sway.
Here dimly, through life's shadowy glass,
We strain our infant eyes;
Soon shall the earth-born vapours pass,
And light, unclouded, rise;
Then HOPE shall sink in changeless doom,
Then FAITH's bright race be o'er,
But Thou, Eternal Love, shalt bloom
More glorious than before. WM. PETER.

WERE we as rich in charity of deed
As gold — what rock would bloom not with the seed?
We give our alms and cry "What can we more?"
One hour of time were worth a load of ore!
Give to the ignorant our own wisdom! — give
Sorrow our comfort! — lend to those who live
In crime, the counsels of our virtue! — share
With souls our souls, and Satan shall despair!
Alas! what converts one man, who would take
The cross, and staff, and house with Guilt, could make!
SIR E. B. LYTTON.

SEARCH the material tribes of earth, sea, air,
And the fierce SELF, which strives and slays, is there;
What but that SELF to man doth Nature teach?
Where the charmed link that binds the all to earth?
Where the sweet law, (doth Nature boast its birth?)
"Good will to man and charity on earth."

SIR E. B. LYTTON.

AND where the natural halts, where cramped, confined,
The seen horizon bounds the baffled mind,
The Inspired begins — the onward march is given;
Bridging all space, nor ending e'en in Heaven!
There, veiled on earth, we mark, divinely clear,
Duty and end — the There explains the Here!
We see the link that binds the future band,
Foeman with foeman gliding hand in hand;
And feel that hate is but an hour's — the son
Of earth, to perish when the earth is done —
But love eternal, and we turn below,
To hail the brother, where we loathed the foe.

SIR E. B. LYTTON.

THE blessings which the poor and weak can scatter
Have their own season. 'T is a little thing
To give a cup of water; yet its draught
Of cool refreshment, drained by fevered lips,
May give a shock of pleasure to the frame
More exquisite than when nectarean juice
Renews the life of joy in happiest hours.
It is a little thing to speak a phrase
Of common comfort, which by daily use
Has almost lost its sense; yet on the ear
Of him who thought to die unmourned, 't will fall
Like choicest music; fill the glazing eye
With gentle tears; relax the knotted hand
To know the bonds of fellowship again.

TALFOURD.

He who the lily clothes in simple glory,
He who doth hear the raven's cry for food,
Hath on our hearts with hand invisible,
In signs mysterious, written that alone
Our *hearts* may read.

R. H. Dana.

Send thy good before thee, man,
 The whilst thou may, to Heaven:
For better is one alms before,
 Than bin after seven.

Old English Rhyme.

Who gives, constrained, but his own fear reviles;
Not thanked, but scorned; nor are they gifts, but spoils

Denham

Great minds, like Heaven, are pleased in doing good,
Though the ungrateful subjects of their favours
Are barren in return.

Nicholas Rowe.

Largely Thou givest, gracious Lord,
Largely Thy gifts should be restored;
Freely Thou givest, and Thy word
 Is "Freely give."
He only who forgets to hoard
 Has learned to live.

Keble.

Cheap gifts best fit poor givers. We are told
Of the lone mite, and cup of water cold,
That, in their way, approved the offerer's zeal.
True love shows costliest where the means are scant,
And, in her reckoning, they abound, who want.

Charles Lamb.

The consciousness of wrong, in wills not evil
Brings charity.

Leigh Hunt.

WHEN prophecies shall fail,
When tongues shall cease, when knowledge is no more,
And the Great Day is come, thou by the throne
Shalt sit triumphant. GLYNN.

WITH a look of sad content,
Her mite within the treasure heap she cast;
Then, timidly as bashful twilight, stole
From out the temple. But her lowly gift
Was witnessed by an eye whose mercy views,
In motive, all that consecrates a deed
To goodness, so he blessed the Widow's Mite.
ROBERT MONTGOMERY.

WHAT though to poverty's imploring voice
I give my earthly goods; though to the pile
I yield my body, if thy genuine love
Inspire not, this alike is void and vain.
C. P. LAYARD.

THOU, mild and gentle nature, art estranged
From envy, hatred, insolence, or pride;
Thou seekest not thy own, but others' weal;
Slow to reprove, but studious to applaud,
And from the eyes of malice to conceal
The weakness thou lamentest to behold:
For thou of each forgiv'st and hop'st the best,
Forbearing and forgiving every ill.
C. P. LAYARD.

THE time shall come when prophecy itself,
And all the knowledge which exalts mankind,
Shall lose their use; these, while the state of man
In imperfection lies, by Heaven are made
To compass ends sublime; but when that state

Imperfect, for perfection shall be changed,
Shall fade away, and boast that use no more.
But, subject to no change, through endless time
Shall Faith, and Hope, and Charity endure;
And thou, O Charity, of these the chief,
In high pre-eminence shalt ever reign!

C. P. Layard.

When constant Faith and holy Hope shall die,
One lost in certainty, and one in joy,
Then, thou more happy power, fair Charity!
Triumphant sister! greatest of the three!
Thy office and thy nature still the same,
Lasting thy lamp, and unconsumed thy flame,
Shall stand before the host of Heaven confest,
For ever blessing, and for ever blest! Prior.

Give credit to thy mortal brother's heart
For all the good that in thine own hath part.

Mrs. Norton.

Not soon provoked, she easily forgives;
And much she suffers, as she much believes.
Soft peace she brings wherever she arrives,
She builds our quiet as she forms our lives;
Lays the rough paths of peevish nature even,
And opens in each heart a little heaven. Prior.

CHILDHOOD—CHILDREN.

HAVE ye never read, Out of the mouths of babes and sucklings thou hast perfected praise? MATTHEW, xxi, 16.

Verily I say unto you, except ye be converted, and become as little children, ye shall not enter into the kingdom of Heaven. MATTHEW, xviii, 3.

Suffer little children to come unto me, and forbid them not, for of such is the kingdom of Heaven. MATTHEW, xix, 14.

Take heed that ye despise not one of these little ones; for I say unto you, That in Heaven these angels do always behold the face of my Father which is in Heaven. MATTHEW, xviii, 10.

THE child between her parents knelt,
Who prayed the more to God above,
Because so close to them they felt
The dearest gift of Heavenly love.

JOHN STERLING.

A CHERUB might mistake our rosy boy
For a reposing mate! ARTHUR C. COXE.

To her new beauty largely given
From deeper fountains, looked and smiled,
And, like a morning dream from heaven,
The woman gleamed within the child.

JOHN STERLING.

THERE are smiles and tears in the mother's eyes,
For her new-born infant beside her lies.
O, hour of bliss! when the heart o'erflows
With rapture a mother only knows.
Let it gush forth in words of fervent prayer;
Let it swell up to heaven for her precious care.

HENRY WARE, JR.

W. Finden

CHILDREN OF THE SKY.

How soft and fresh he breathes!
Look, he is dreaming! Visions sure of joy
Are gladdening his rest; and ah who knows
But waiting angels do converse in sleep
With babes like this! ARTHUR C. COXE.

AT his first aptness the maternal love
Those rudiments of wisdom did improve;
The tender age was pliant to command;
Like wax it yielded to the forming hand:
True to the artificer, the laboured mind
With ease was pious, generous, just, and kind;
Soft for impression, from the first prepared,
Till virtue, with long exercise, grew hard;
With every act confirmed and made at last,
So durable as not to be effaced,
It turned to habit; and from vices free,
Goodness resolved into necessity. DRYDEN.

CHILD, there is One, the High above all Height,
Who doth not scorn thee—
Ever, from Him, may beams of Heavenly light
Comfort,—but warn thee—
That, from youth's innocence each proud removal
Is a departure from His blest approval.
H. H. WELD.

I REMEMBER, I remember
The fir-trees dark and high,
I used to think their tiny tops
Were close against the sky:
It was a childish ignorance,
But now 'tis little joy,
To know I'm farther off from heaven
Than when I was a boy! T. HOOD.

Blessed Jesus ever loved to trace
The innocent brightness of an infant's face;
He raised them in His holy arms;
He blessed them from the world and all its harms:
Heirs though they were of sin and shame,
He blessed them in His own, and in His Father's Name

Keble.

Christian! thy dream is now — it was not then:
O, it were strange if childhood were a dream.
Strife, and the world, are dreams: to wakeful men
Childhood and home as jealous angels seem:
Like shapes and hues that play in clouds at even,
They have but shifted from thee into Heaven!

F. W. Faber.

When little tripping children follow God,
And leave old doting sinners to his rod,
'Tis like those days wherein the young ones cried,
Hosanna! while the old ones did deride.

Bunyan.

Woe worth the worldly wisdom,
That, in its iron mood,
Would teach that young heart hardness,
And deem such hardness good;
The stoic's stern enduring
Is no lesson of our God;
He would not have his children
Despise the chastening rod.

Anonymous.

The Lord of Heaven, who, from his throne above,
Governs the universe, yet deigns to hear
The praise which from the mouths of sucklings flows,
And from the lisping babe ordaineth strength.

C. P. Layard.

How oft, heart-sick and sore,
I've wished I were, once more,
A little child! MRS. SOUTHEY.

"SUFFER these little ones to come to me,"
Was the command of Him who, on the cross,
Bowed His anointed head, and with his blood
Purchased redemption for our fallen race—
And blessed they, who to that holy task
Devote the energies of their young years,
Teaching, with pious care, the dawning light
Of infant intellect to know the Lord.
C. HUNTINGDON.

CHRISTIANS—CHRISTIANITY.

AND the disciples were called Christians first in Antioch. ACTS, xi, 26.

Yet if any man suffer as a Christian, let him not be ashamed; but let him glorify God on this behalf. I. PETER, iv, 16.

For even hereunto were ye called; because Christ also suffered for us, leaving us an example, that we should follow His steps:

Who did no sin, neither was guile found in his mouth:

Who, when He was reviled, reviled not again; when He suffered, he threatened not; but committed Himself to Him that judgeth righteously. I. PETER, ii, 21, 22, 23.

Adorn the doctrine of God our Saviour in all things. TITUS, ii, 10.

Stand fast, therefore, in the liberty wherewith Christ hath made you free. GALATIANS, v, 1.

Walk worthy of the vocation wherewith ye are called. EPHESIANS, iv, 1.

BEHOLD His life, and learn from Him to live;
In death still greater view thy dying Lord,
And imitate that worth thou canst not reach.
Smooth are His paths, and to conduct thy feet,
The Gospel's holy light around thee sheds
Its mild effulgence. WILLIAM BOLLAND.

To be the humble follower of Him,
Who left the bliss of Heaven, to be for us
A man on earth in spotless virtue living
As man ne'er lived; such words of comfort speaking,
To raise, and elevate, and cheer the heart,
As man ne'er spake; and suffering poverty,
Contempt, and wrong, and pain, and death itself,
As man ne'er suffered. JOANNA BAILLIE.

HE that alone would wise and mighty be,
Commands that others love, as well as He.
Love as He loved! how can we soar so high?
He can add wings when He commands to fly.
Nor should we be with this command dismayed,
He that examples gives, will give His aid;
For He took flesh, that where His precepts fail,
His practice as a pattern might prevail.

WALLER.

THE Christian's faith had many mysteries too.
The uncreated Holy Three in One;
Divine Incarnate, Human in Divine;
The inward call; the Sanctifying Dew;
Coming unseen, unseen departing thence;
Anew creating all, and yet not heard;
Compelling, yet not felt: — mysterious these;
Not that Jehovah to conceal them wished;
Not that Religion wished. The Christian faith,
Unlike the timorous creeds of Pagan priest,
Was frank, stood forth to view, invited all
To prove, examine, search, investigate,
And gave herself a light to see her by.
Mysterious these — because too large for eye
Of man, too long for human arm to mete.

POLLOK.

O ANTIOCH, thou teacher of the world!—
From out thy portals passed the feet of those,
Who, banished and despised, have made thy name
The next in rank to proud Jerusalem.
Within thy gates the persecuted few,
Who dared to rally round the Holy Cross,
And worship Him whose sacred form it bore,
Were first called Christians. In thy sad conceit,
Thou mad'st a stigma of reproach and shame,
This noblest title of the sons of earth:
While, save for this, thy name were scarcely known,
Except among the mouldering vestiges
Of dim antiquity. So doth our God
Make all men's folly ever praise His name.

J. L. CHESTER.

BUT for that contention and brave strife
The Christian hath to enjoy, the future life,
He were the wretchedest of the race of men;
But as he soars at that, he bruiseth then
The serpent's head; gets above death and sin,
And, sure of Heaven, rides triumphing in.

BEN JONSON.

WITH force of arms we nothing can,
  Full soon were we down-ridden;
But for us fights the proper man,
  Whom God himself hath bidden.
Ask ye, who is the same? Christ Jesus is His name,
The Lord Zebaoth's Son, He, and no other one,
  Shall conquer in the battle.

MARTIN LUTHER

ALL faiths beside, or did by arms ascend;
Or sense indulged has made mankind their friend:
This only doctrine does our lusts oppose;
Unfed by nature's soil, in which it grows;

Cross to our interests, curbing sense and sin;
Oppressed without, and undermined within,
It thrives through pain, its own tormentors tires;
And with a stubborn patience still aspires.
To what can reason such effects assign,
Transcending nature, but to laws divine,
Which in that sacred volume are contained,
Sufficient, clear, and for that use ordained?

DRYDEN.

WELL hast thou fought
The better fight, who, singly, hast maintained
Against revolted multitudes the cause
Of truth, in word mightier than they in arms;
And for the testimony of truth hast borne
Universal reproach, far worse to bear
Than violence.

MILTON.

THE CHURCH.

THE Church of the Living God, the Pillar and Ground of the truth. I. TIMOTHY, iii, 15.

And God hath set some in the Church, first, apostles, secondarily, prophets, thirdly teachers. I. CORINTHIANS, xii, 28.

Whatsoever thou shalt bind on earth, shall be bound in Heaven: and whatsoever thou shalt loose on earth shall be loosed in Heaven. MATTHEW, xvi, 19.

Lo, I am with you alway, even unto the end of the world. MATTHEW, xxviii, 20.

Not forsaking the assembling of ourselves together, as the manner of some is. HEBREWS, x, 25.

And hath put all things under His feet, and gave them to be head over all things to the Church, which is His Body; the fulness of Him that filleth all in all. EPHESIANS, i. 22, 23.

————THY best type, Desire
Of the sad heart, — the Heaven-ascending spire!

SIR E. B. LYTTON.

THE groves were God's first temples. Ere man learned
To hew the shaft, and lay the architrave,
And spread the roof above them, — ere he framed
The lofty vault, to gather and roll back
The sound of anthems; in the darkling wood,
Amidst the cool and silence, he knelt down,
And offered to the Mightiest solemn thanks
And supplication. WM. C. BRYANT.

CLAD in a robe of pure and spotless white,
The youthful bride, with timid steps, comes forth
To greet the hand to which she plights her troth,
Her soft eyes radiant with a strange delight.
The snowy veil which circles her around,
Shades the sweet face from every gazer's eye,
And thus enwrapt, she passes calmly by —
Nor casts a look, but on the unconscious ground.
So should the Church, the bride elect of Heaven, —
Remembering whom she goeth forth to meet,
And with a truth that cannot brook deceit,
Holding the faith which unto her is given —
Pass through this world, which claims her for a while,
Nor cast about her longing look nor smile.
MRS. NEAL.

THERE is a joy which angels well may prize:
To see, and hear, and aid God's worship, when
Unnumbered tongues, a host of Christian men,
Youths, matrons, maidens, join. Their sounds arise
Like many waters; now glad symphonies
Of thanks and glory to one God; and then,
Seal of the social prayer, the loud Amen!
Faith's common pledge, contrition's mingled cries.
BP. MANT.

Some there are
Who hold it meet to linger now at home,
And some o'er fields and the wide hills to roam,
And worship in the temple of the air!
For me, not heedless of the lone address,
Nor slack to meet my Maker on the height,
By wood, or living stream; yet not the less
Seek I His presence in each social rite
Of His own temple: *that* He deigns to bless,
There still He dwells, and that is His delight.

Bp. Mant.

Let vain or busy thoughts have there no part;
Bring not thy plots, thy plough, thy pleasure thither.
Christ purged His temple — so must thou thy heart.
All worldly thoughts are but thieves met together
To cozen thee. Look to thy action well,
For churches either are our heaven or hell.

George Herbert.

How reverend is the face of this tall pile,
Whose ancient pillars rear their marble heads,
To bear aloft its arched and ponderous roof,
By its own weight made steadfast and immovable,
Looking tranquillity. It strikes an awe
And terror on my aching sight; the tombs
And monumental caves of death look cold,
And shoot a chillness to my trembling heart.

Congreve.

To thee the churches here rejoice,
The solemn organs aid the voice;
To sacred roofs the sound we raise,
The sacred roofs re-sound Thy praise;
And while our notes in one agree,
Oh! bless the church that sings to Thee!

Parnell.

O, PRAYER is good when many pour
  Their voices in one solemn tone;
Conning their sacred lessons o'er,
  Or yielding thanks for mercies shown.
'Tis good to see the quiet train
  Forget their worldly joy and care,
While loud response, and choral strain,
  Re-echo in the House of Prayer. ELIZA COCK.

So shall her holy bounds increase,
With walls of praise and gates of peace;
So shall the Vine which martyr tears
And blood sustained, in other years,
    With fresher life be clothed upon;
And to the world in beauty show
Like the rose-plant of Jericho,
  And glorious as Lebanon. J. G. WHITTIER

I LOVE to hear the sound of holy bell,
And peaceful men, their praises lift to Heaven.
JOANNA BAILLIE.

THE solemn scene
The sun, through storied panes, surveys with awe,
And bashfully withholds each bolder beam.
SMART.

CONSCIENCE.

THEIR conscience also bearing witness, and their thoughts the meanwhile accusing or else excusing one another. ROMANS, ii, 15.

Happy is he that condemneth not himself, in that thing which he alloweth. ROMANS, xiv, 22.

Holding the mystery of the faith in a pure conscience. I. TIMOTHY, iii, 9.

For, if our heart condemn us, God is greater than our heart and knoweth all things.

Beloved, if our heart condemn us not, then have we confidence toward God. I. JOHN, iii. 20, 21.

DIVINE authority, within man's breast,
Brings every thought, word, action, to the test;
Warns him or prompts, approves him or restrains,
As Reason or as passion takes the reins.
Heaven from above, and Conscience from within,
Cries in his startled ear,—Abstain from sin!

COWPER.

SKEPTIC, whoe'er thou art, tell, if thou knowest,
Why every nation, every clime, though all
In laws, in rites, in manners disagree,
With one consent expect another world
Where wickedness shall weep? Why in each breast
Is placed a friendly monitor, that prompts,
Informs, directs, encourages, forbids?
Tell, why on unknown evil grief attends,
Or joy on secret good? Why Conscience acts
With tenfold force, when sickness, age, or pain
Stands tottering on the precipice of death?
Or why such horror gnaws the guilty soul
Of dying sinners, while the good man sleeps
Peaceful and calm, and with a smile expires?

GLYNN.

Lest too powerful passions should propel
Headlong to acts immoral, nor allow
Time for slow Reason to deduce a rule
To curb their mad career, Conscience kind Heaven
Appointed her assistant; Conscience, quick
To heed the call of duty, to discern
'Twixt right and wrong, and bias to the best.

William Gibson.

For though the plain judge, Conscience, makes no show,
But silently to her dark session comes,
Not as red law does to arraignment go,
Or war to execution, with loud drums;

Though she on hills sets not her gibbets high,
Where frightful law sets hers; nor bloody seems,
Like war in colours spread, yet secretly
She does her work, and many men condemns;

Chokes in the seed what law, till ripe, ne'er sees;
What law would punish, Conscience can prevent;
And so the world from many mischiefs frees;
Known by her cures, as law by punishment.

Sir William Davenant.

There is a kind of conscience some men keep,
Is like a member that 's benumbed with sleep;
Which, as it gathers blood, and wakes again,
It shoots, and pricks, and feels, as big as ten.

Quarles.

So gnaws the grief of conscience evermore,
And in the heart it is so deep ygrave,
That they may never sleep nor rest therefor,
Nor think one thought but on the dread they have.

Earl of Dorset.

THE soul's rough file that smoothness does impart:
The hammer that does break the stony heart!
The worm that never dies! the "thorn within,"
That pricks and pains! the whip and scourge of sin!
The voice of God in man! which without rest
Does softly cry within a troubled breast—
"To all temptations is that soul set free
That makes not to itself a curb of me."

SIR E. SHERBURNE.

FROM behind her secret stand,
The sly informer minutes every fault,
And her dread diary with horror fills.
Not the gross act alone employs her pen:
She reconnoitres fancy's airy band,
Our dawning purposes of heart explores,
And steals our embryos of iniquity.

YOUNG.

YET still there whispers the small voice within,
Heard through gain's silence, and o'er glory's din;
Whatever creed be taught, or land be trod,
Man's conscience is the oracle of God.

BYRON.

STUDY conscience more than thou wouldst fame;
Though both be good, the latter yet is worst,
And ever is ill got, without the first.

BEN JONSON.

CONSOLATION.

THE Lord God will wipe away tears from all faces; and the rebuke of His people shall He take away from off all the earth; for the Lord hath spoken it. ISAIAH, xxxv, 8.

I, even I, am He that comforteth you: who art thou, that thou shouldest be afraid of man that shall die, and of the Son of Man which shall be made as grass, and forgettest he Lord thy Maker? ISAIAH, lxi, 12.

Yea, though I walk through the valley of the shadow of death, I will fear no evil: for Thou art with me; thy rod and thy staff they comfort me. PSALM xxiii, 4.

This is my comfort in my affliction, for thy word hath quickened me. PSALM cxix, 50.

Blessed be God, even the Father of our Lord Jesus Christ, the Father of mercies, and the God of all comfort;

Who comforteth us in all our tribulation, that we may be able to comfort them which are in any trouble, by the comfort wherewith we ourselves are comforted of God. I. THESSALONIANS, i, 3, 4.

THE soul reposing on assured relief,
Feels herself happy amidst all her grief;
Forgets her labour as she toils along,
Weeps tears of joy, and bursts into a song.

COWPER.

DREAD Omnipotence alone,
  Can heal the wound He gave;
Can point the brim-full, grief-worn eyes,
  To scenes beyond the grave.

BURNS.

THUS ever in the steps of grief,
  Are sown the precious seeds of joy;
Each fount of Marah hath a leaf,
  Whose healing balm we may employ.
Then, 'mid life's fitful, fleeting day,
  Look up! the sky is bright above!
Kind voices cheer thee on thy way!
  Faint spirit! Trust the God of Love!

MISS A. D. WOODBRIDGE.

FRIENDS counsel quick dismission of our grief;
Mistaken kindness! Our hearts heal too soon.
Are they more kind than He who struck the blow?
Who bid it do His errand in our hearts,
And banish peace till nobler guests arrive,
And bring it back, a true and endless peace?
Calamities are friends. YOUNG.

And what is want? 'Tis virtue's test:
What weakness? An escape from pride:
That life on earth may be the best
In which, by woe, the soul is tried:
For He whose word is ever sure,
Hath said that "Blessed are the Poor."
H. H. WELD.

There is a haven yet to rest my soul on,
In midst of all unhappiness, which I look on
With the same comfort as a distressed seaman
Afar off views the coast he would enjoy,
When yet the seas do toss his reeling barque,
'Twixt hope and danger. SHIRLEY.

THERE is no gloom on earth, for God above
Chastens in love;
Transmitting sorrow into golden joy,
Free from alloy.
His dearest attribute is still to bless,
And man's most welcome hymn is grateful cheerfulness.
HORACE SMITH.

OUT of my penitence there has grown hope;
I trust and raise my suppliant eyes to Heaven,
And when my soul desponds, I meekly say,
"I know that my Redeemer liveth."
MISS LANDON.

ALL hope on earth for ever fled,
  A higher hope remaineth;
For while His wrath is o'er me shed,
  I know my Saviour reigneth.
The worm may waste the withering clay,
  When flesh and spirit sever;
My soul shall see eternal day,
  And dwell with God for ever!

THOMAS DALE.

VIRTUE, on herself relying,
  Every passion hushed to rest,
Loses every pain of dying,
  In the hope of being blest.
Every added pang she suffers
  Some increasing good bestows,
And every shock that malice offers,
  Only rocks her to repose.

GOLDSMITH.

So, Christian! though gloomy and sad be thy days,
  And the tempest of sorrow encompass thee black;
Though no sunshine of promise or hope sheds its rays
  To illumine and cheer thy life's desolate track:
Though thy soul writhes in anguish, and bitter tears flow
  O'er the wreck of fond joys from thy bleeding heart riven,
Check thy murmuring sorrows, thou lorn one, and know
  That the chastened on earth are the purest for Heaven;
And remember, though gloomy thy present may be,
That "the Master is coming," and coming to thee.

S. D. PATTERSON.

IN the dark winter of affliction's hour,
When summer friends and pleasures haste away,
And the wrecked heart perceives how frail each power
It made a refuge, and believed a stay;
When man, all wild and weak is seen to be—
There's none like Thee, O Lord! there's none like Thee!

Thou in adversity canst be a sun;
Thou hast a healing balm, a sheltering tower,
The peace, the truth, the life, the love of One,
Nor wound, nor grief, nor storm can overpower
Gifts of a King; gifts, frequent and yet free,—
There's none like Thee, O Lord! none, none like Thee!

MISS JEWSBURY.

THANK God, bless God, all ye who suffer not
More grief than ye can weep for. That is well—
That is light grieving! lighter none befel,
Since Adam forfeited the primal lot.
Tears! what are tears? The babe weeps in its cot,
The mother singing: at her marriage bell
The bride weeps: and before the oracle
Of high-faned hills, the poet hath forgot
That moisture on his cheeks. Commend the grace,
Mourners who weep! Albeit, as some have done,
Ye grope, tear-blinded, in a desert place,
And touch but tombs,—look up! Those tears will run,
Soon, in long rivers, down the lifted face,
And leave the vision clear, for stars and sun.

MISS BARRETT.

WHY should my fond, ungrateful heart complain?
What have I lost, of excellent and fair,
Of kind or good, that Thou canst not repair?
What have I lost of truth or amity,
But what derived its gentle source from Thee?
What is there here of excellence or grace,
That one bright smile from Thee would not efface?

MRS. STEELE.

THEY who die in Christ are bless'd—
  Ours be, then, no thought of grieving!
Sweetly with their God they rest,
  All their toils and troubles leaving:

So be ours the faith that saveth,
Hope that every trial braveth,
Love that to the end endureth,
And, through Christ, the crown secureth!

Bp. Doane.

Raise it to Heaven when thine eye fills with tears,
For only in a watery sky appears
The bow of light; and from th' invisible skies
Hope's glory shines not, save through weeping eyes.

Frances Ann Kemble.

And when Time sweet opiates flings
From his swift, invisible wings,
Bearing from the heart away
Some slight anguish day by day;
Grief, through Memory's medium scanned,
  Mellow, sweet, and soft appears;
Though no smile the Past demand,
  Still it does not ask for tears.

And, when better still than this,
Comes Religion's soothing kiss,
Breathing on the wounded heart
Balm no other can impart,
Grief thenceforth is grief no more;
  All its power on earth shall cease,
But shall give, when life is o'er,
  Birth to deathless joy and peace. J. H. Clinch.

(*See also* Patience, Resignation.)

CONTENT.

But Godliness, with contentment, is great gain.
For we brought nothing into this world, and it is certain we can carry nothing out.
And, having food and raiment, let us be therewith content. I. Timothy, vi, 6, 7, 8.
I have learned, in whatsoever state I am, therewith to be content. Philippians, iv, 11.
Let your conversation be without covetousness; and be ye content with such things as ye have: for He hath said, I will never leave thee, nor forsake thee. Hebrews, xiii, 5.

Who God doth late and early pray,
More of His grace than gifts to lend;
And entertains the harmless day
With a religious book or friend;—
This man is freed from servile bands
Of hope to rise, or fear to fall;
Lord of himself, though not of lands,
And, having nothing, yet hath all.

Henry Wotton.

Take well whate'er shall chance, though bad it be,
Take it for good, and 't will be good to thee.

Thomas Randolph.

Think'st thou the man whose mansions hold
The worldling's pomp, and miser's gold,
Obtains a richer prize
Than he, who, in his cot at rest,
Finds, heavenly peace a willing guest,
And bears the promise in his breast
Of treasure in the skies?

Mrs. Sigourney.

Poor and content is rich and rich enough.

Shakspeare

conscience is my crown,
ontented thoughts my rest;
ıy heart is happy in itself,
My bliss is in my breast.

Enough I reckon wealth,
A mean the surest lot;
That lies too high for base contempt,
Too low for envy's shot. ROBERT SOUTHWELL.

LARGE scope of pleasure drowns us like a flood,
To rest in little is our greatest good.
SIR JOHN BEAUMONT.

LUXURY and pomp
Are but the splendid cover of distress
Rankling within; while conscience, ever gay,
And placid resignation to his lot,
Cheer the poor tattered pilgrim, and derive
A flavour to his casual homely meal,
The rich man's laboured dainties cannot yield.
GEORGE BALLY.

YET oft we see that some in humble state,
Are cheerful, pleasant, happy, and content:
When those, indeed, who are of higher state,
With vain additions do their thoughts torment.
The one would to his mind his fortune bind,
The other to his fortune frames his mind.
LADY CAREW.

MUCH will always wanting be
To him who much desires. Thrice happy he
To whom the wise indulgency of heaven,
With sparing hand, but just enough has given.
COWLEY.

THOUGH still thou get'st, yet is thy want not spent,
But, as thy wealth, so grows thy wealthy itch;
But with my little I have much content—
Content hath all; and who hath all, is rich:
  Then this in reason thou must needs confess—
  If I have little, yet that thou hast less.

Whatever man possesses, God hath lent,
And to his audit liable is, ever,
To reckon how, and when, and where he spent;
Then this thou bragg'st—thou art a great receiver:
  Little my debt, when little is my store—
  The more thou hast, the debt still grows the more.

PHINEAS FLETCHER.

WHO hath the mean with a contented mind,
Most perfect bliss his God hath him assigned.

THOMAS BLENNERHASSET.

THE wise example of the heavenly lark,
  Thy fellow-poet, mark;—
Above the clouds let thy proud music sound,
  Thy humble nest build on the ground. COWLEY.

CONTRITION—SORROW FOR SIN.

The Lord is nigh unto them that are of a broken heart; and saveth such as be of a contrite spirit. PSALM xxiv, 18.

I will declare mine iniquity; I will be sorry for my sin. PSALM xxxviii, 18.

The sacrifices of God are a broken spirit; a broken and a contrite heart, O God, Thou wilt not despise. PSALM li, 17.

Now I rejoice, not that ye were made sorry, but that ye sorrowed to repentance; for ye were made sorry after a godly manner, that ye might receive damage by us in nothing.

For Godly sorrow worketh repentance to salvation not to be repented of: but the sorrow of the world worketh death. II. CORINTHIANS, vii, 9, 10.

To this man will I look, even to him that is poor and of a contrite spirit, and trembleth at my word. ISAIAH, lxvi, 2.

Thus saith the high and lofty One that inhabiteth eternity, whose name is Holy: I dwell in the high and holy place, with him also that is of a contrite and humble spirit, to revive the spirit of the humble, and to revive the heart of the contrite ones. ISAIAH, lvii, 17.

ALL powerful is the penitential sigh
Of true contrition; like the placid wreaths
Of incense, wafted from the righteous shrine
Where Abel ministered, to the blest seat
Of Mercy, an accepted sacrifice,
Humiliation's conscious plaint ascends.

SAMUEL HAYES.

Lo! through the gloom of guilty fears,
My faith discerns a dawn of grace;
The Sun of Righteousness appears
In Jesus' reconciling face.

My suffering, slain, and risen Lord!
In deep distress I turn to thee—
I claim acceptance, in thy word,
My God! My God! forsake not me!

JAMES MONTGOMERY.

If, gracious God, in life's green, ardent year,
A thousand times thy patient love I tried;
With reckless heart, with conscience hard and sere,
Thy gifts perverted, and thy power defied:
O grant me, now that wintry snows appear
Around my brow, and youth's bright promise hide,—
Grant me with reverential awe to hear
Thy holy voice, and in thy word confide!
Blot from my book of life its early stain!
Since days misspent will never more return,
My future path do thou in mercy trace;
So cause my soul with pious zeal to burn,
That all the trust which in thy name I place,
Frail as I am, may not prove wholly vain.

PIETRO BEMBO.

'Tis well to be a mourner, well to feel
My glad hope die;
And sicken at the tears that daily steal
O'er the dimmed eye,
If this strong desolation should reveal
Where my sins lie.

E. L. MONTAGUE.

The very rod,
If we but kiss it as the stroke descendeth,
Distilleth oil to allay the inflicted smart,
And "peace that passeth understanding" blendeth
With the deep sighing of the contrite heart.

MRS. SOUTHEY.

My fears of danger, while I breathe,
My dread of endless hell beneath,
My sense of sorrow for my sin,
To springing comfort change within;
Change all my sad complaints for ease,
To cheerful notes of endless praise.

PARNELL.

LORD, have mercy when we strive
To save, through Thee, our souls alive!
When the pampered flesh is strong,
When the strife is fierce and long;
When our wakening thoughts begin
First to loathe their cherished sin,
And our weary spirits fail,
And our aching brows are pale,
Oh, then have mercy, Lord! H. H. MILMAN

HE can, He will, from out the dust,
Praise the blest spirits of the just;
Heal every wound, hush every fear,
From every eye wipe every tear;
And place them where distress is o'er,
And pleasures dwell forevermore. BP. MANT.

I SUFFER now for what hath former been,
Sorrow is held the eldest son of sin.
JOHN WEBSTER.

THE All-seeing Power,
To whom each secret from the human view
Removed, lies open, sanctifies alone
The offering of a contrite heart. SAMUEL HAYES.

(*See also* REPENTANCE.)

COURAGE.

The wicked flee when no man pursueth, but the righteous are bold as a lion. PROVERBS, xxviii, 1.

So that we may boldly say, The Lord is my helper, and I will not fear what man shall do unto me. HEBREWS, xiii, 6.

Fear not them which kill the body, but are not able to kill the soul: but rather fear Him which is able to destroy both soul and body in Hell. MATTHEW, x, 28

Say to them that are of a fearful heart, Be strong, fear not: behold, your God will come with vengeance, even God with a recompense; He will come and save you. ISAIAH, xxxv, 4.

Hearken unto me, ye that know righteousness, the people in whose heart is my law; fear ye not the reproach of men, neither be ye afraid of their revilings.

STAND but your ground, your ghostly foes will fly—
Hell trembles at a heaven-directed eye;
Choose rather to defend than to assail—
Self-confidence will in the conflict fail:
When you are challenged, you may dangers meet—
True courage is a fixed, not sudden heat;
Is always humble, lives in self-distrust,
And will itself into no danger thrust.
Devote yourself to God, and you will find
God fights the battles of a will resigned.
Love Jesus! Love will no base fear endure—
Love Jesus! And of conquest rest secure.

BISHOP KEN.

THE strength of man sinks in the hour of trial;
But there doth live a Power, that to the battle
Girdeth the weak.

JOANNA BAILLIE.

WHO the Creator love, created might
Dread not; within their tents no terrors walk.

COLERIDGE.

Thy life's a warfare, thou a soldier art,
Satan's thy foeman, and a faithful heart
Thy two-edged weapon, patience is thy shield,
Heaven is thy chieftain, and the world thy field.
To be afraid to die, or wish for death,
Are words and passions of despairing breath:
Who doth the first, the day doth faintly yield;
And who the second, basely flies the field.

Francis Quarles.

Fear to do base, unworthy things, is valour;
If they be done to us, to suffer them,
Is valour too. Ben Jonson.

In the good man's breast,
Justice and piety, with valour reign;
He, though the fabric of the shaken world
Should burst in thundering ruin o'er his head,
Calm and unawed would view the crushing wreck,
Nor shudder at destruction; but to brave
The wrath of Heaven, or rashly to intrude,
Spotted with guilt, into his Maker's sight;
Or lift for mercy, a rebellious hand
Dyed with a brother's gore, he justly fears;
Yet, in himself collected, will defy
The taunt of malice, or that groundless right
The weakest, lightest of mankind assume
To brand with infamy his injured name,
And scorn the coward, daring to forgive.

C. P. Layard.

That man alone is truly brave, whose soul
By virtue tutored, by religion swayed,
At their tribunal every impulse scans.

Samuel Hayes.

THAT courage which the vain for valour take,
Who proudly danger seek for glory's sake,
Is impudence; and what they rashly do,
Has no excuse, but that 't is madness too.
SIR WILLIAM DAVENANT.

CREATION.

IN the beginning, God created the heavens and the earth. GENESIS, i, 1.

In six days the Lord made heaven and earth, the sea, and all that in them is. EXODUS, xx, 11.

In the beginning was the Word, and the Word was with God, and the Word was God.

The same was in the beginning with God.

All things were made by Him, and without Him was nothing made that was made. JOHN, i, 1, 2, 3.

Let them praise the name of the Lord, for He commanded, and they were created. PSALM, cxlviii, 5.

O, all ye works of the Lord, bless ye the Lord, praise Him and exalt Him above all for ever. SONG OF THE THREE CHILDREN.

"LET there be light!" The Eternal spoke,
And from the abyss where darkness rode,
The earliest dawn of Nature broke,
And Light around Creation flowed.
The glad earth smiled to see the day,
The first-born day, come blushing in;
The young day smiled to shed its ray
Upon a world untouched by sin.
C. F. HOFFMAN.

MY heart is awed within me, when I think
Of the great miracle that still goes on,
In silence, round me — the perpetual work
Of thy creation, finished, yet renewed
For ever
WM. C. BRYANT.

THE Hand that built the palace of the sky,
Formed the light wings that decorate a fly;
The Power that wheels the circling planets round,
Rears every infant floweret on the ground;
That Bounty which the mightiest beings share,
Feeds the least gnat that gilds the evening air.

JAMES MONTGOMERY.

THEN moved upon the waveless deep
  The quickening Spirit of the Lord;
And broken was its pulseless sleep
  Before the Everlasting Word!
"Let there be Light!" and listening earth,
  With tree, and plant, and flowery sod,
"In the beginning" sprang to birth,
  Obedient to the voice of God.

W. H. BURLEIGH.

WITH what an awful world-revolving power
Were first the unwieldy planets launched along
The illimitable void! Thus to remain,
Amid the flux of many thousand years,
That oft has swept the toiling race of men
And all their laboured monuments away,
Firm, unremitting, matchless, in their course;
To the kind tempered change of night and day,
And of the seasons, ever stealing round,
Minutely faithful: such the All-perfect Hand,
That poised, impels, and rules, the steady whole.

THOMSON.

WHEN the Almighty Fiat, from the gloom
Of chaos drawn to light, had now arranged
The jarring seeds, the last, the most sublime
Of all His works, was Man called forth; to him
The Sovereign Word gave empire o'er the whole.

SAMUEL HAYES.

IN the Beginning primal darkness flung
  Her veil o'er chaos, void and formless all;
The brooding Spirit o'er the waters hung;
  The Father's fiat moved the empty pall:
"Let there be Light!" Forthwith Creation sprung
  Glad into being. Thy Creating Love,
Lord, I believe! Mine unbelief remove!

H. H. WELD.

CONFUSION heard His voice, and wild uproar
Stood ruled, stood vast infinitude confined;
Till, at His second bidding, darkness fled,
Light shone, and order from disorder sprung:
Swift to their several quarters hasted then
The cumbrous elements, Earth, Flood, Air, Fire;
And this ethereal quintessence of Heaven
Flew upward, spirited with various forms,
That rolled orbicular, and turned to stars
Numberless, as thou seest, and how they move:
Each had his place appointed, each his course.

MILTON.

THE CROSS.

BUT God forbid that I should glory, save in the Cross of our Lord Jesus Christ, by whom the world is crucified unto me, and I unto the world. GALATIANS, vi, 14.

And he that taketh not his cross, and followeth after me, is not worthy of me. MATTHEW, x, 38.

For the preaching of the cross is, to them that perish, foolishness; but unto us, which are saved, it is the power of God. 1. CORINTHIANS, i, 18.

THE way to bliss lies not on a bed of down,
And he that had no cross deserves no crown.

FRANCIS QUARLES.

THERE, where the cross in hoary ruin nods,
  And weeping yews o'ershade the lettered stones;
While midnight silence wraps these dark abodes,
  And soothes me, wand'ring o'er my kindred bones;
Let kindled fancy view the glorious morn,
  When from the bursting graves the dust shall rise,
All nature smiling; and, by angels borne,
  Messiah's cross, far blazing o'er the skies.

MICKLE.

CAST up thy tearful eyes
To where thy Lord and Love was crucified;
So shall the world, and all its vanities
Appear like dross — ambition, lust, and pride,
Shall far, far off their baleful powers remove,
And in the pure, unspotted mind
Nothing remain behind,
But adoration, ecstacy, and love.

JAMES SCOTT.

IF the wanderer his mistake discern,
Judge his own ways, and sigh for a return,
Bewildered once, must he bewail his loss
For ever and for ever? No — the cross!
There, and there only, (though the Deist rave
And Atheist, if earth bear so base a slave);
There, and there only, is the power to save.
There no delusive hope invites despair;
No mockery meets you, no delusion there;
The spells and charms that blinded you before,
All vanish there, and fascinate no more.

COWPER

OR if, at times, wild storms shall hover, dark,
Still fix thy gaze upon that hallowed mark
Which gilds the tempest with hope's bow divine —
Cling to the Cross, and conquer in that sign.

B. D. WINSLOW.

GUIDE me there, for here I burn
To make my Saviour some return.
I'll rise (if that will please thee, still,
And sure I've heard thee own it will;)
I'll trace His steps and bear my cross,
Despising every grief and loss;
Since He, despising pain and shame,
First took up His, and did the same. PARNELL.

How blessed the man, how fully so,
As far as man is blessed below,
Who, taking up his cross, essays,
To follow Jesus all his days. PARNELL.

THE cross once seen is death to every vice:
Else He that died there suffered all His pain,
Bled, groaned, and agonized, and died, in vain.
COWPER.

THROUGH cross to crown! And, through the spirit's life,
Trials untold assail with giant strength.
Good cheer! good cheer! Soon ends the bitter strife,
And thou shalt reign, in peace, with Christ, at length.
ROSEGARTEN.

MY trust is in the Cross, there lies my rest,
My fast, my sole delight.
Let cold-mouthed Boreas, or the hot-mouthed East,
Blow till they burst with spite;
Let earth and hell conspire their worst, their best,
And join their twisted might;
Let showers of thunderbolts dart round and round me,
And troops of fiends surround me:
All this may well confront; all this shall ne'er confound me. FRANCIS QUARLES.

My soul is caught:
Heaven's sovereign blessings, clustering from the cross,
Rush on her in a throng, and close her round,
The prisoner of amaze! — In His blessed life
I see the path, and, in His death, the price,
And in His great ascent, the proof supreme
Of immortality. YOUNG.

(*See also* ATONEMENT, CRUCIFIXION, REDEMPTION.)

THE CRUCIFIXION.

CHRIST our passover is sacrificed for us: Therefore let us keep the feast, not with old leaven, neither with the leaven of malice and wickedness; but with the unleavened bread of sincerity and truth. I. CORINTHIANS, v, 7, 8.

But we preach Christ crucified, unto the Jews a stumbling-block, and unto the Greeks foolishness;

But unto them which are called, both Jews and Greeks, Christ the power of God, and the wisdom of God. I. CORINTHIANS, i, 23, 24.

For if the blood of bulls and of goats, and the ashes of a heifer sprinkling the unclean, sanctifieth to the purifying of the flesh:

How much more shall the blood of Christ, who through the eternal spirit offered himself without spot to God, purge your conscience from dead works to serve the Living God? HEBREWS, ix, 12, 13.

Christ was once offered to bear the sins of many; and unto them that look for Him shall he appear the second time, without sin, unto salvation. HEBREWS, ix, 28.

For by one offerin' He hath perfected for ever them that are sanctified. HEBREWS, x, 14.

Let us go forth therefore unto Him without the camp, bearing His reproach. HEBREWS, xiii, 13.

He dies; in whose high victory,
The slayer, death himself, shall die.
He dies; by whose all-conquering tread
Shall yet be crushed the serpent's head;
From his proud throne to darkness hurled,
The god and tempter of this world.

He dies; creation's awful Lord,
Jehovah, Christ, Eternal Word!
To come in thunder from the skies;
To bid the buried world arise;
The earth His footstool, heaven His throne;—
Redeemer! may Thy will be done! CROLY.

WELL may the cavern depths of earth
Be shaken, and her mountains nod;
Well may the sheeted dead come forth
To gaze upon a suffering God!
Well may the temple-shrine grow dim,
And shadows veil the Cherubim,
When He, the chosen One of Heaven,
A sacrifice for guilt is given! J. G. WHITTIER.

WHEN with deep agony His heart was racked,
Not for Himself the tear-drop dewed His cheek,
For *them* He wept, for *them* to Heaven He prayed,—
His persecutors—"Father, pardon them;
They know not what they do." CHARLES LAMB.

BEHOLD Him now
Suspended on the cross! On His pale brow
Hang the cold drops of death; through every limb
The piercing torture rages; every nerve
Stretched with excess of pain, trembles convulsed.
Now look beneath, and view the senseless crowd;
How they deride His sufferings, how they shake
Their heads contemptuous, while the bitter taunt,
More bitter than the gall they gave, insults
The agony of Him on whom they gaze.
But hark! He speaks, and the still hovering breath
Wafts His last prayer to all-approving Heaven:
"Forgive them, for they know not what they do!"
C. P. LAYARD.

SEE where man's voluntary sacrifice
Bows His meek head, the God eternal dies!
Fixed to the Cross His bleeding arms are bound,
While copious Mercy streams from every wound.

BP. LOWTH.

LOVELY was the death
Of Him whose life was love! Holy, with power,
He on the thought-benighted skeptic beamed
Manifest Godhead. COLERIDGE.

UPON the Cross He hung, and bowed the head,
And prayed for them that smote, and them that curst
And, drop by drop, His slow life-blood was shed,
And His last hour of suffering was His worst.

H. H. MILMAN.

THOU who for me didst feel such pain,
Whose precious blood the cross did stain,
Let not those agonies be vain. ROSCOMMON.

THE sun beheld it — No, the shocking scene
Drove back his chariot: midnight veiled his face;
Not such as this; not such as nature makes;
A midnight nature shuddered to behold;
A midnight new! a dread eclipse (without
Opposing spheres,) from her Creator's frown!
Sun! didst thou fly thy Maker's pain? or start
At that enormous load of human guilt,
Which bowed His blessed head; o'erwhelmed his cross;
Made groan the centre; burst earth's marble womb
With pangs, strange pangs! delivered of her dead?
Hell howled, and Heaven that hour let fall a tear;
Heaven wept that man might smile! Heaven bled that man
Might never die! YOUNG.

THOU palsied earth, with noon-day night o'erspread!
Thou sickening sun, so dark, so deep, so red!
Ye hovering ghosts, that throng the starless air,
Why shakes the earth? Why fades the light? Declare!
Are those His limbs, with ruthless scourges torn?
His brows, all bleeding with the twisted thorn?
His the pale form, the meek, forgiving eye,
Raised from the cross in patient agony?

BP. HEBER.

YET not with man His Holiness could plead;
His own familiar friend a foe He found.
Pagans and Priests uniting in the deed,
His limbs they scourged, His brows with thorns they bound.
In mocking purple, with a sceptre reed,
"Behold the Man!" Thy Patient, Suffering Love,
Lord, I believe! Mine unbelief remove!

The burden of our sin upon Him fell;
Between two thieves they led the Just to death.
The sun withdrawn, rocks rent, and earthquakes, tell
The world-weight value of His passing breath.
His body to the grave, His soul to Hell
For us descend. Thy Saving, Dying Love,
Lord, I believe! Mine unbelief remove!

H. H. WELD.

(*See also* REDEMPTION, ATONEMENT, CROSS.)

DAVID.

He chose David also, his servant, and took him from the sheepfolds:

From following the ewes great with young, he brought him to feed Jacob his people, and Israel his inheritance. PSALM lxxviii, 70, 71.

Blessed be the Lord God of Israel, for He hath visited and redeemed His people,

And hath raised up a horn of salvation for us, in the house of His servant David LUKE, i, 68, 69.

For David speaketh concerning Him, I foresaw the Lord always before my face. ACTS, ii, 25.

All things must be fulfilled which were written in the law of Moses, and in the prophets, and in the Psalms, concerning me. LUKE, xxiv, 44.

David, the son of Jesse, the man who was raised up on high, the anointed of the God of Jacob, the sweet Psalmist of Israel. II. SAMUEL, xxiii, 1.

ONE struggle of might, and the giant of Gath,
With a crash like the oak in the hurricane's path,
And a clangour of arms, as of hosts in the fray,
At the feet of the stripling of Ephratah lay.

A hush of amazement; — a calm as of death,
When the watcher lists long for that spasm-drawn breath,
Then a shout like the roll of artillery rose,
And the armies of Israel swept on their foes.

For a space the Philistines had paused, as in doubt,
Ere the Israelite triumph rang gloriously out;
Then, scattering his arms on the mountains, he fled,
Till the valley of Elah was strewn with the dead.

The carnage moved on, and alone in the vale,
The Shepherd knelt down by the dead in his mail,
And there, with his arm on that still reeking sword,
Poured forth his thanksgiving in prayer to the Lord.

From "CAPRICES."

And lo! the glories of the illustrious line
At their first dawn with ripened splendours shine.
In David all expressed; the good, the great,
The king, the hero, and the man, complete.
Serene he sits, and sweeps the golden lyre,
And blends the prophet's with the poet's fire.
See, with what art he strikes the vocal strings,
The God his theme, inspiring what he sings!

Bp. Lowth.

A prince,
With every gift adorned, and framed alike
To dare the horrors of the tented field,
While battle rolled against his side, or grace
The gentle arts of peace. William Hodson.

Amidst the royal race, see Nathan stand:
Fervent he seems to speak, and lifts his hand;
His looks the emotion of his soul disclose,
And eloquence from every gesture flows.
Such, and so stern he came, ordained to bring
The ungrateful mandate to the guilty king:
When, at his dreadful voice, a sudden smart
Shot through the trembling monarch's conscious heart,
From his own lips condemned, severe decree,
Had his God proved as stern a Judge as he.

Bp. Lowth.

Wide he extends
His royalties, and still the throne adorns
With piety and mercy. Loved and feared,
Twice twenty years, with equitable hand,
He sways the sceptre; then in peace repose
His ashes, but his name lives evermore.

Charles Hoyle.

SEE Judah's promised king, bereft of all;
Driven out an exile from the face of Saul.
To distant caves the lonely wanderer flies,
To seek that peace a tyrant's frown denies.
Hear the sweet accents of his tuneful voice;
Hear him, o'erwhelmed with sorrows, yet rejoice;
No womanish or wailing grief has part,
No, not a moment, in his royal heart;
'Tis manly music, such as martyrs make,
Suffering with gladness for a Saviour's sake;
His soul exults; hope animates his lays;
The sense of mercy kindles into praise;
And wilds, familiar with the lion's roar,
Ring with ecstatic sounds unheard before. COWPER.

THY living lyre alone, whose dulcet sounds
In gentlest murmurs floating on the air,
Could calm the fury of the woe-struck king,
And soothe the agony which pierced his heart.
Or when thou swept the master strings, and rolled'st
The deep impetuous tide along with more
Than mortal sound, could'st raise his raptured soul
To ecstacy; or from the tortured strings
Harsh discord shaking, sink him in the gulph
Of dire despair, while horror chilled his blood,
And from each pore the agonizing sweat
Distilled; that deep-toned lyre alone can sing
Thy fervent piety, thy glowing zeal.

WILLIAM HODSON.

DEATH.

All go unto one place; all are of dust, and all turn to dust again. Ecclesiastes iii, 20.

All flesh shall perish together, and man shall turn again into dust. Job, xxxiv, 15.

Then shall the earth return unto the dust as it was, and the spirit unto God who gave it. Ecclesiastes, xii, 7.

Let me die the death of the righteous, and let my last end be like his! Numbers, xxiii, 10.

Blessed are the dead which die in the Lord from henceforth: yea, saith the Spirit, that they may rest from their labours; and their works do follow them. Revelations, xiv, 13.

What man is he that liveth, and shall not see death? Shall he deliver his soul from the hand of the grave? Psalm, lxxxix, 48.

Precious in the sight of the Lord is the death of his saints. Psalm, cxvi, 15.

Forasmuch then as the children are partakers of flesh and blood, He also himself likewise took part of the same; that through death He might destroy him who had the power of death, that is, the devil;

And deliver them who, through fear of death, were all their lifetime subject to bondage. Hebrews, ii, 14, 15.

O death, where is thy sting? O grave, where is thy victory?

The sting of death is sin; and the strength of sin is the law.

But thanks be to God, which giveth us the victory, through our Lord Jesus Christ. I Corinthians, xv, 55, 56, 57.

It matters not, how, or when I die;
But I lift, O God! my humble prayer,
That my hand from my brother's blood be clear;
Like the righteous man's let my spirit flee,
And like his, like his, let my last end be.

R. M. Charlton.

All at rest now — all dust! — wave flows on wave;
But the sea dries not! — what to us the grave?
It brings no real homily; we sigh,
Pause for awhile and murmur, "all must die!"
Then rush to pleasure, action, sin once more,
Swell the loud tide, and fret unto the shore.

Sir E. Bulwer Lytton.

O WHAT is death? 'T is life's last shore,
Where vanities are vain no more!
Where all pursuits their goal obtain,
And life is all retouched again;
Where, in their bright results, shall rise
Thoughts, virtues, friendships, griefs, and joys.

LEIGH RICHMOND.

THE lovely bud, so young and fair,
Called hence by early doom,
Just came to show how sweet a flower
In paradise would bloom.

LEIGH RICHMOND.

DEATH has no terrors for the Christian's soul,
His sting's extracted, and his mighty dart
Was blunted by its task on Calvary.

JOSEPH H. WYTHES.

THE man, how wise, who, sick of gaudy scenes,
Is led by choice to take his favourite walk
Beneath death's gloomy, silent cypress shades,
Unpierced by vanity's fantastic ray!
To read his monuments, to weigh his dust,
Visit his vaults, and dwell among the tombs!

YOUNG.

COLD hand, I touch thee! Perished friend! I know
What years of mutual joy are gone with thee;
And yet from those benumbed remains there flow
Calm thoughts, that first with chastened hopes agree.

How strange is Death to Life! and yet how sure
The law which dooms all living things to die!
Whate'er is outward cannot long endure,
And all that lasts, eludes the subtlest eye.

JOHN STERLING.

ON a snow-white couch,
Wrapped in the pure habiliments of death,
Was laid an infant. Like a form of wax
It was, so fair, even to transparency,
And beautifully moulded. But the lips
Were livid, and the eyes closed heavily,
In the eternal sleep. LYDIA JANE PEIRSON.

WE weep, though not in bitterness,
Ours are not tears of gloom;
No thoughts, but those of tenderness,
Shall glisten round his tomb;
No painful recollections rise —
His morn — it dawned so blest,
And, ere a cloud had dimmed its skies,
Sweet lamb, he was at rest. WM. PETER.

HAPPY the babe, who, privileged by fate
To shorter labour, and a lighter weight,
Received but yesterday the gift of breath,
Ordered to-morrow to return to Death. PRIOR.

'TIS not the stoic's lessons got by rote,
The pomp of words, and pedant dissertations,
That can sustain thee in that hour of terror;
Books have taught cowards to talk nobly of it,
But when the trial comes, they stand aghast;
Hast thou considered what may happen after it?
How thy account may stand, and what to answer?
NICHOLAS ROWE.

LEAVES have their time to fall,
And flowers to wither at the North wind's breath,
And stars to set — but all,
Thou hast all seasons for thine own, O Death!
MRS. HEMANS

Ere sin could blight, or sorrow fade,
  Death came with friendly care,
The opening bud to Heaven conveyed,
  And bade it blossom there. Coleridge.

My joy is — death;
Death, at whose name I oft have been afeard,
Because I wished this world's eternity.
Shakspeare.

Death gives us more than was in Eden lost.
The king of terrors is the Prince of Peace.
Young.

Soon as man, expert from time, has found
The key of life, it opes the gates of death.
Young

Whatever farce the boastful hero plays,
Virtue alone has majesty in death;
And, greater still, the more the tyrant frowns.
Young

On this side, and on that, men see their friends
Drop off, like leaves in autumn; yet launch out
Into fantastic schemes, which the long-livers,
In the world's hale and undegenerate days,
Could scarce have leisure for; fools that we are!
Never to think of death, and of ourselves,
At the same time! As if, to learn to die
Were no concern of ours! Blair

A death-bed's a detector of the heart;
Here tired dissimulation drops her mask,
Through life's grimace, that mistress of the scene.
Young.

Behold the inexorable hour at hand!
Behold the inexorable hour forgot!
And to forget it, the chief aim of life;
Though well to ponder it is life's chief end.
Young.

Death is, no doubt, in every place the same;
Yet nature casts a look towards home, and most,
Who have it in their power, choose to expire
Where first they drew their breath. Lillo.

Is that a death-bed where the Christian lies?
Yes, but not his: 'Tis death itself there dies.
Coleridge.

O Death! Thou great invisible,
  Pale monarch of the unending Past,
Who shall thy countless trophies tell,
  Or when shall be the last!
By thee high thrones to earth are flung—
  By thee the sword and sceptre rust—
By thee the beautiful and young
  Lie mouldering in the dust.
Into thy cold and faded reign
  All glorious things of earth depart;
The fairest forms are early slain,
  And quenched the fiery heart.
But in yon world thou hast not been,
  Where joy can fade, nor beauty fall:
O, mightiest of the things unseen,
  Save One that ruleth all! Geo. H. Colton.

Sure the last end
Of the good man is peace. How calm his exit!
Night dews fall not more calmly on the ground,
Nor weary, worn-out winds expire so soft. Blair.

Men may live fools, but fools they cannot die.
Young.

When the good man yields his breath,
(For the good man never dies,)
Bright, beyond the gulf of death,
To the land of promise lies!
James Montgomery.

Kneel down by the dying sinner's side,
And pray for his soul through Him who died.
Large drops of anguish are on his brow—
O, what are earth and its pleasures now!
And what shall assuage his dark despair,
But the penitent cry of humble prayer?
Henry Ware, Jr.

Hear the last words the believer saith.
He has bidden adieu to his earthly friends;
There is peace in his eye that upward bends;
There is peace in his calm, confiding air;
For his last thoughts are God's, his last words, .prayer
Henry Ware, Jr.

Our God, to call us homeward,
His only Son sent down;
And now, still more to tempt our hearts,
Has taken up our own. Thomas Ward.

And I am glad that he has lived thus long,
And glad that he has gone to his reward:
Nor deem that kindly Nature did him wrong,
Softly to disengage the vital cord.
When his weak hand grew palsied, and his eye
Dark with the mists of age, it was his time to die.
Wm. C. Bryant.

AND her last fond, lingering look is given
To the love she leaves, and then to Heaven.
As if she would bear that love away,
To a purer world, and a brighter day.
J. G. PERCIVAL.

BUT O, how frightful is the pain, when death shall read our doom,
To find that all our hopes are vain, and crumble in the tomb;
To have no precious word of love thrill on the failing breath,
And see no arm around, above, to strengthen us for death!
C. M. F. DEEMS.

THE dead,
The only beautiful, who change no more;
The only blest, the dwellers on the shore
Of Spring fulfilled. The dead! — whom call we so?
They that breathe purer air, that feel, that know,
Things wrapt from us. MRS. HEMANS.

DUST to its narrow house beneath!
Soul to its place on high!
They that have seen thy look in death,
No more may fear to die. MRS. HEMANS.

DEATH'S but a path that must be trod,
If men would ever pass to God. PARNELL.

HEAVEN gives us friends to bless the present scene;
Resumes them to prepare us for the next. YOUNG.

THY skeleton hand
Shows to the faint of spirit the right path,
And he is warned, and fears to step aside.
Thou settest between the ruffian and his crime
Thy ghastly countenance, and his slack hand
Drops the drawn knife. WM. C. BRYANT.

Deliverer!
God hath anointed thee to free the oppressed,
And crush the oppressor. Wm. C. Bryant.

Thus from the first of time, thou hast been found
On virtue's side; the wicked, but for thee,
Had been too strong for the good; the great of earth
Had crushed the weak, for ever.

Wm. C. Bryant.

Is this death's seal? The impression, O, how fair!
Look what a radiant smile is playing there!
That was the soul's farewell: — the sacred dust
Awaits the resurrection of the just.

Geo. B. Cheever.

This world death's region is, the other, life's:
And here it should be one of our first strifes,
So to front death, as each might judge us past it:
For good men but see death, the others taste it.

Ben Jonson.

(*See also* The Grave, The Departed.)

THE DELUGE—NOAH.

By faith Noah, being warned of God of things not seen as yet, moved with fear, prepared an ark to the saving of his house; by the which he condemned the world, and became heir of the righteousness which is by faith. HEBREWS, xi, 7.

God spared not the old world, but saved Noah, the eighth person, a preacher of righteousness, bringing in the flood upon the world of the ungodly. II. PETER, ii, 5.

For as in the days that were before the flood they were eating and drinking, marrying, and giving in marriage, until the day that Noe entered into the ark,

And knew not until the flood came and took them all away; so shall also the coming of the Son of Man be. MATTHEW, xxiv, 38, 39.

And it shall come to pass, when I bring a cloud over the earth, that the bow shall be seen in the cloud:

And I will remember my covenant, which is between me and you, and every living thing of all flesh; and the waters shall no more become a cloud to destroy all flesh. GENESIS, ix, 14, 15.

THE hills beneath the swelling waters stood,
And all the globe of earth was but one flood.

SANDYS.

THE rainbow bending in the sky,
  Bedecked with sundry hues,
Is like the seat of God on high,
  And seems to tell these news:—
That as, thereby, He promised
  To drown the world no more,
So, by the blood which Christ has shed,
  He will our souls restore. GEORGE GASCOIGNE.

ALL now was turned to jollity and game,
To luxury and riot, feast and dance,
Marrying or prostituting, as befel,
Rape or adultery, where passing fair
Allured them: thence from cups to civil broils.

MILTON.

SUNK beneath the wave,
The guilty share an universal grave;
One wilderness of waters rolls in view,
And heaven and ocean wear one turbid hue;
Still stream unbroken torrents from the skies,
Higher, beneath, the inundations rise;
A lurid twilight glares athwart the scene,
Now thunders peal, faint lightnings flash between.

JAMES MONTGOMERY.

HE preached
Conversion and repentance, as to souls
In prison under dangers imminent:
But all in vain, which, when he saw, he ceased
Contending, and removed his tents far off.
Then from the mountain hewing timbers tall,
Began to build a vessel of huge bulk.

MILTON.

METHINKS I see a distant vessel ride,
A lonely object on the shoreless tide;
Within whose ark the innocent have found
Safety, when stayed destruction ravens round;
Thus, in the hour of vengeance, God, who knows
His servants, spares them, while He smites His foes.

JAMES MONTGOMERY.

SUCH thou hast shone, bright rainbow! when the sky
Has clothed in clouds its blue serenity;
And such shall shine, while, grateful for the vow,
All nations of the earth to heaven shall bow.
Curbing the tempest on its thunder path,
Chaining the boisterous billows in their wrath;
Mystic symbol of thy Maker's might!
Girdle of beauty! coronal of light!
God's own blest handmark, mystic, sure, sublime,
Graven in glory to the end of time!

ANONYMOUS.

AND now, the thickening sky
Like a dark ceiling stood; down rushed the rain
Impetuous, and continued till the earth
No more was seen. The floating vessel swam
Uplifted, and secure with beaked prow,
Rode tilting o'er the waves: all dwellings else
Flood overwhelmed, and them, with all their pomp,
Deep under water rolled; sea covered sea,
Sea without shore: and in their palaces,
Where luxury late reigned, sea monsters whelped
And stabled. Of mankind, so numerous late,
All left in one small bottom swam imbarked.

MILTON

THE DEPARTED.

BUT now he is dead, wherefore should I fast? Can I bring him back again? I shall go to him, but he shall not return to me. II. SAMUEL, xii, 23.

Is it well with the child? And she answered, It is well. II. KINGS, iv, 26.

Weep not for the dead, neither bemoan him; but weep sore for him that goeth away for he shall return no more, nor see his native country. JEREMIAH, xxii, 10.

But I would not have you to be ignorant, brethren, concerning them which are asleep, that ye sorrow not, even as others which have no hope.

For if we believe that Jesus died and rose again, even so also them which sleep in JESUS, will God bring with him. I. THESSALONIANS, iv, 13, 14.

GOD gives us ministers of love
  Which we regard not, being near;
Death takes them from us,—then we feel
  That angels have been with us here!
As mother, sister, friend, or wife,
  They guide us, cheer us, soothe our pain;
And when the grave has closed between
  Our hearts and theirs, we love — in vain!

JAMES ALDRICH.

UNGRATEFUL shall we grieve their hovering shades,
Which wait the revolution in our hearts?
Shall we disdain their silent, soft address,
Their posthumous advice and pious prayer?

YOUNG.

I SOMETIMES deem their pleasant smiles
  Still on me sweetly fall,
Their tones of love I faintly hear
  My name in sadness call.
I know that they are happy
  With their angel plumage on,
But my heart is very desolate,
  To think that they are gone.

PARK BENJAMIN.

  O, WEEP not for the dead!
Rather, O rather give the tear
To those that darkly linger,
  When all besides are fled:
Weep for the spirit withering
In its cold, cheerless sorrowing;
Weep for the young and lovely one
That ruin darkly revels on;
    But never be a tear-drop shed
    For them, the pure, enfranchised dead.

MRS. MARY E. BROOKS.

EACH friend by fate snatched from us, is a plume
Plucked from the wing of human vanity,
Which makes us stoop from our aerial heights,
And, damped with omen of our own decease,
On drooping pinions of ambition lowered,
Just skim earth's surface, ere we break it up;
O'er putrid earth to scratch a little dust,
And save the world a nuisance.

YOUNG.

WE grieve to think, our eyes no more
  That form, those features loved, shall trace:
But sweet it is, from memory's store
  To call each fondly cherished grace,
  And fold them in the heart's embrace.
No bliss 'mid worldly crowds is bred,
Like musing on the sainted dead. BP. MANT.

THE friends gone there before me,
  Are calling from on high,
And happy angels o'er me,
  Tempt sweetly to the sky;
"Why wait," they say, "and wither,
  'Mid scenes of death and sin?
O, rise to glory hither,
  And find true life begin." BRITISH MAGAZINE.

BUT when I go
To my lone bed, I find no mother there;
And weeping kneel, to say the prayer she taught;
Or when I read the Bible that she loved,
Or to her vacant seat at Church draw near,
And think of her, a voice is in my heart,
Bidding me early seek my God, and love
My Blessed Saviour; and that voice is her's,
I know it is, because these were the words
She used to speak so tenderly, with tears,
At the still twilight hour, — or when we walked
Forth in the Spring, among rejoicing birds,
Or peaceful talked beside the Winter hearth.
MRS. SIGOURNEY.

SAY, who can mourn
Over the smitten idol, by long years
Cemented with his being, yet perceive
No dark remembrance that he fain would blot,

Troubling the tear? If there were no kind deed
Omitted, no sweet, healing word of love
Expected, yet unspoken; no light tone
That struck discordant on the shivering nerve,
For which the weeper fain would rend the tomb
To cry, "Forgive." O, let him kneel and praise
God amid all his grief. MRS. SIGOURNEY.

DEAR, beauteous Death, the jewel of the just,
  Shining no where but in the dark,
What mysteries do lie beyond thy dust,
  Could man outlook that mark!
He that hath found some fledg'd bird's nest may know
  At first sight, if the bird be flown;
But what fair field or grove he sings in now,
  That is to him unknown. HENRY VAUGHAN.

(*See also* DEATH, GRAVE, &c.)

DEVOTION—HOLY DESIRES.

;ood to be zealously affected always in a good thing. GALATIANS, iv, 18.
out man, and one that feared God with all his house, which gave much alms to
ıle, and prayed to God alway. ACTS, x, 2.
ul thirsteth for God, for the living God: when shall I come and appear before
SALM xlii, 2.
ech you therefore, brethren, by the mercies of God, that ye present your bodies
sacrifice, holy, acceptable unto God, which is your reasonable service. ROMANS

:e evermore. Pray without ceasing. In everything give thanks: for this is the
God, in Christ Jesus, concerning you. I. THESSALONIANS, v, 16, 17, 18.
nt in spirit, serving the Lord. ROMANS, xii, 11.
e are bought with a price, therefore glorify God in your body, and in your spirit
.re God's. I. CORINTHIANS, vi, 20.

O, THAT mine eye might closed be
To what concerns me not to see;
That deafness might possess mine ear
To what concerns me not to hear;

That Truth my tongue might always tie
From ever speaking foolishly;
That no vain thought might ever rest,
Or be conceived, in my breast;
That by each word, and deed, and thought,
Glory may to my God be brought!

THOMAS ELLWOOD.

DEVOTION, when lukewarm, is undevout;
But when it glows, its heat is struck to heaven:
To human hearts her golden harps are strung;
High Heaven's orchestra chants Amen to man.

YOUNG.

LET there be light!
Devotion on her bended knee,
When doubt and darkness will not flee,
Lifts up this earnest prayer to Thee,
Great Infinite;
And reason, blighted by the fall,
When truth heeds not her earnest call,
Offers, in fervent, feverish grief,
This, her petition for relief.

From "CAPRICES."

MAN at home, within himself, may find
The Deity immense, and in that frame
So fearfully, so wonderfully made,
See and adore His providence and power.
I see, and I adore! O God most bounteous!
O Infinite of goodness and of glory!
The knee that Thou hast shaped, shall bend to Thee;
The tongue which Thou hast tuned, shall chant Thy praise.
And Thine own image, the immortal soul,
Shall consecrate herself to Thee, for ever!

CHRISTOPHER SMART.

O, FOR a message from above
 To bear my spirits up!
Some pledge of my Creator's love
To calm my terrors, and support my hope!
 Let waves and thunders mix and roar,
Be Thou my God, and the whole world is mine:
 While Thou art Sovereign I'm secure;
 I shall be rich till Thou art poor;
For all I fear, and all I wish, Heaven, Earth, and
 Hell, are thine.

WATTS.

BEAUTY;—may that of holiness be mine;
May power be given me to o'ercome the world;
For Pleasure, may I have a hand to pour
The oil and wine upon another's wound!
For Honour, may I bear my Saviour's cross;
For Splendour, light that from His follower beams;
And be my Glory His approving smile;
My Fame, the world's reproaches for His sake;
My Wealth, a conscience where no rust corrodes—
One that may look into a coming world,
As nature shall dissolve, and feel secure!
With these to aid me in the mortal strife,
May I, the palm of victory o'er the grave,
Make my immortal prize!

HANNAH F. GOULD.

O, I AM weary of this sinful life!
 Weary of error, and yet erring still,
 Knowing, yet doing not Thy holy will,
O, I am weary of this endless strife!

I ask not that Thou take me from the earth,
 But keep me from its evils—guide my feet,
 And give me strength its many cares to meet—
To act all worthy of my heavenly birth.

MARY J. REED.

EARTH—THE WORLD.

BE not conformed to this world, but be ye transformed by the renewing of your mi that ye may prove what is that good, and acceptable, and perfect will of God. ROMA xii, 2.

The friendship of the world is enmity with God: whosoever therefore will be a frie of the world, is the enemy of God. JAMES, iv, 4.

What shall it profit a man, if he shall gain the whole world, and lose his own so MARK, iii, 36.

If the world hate you, ye know that it hated me before it hated you.

If ye were of the world, the world would love his own: but because ye are not of world, but I have chosen you out of the world, therefore the world hateth you. Jo xv, 18, 19.

The cares of this world, and the deceitfulness of riches, and the lusts of other thi entering in, choke the word, and it becometh unfruitful. MARK, ix, 19.

THE world's a school
Of wrong, and what proficients swarm around
We must or imitate or disapprove;
Must 'list as their accomplices or foes;
That stains our innocence, this wounds our peace.

YOUNG.

PASS on, relentless world! I grieve
No more for all that thou hast riven;
Pass on, in God's name, only leave
The things thou never yet hast given—
A heart at ease, a mind at home,
Affections fixed above thy sway,
Faith set upon a world to come,
And patience through life's little day.

GEORGE LUNT.

THE world is too much with us; late and soon,
Getting and spending, we lay waste our powers.

WORDSWORTH.

EARTH'S cup
Is poisoned; her renown, most infamous;
Her gold, seem as it may, is really dust;
Her titles, slanderous names; her praise, reproach;
Her strength, an idiot's boast; her wisdom, blind;
Her gain, eternal loss; her hope, a dream;
Her love, her friendship, enmity with God;
Her promises, a lie; her smile, a harlot's;
Her beauty, paint, and rotten within; her pleasures,
Deadly assassins masked; her laughter, grief;
Her breasts, the sting of death; her total sum,
Her all, most total vanity. POLLOK.

I BELIEVE this earth on which we stand
Is but the vestibule to glorious mansions,
Through which a moving crowd for ever press.
JOANNA BAILLIE.

THE world and Christ have different measurements:
While He has said that, Blessed are the meek,
Who in forgiveness their avengement seek,
The world applauds a coward who resents
A scornful word — whose craven spirit fears
His Maker's anger less than man's disdainful leers.
THOMAS MCKELLAR.

A PUFF of honour fills the mind,
And yellow dust is solid good;
Thus, like the ass of savage kind,
We snuff the breezes of the wind,
Or steal the serpent's food.
Could all the choirs
That charm the poles
But strike one doleful sound,
'T would be employed to mourn our souls;
Souls that were formed of sprightly fires
In floods of folly drowned.

Souls made of glory seek a brutal joy;
  How they disclaim their heavenly birth,
Melt their bright substance down with drossy earth,
And hate to be refined from that impure alloy.

WATTS.

AND had earth, then, no joys? no native sweets,
No happiness, that one who spoke the truth,
Might call her own? She had, true native sweets,
Indigenous delights, which up the Tree
Of Holiness, embracing as they grew,
Ascended, and bore fruit of heavenly taste.

POLLOK.

WHAT is this world?
What but a spacious burial-field, unwalled,
Strewed with death's spoils, the spoils of animals,
Savage and tame, and full of dead men's bones?
The very turf on which we tread once lived,
And we that live must lend our carcasses,
To cover our own offspring: in their turns,
They too must cover theirs.

BLAIR.

THERE'S nothing here but what as nothing weighs;
The more our joy, the more we know it vain;
And by success are tutored to despair.
Nor is it only thus, but must be so.
Who knows not this, though grey, is still a child;
Loose then from earth the grasp of fond desire,
Weigh anchor, and some happier clime explore.

YOUNG.

LEAN not on earth; 'twill pierce thee to the heart;
A broken reed at best, but oft a spear:
On its sharp point peace bleeds, and hope expires.

YOUNG.

VIRTUE, for ever frail as fair below,
Her tender nature suffers in the crowd,
Nor touches on the world without a stain;
The world's infectious. YOUNG.

SOMETIMES we feel the wish across the mind,
That we should join with God, and give the world
The go-by; but the world meantime turns round,
And peeps us in the face, the wanton world;
We feel it gently pressing down our arm,
The arm we raised to do for truth such wonders;
We feel it softly bearing on our side;
We feel it touch and thrill us through the body;
And we are fools, and there's an end of us.

J. P. BAILEY.

THE world, in all its boasted grandeur proud,
In all its stores of dazzling splendour bright,
Is but a transient, unsubstantial cloud,
Which the sun skirts with momentary light:
Anon, the assailing winds impetuous rise,
Black lowers the tempest in the sullen sky
Before the driving blast the vision dies,
And all the vivid tints of splendour fly:
Pass but a moment, every ray is gone;
Nor e'en a vestige left where the bright glories shone.

And shall we, for this visionary gleam,
Degenerate, swerve from Heaven's immortal plan?
Give up, for vanity's light, airy dream,
The nobler heritage reserved for man?
Though rocks their cragged heads in ambush hide,
Though storms and tempests sweep the angry main,
While Hope's fair star shines forth, auspicious guide,
E'en tempests, storms, and rocks oppose in vain.
Safe, 'mid the ocean's iterated force,
The sacred vessel shapes her Heaven-directed course.

SAMUEL HAYES.

ETERNITY—IMMORTALITY.

As touching the resurrection of the dead, have ye not read that which was spoken unto you, by God, saying,

I am the God of Abraham, and the God of Isaac, and the God of Jacob? God is not the God of the dead, but of the living. MATTHEW, xxii, 31, 32.

Our Saviour Jesus Christ hath abolished death, and hath brought life and immortality to light through the Gospel. II. TIMOTHY, i, 10.

This corruption must put on incorruption, and this mortal must put on immortality I. CORINTHIANS, xv, 53.

WE strive with earthly imagings,
To reach and understand
The wondrous and the fearful things
Of an eternal land.

But soon the doubt, the toil, the strife
Of earth shall all be done,
And knowledge of our endless life
Be in a moment won. OTWAY CURRY.

As trees beneath the soil must shoot,
Before they form the grove,
So man in earth must spread his root,
That hopes to bloom above. THOMAS WARD.

WHY shrinks the soul
Back on herself, and startles at destruction?
'Tis the Divinity that stirs within us;
'Tis Heaven itself that points out an hereafter,
And intimates eternity to man. ADDISON.

WHO reads his bosom reads immortal life;
Or nature there, imposing on her sons,
Has written fables; man was made a lie. YOUNG.

'Tis immortality deciphers man,
And opens all the mysteries of his make.
Without it, half his instincts are a riddle,
Without it, all his virtues are a dream. Young.

Man's soul immortal is; whilst here they live,
The purest minds for perfect knowledge strive;
Which is the knowledge of that glorious God,
From whom all life proceeds: in this abode
Of flesh, the soul can never reach so high,
So reason tells us. If the soul then die,
When from the body's bonds she takes her flight,
Her unfulfilled desire is frustrate quite,
And so bestowed in vain! It follows then,
The best desires, unto the best of men,
The Great Creator did in vain dispense;
Or else the soul must live when gone from hence,
And if it live after the body fall,
What reason proves that it must die at all?

Thomas May.

Life is real! Life is earnest!
And the grave is not its goal;
Dust thou art, to dust returnest,
Was not spoken of the soul. Longfellow.

The Eternal Life, beyond the sky,
Wealth cannot purchase, nor the high
And proud estate;
The soul in dalliance laid, — the spirit
Corrupt with sin, — shall not inherit
A joy so great.

Longfellow. *(From the Spanish.)*

Our better nature pineth — let it be!
Thou human soul — earth is no home for thee;
Thy starry rest is in eternity! Miss Landon.

He of the lion-voice, the rainbow-crowned,
Shall stand upon the mountains and the sea,
And swear by earth, by Heaven's throne, and Him
Who sitteth on the throne, there shall be Time
No more, no more! Then veiled Eternity
Shall straight unveil her awful countenance
Unto the reeling world, and take the place
Of seasons, years, and ages. Aye and aye
Shall be the time of day! Miss Barrett

The spirit leaves the body's wondrous frame,
That frame itself a world of strength and skill;
The nobler inmate new abodes will claim,
In every change to Thee aspiring still.

Although from darkness born, to darkness fled,
We know that light beyond surrounds the whole;
The man survives, though the weird corpse be dead,
And He who dooms the flesh, redeems the soul.
John Sterling.

O, listen, man!
A voice within us speaks the startling word,
"Man, thou shalt never die!" Celestial voices
Hymn it around our souls: according harps,
By angel fingers touched, when the mild stars
Of morning sang together, sound forth still
The song of our great immortality! R. H. Dana.

Beyond the purple verge of infinite space,
The immortal soul of man shall live again;
Live where its glories never more may wane,
And where its nobler memories will efface
All thoughts which rend the solemn pall away
That shrouds the meanness of its primal clay.
H. B. Hirst.

THE sun is but a spark of fire,—
A transient meteor in the sky:
The soul, immortal as its Sire,
Shall never die!

JAMES MONTGOMERY

WHEN the vast sun shall veil his golden light
Deep in the gloom of everlasting night;
When wild, destructive flames shall wrap the skies,
When chaos triumphs, and when nature dies;
Man shall alone the wreck of worlds survive,
'Midst falling spheres, immortal man shall live.

MISS WILLIAMS.

YET know, vain skeptics, know the Almighty mind,
Who breathed on man a portion of His fire,
Bade his free soul, by earth nor time confined,
To Heaven, to immortality aspire.

Nor shall the pile of hope His mercy reared,
By vain philosophy be e'er destroyed:
Eternity, by all or wished or feared,
Shall be, by all, or suffered, or enjoyed

WILLIAM MASON.

STILL seems it strange that thou should'st live for ever?
Is it less strange that thou should'st live at all?
This is a miracle, and that no more.
Who gave beginning can exclude an end.
Deny thou art, then doubt if thou shalt be.

YOUNG

(*See also* RESURRECTION, SOUL.)

EVENING—NIGHT—DARKNESS.

He made darkness His secret place; His pavilion round about Him were dark waters, and thick clouds of the skies. Psalm xviii, 11.

Thou makest darkness, and it is night. Psalm civ, 20.

If I say, Surely the darkness shall cover me; even the night shall be light about me.

Yea, the darkness hideth not from Thee; but the night shineth as the day: the darkness and the light are both alike to Thee. Psalm cxxxix, 11, 12.

Day unto day uttereth speech, and night unto night showeth knowledge. Psalm xix, 2.

Then is the time
For those whom wisdom, and whom nature charm,
To steal themselves from the degenerate crowd,
And soar above this little scene of things;
To tread low-thoughted vice beneath their feet,
To soothe the throbbing passions into peace;
And woo lone quiet in her silent walks.

Thomson.

The glorious sun is gone,
And the gathering darkness of night comes on.
Like a curtain from God's kind hand it flows,
To shade the couch where his children repose.
Then kneel, while the watching stars are bright,
And give your last thoughts to the Guardian of night.

Henry Ware, Jr.

Pleasantly comest thou,
Dew of the evening, to the crisp'd up grass;
And the curl'd corn-blades bow,
And the light breezes pass,
That their parch'd lips may feel thee, and expand,
Thou sweet reviver of the fever'd land.

So, to the thirsting soul,
Cometh the dew of the Almighty's love;
And the scathed heart, made whole,
Turneth in joy above,
To where the spirit freely may expand,
And rove, untrammelled, in that "better land."

WM. D. GALLAGHER.

AND when the hours of rest
Come, like a calm upon the mid-sea brine,
Hushing its billowy breast—
The quiet of that moment, too, is thine:
It breathes of him who keeps
The vast and helpless city, while it sleeps.

WM. C. BRYANT.

YET as the stars, the holy stars of night,
Shine out when all is dark,
So would I, cheered by hopes more purely bright,
Tread still the thorny path, whose close is light;
If, but at last, the tossed and weary barque,
Gains the sure haven of her final rest.

LUCY HOOPER.

O, BLESSED Night! that comes to rich and poor
Alike; bringing us dreams that lure
Our hearts to One above! HENRY B. HIRST.

AND still as day concludes in night
To break again with new-born light,
God's wondrous bounty let me find,
With still a more enlightened mind;
When Grace and Love in one agree,
Grace from God and Love from me;
Grace that will from Heaven inspire,
Love that seals it in desire. PARNELL.

Now, with religious awe, the farewell light
Blends with the solemn colouring of the night.

WORDSWORTH.

CLOUDS and thick darkness are thy throne,
Thy wonderful pavilion;
O, dart from thence a shining ray,
And then my midnight shall be day!

THOMAS FLATMAN.

THOUGH light and glory be the Almighty's throne,
Darkness is His pavilion;
From that His radiant beauty, but from thee
He has His terror and His majesty.

NORRIS, *of Bemerton.*

MORN is the time to act, noon to endure;
But O! if thou would'st keep thy spirit pure,
Turn from the beaten path, by worldlings trod,
Go forth at eventide, in heart to walk with God.

MRS. EMBURY.

WHEN day, with farewell beam, delays
Among the opening clouds of even,
And we can almost think we gaze
Through opening vistas into Heaven,
Those hues that mark the sun's decline,
So soft, so radiant, Lord, are Thine!

When night, with wings of starry gloom,
O'ershadows all the earth and skies,
Like some dark, beauteous bird, whose plume
Is sparkling with unnumbered eyes,—
That sacred gloom, those fires divine,
So grand, so countless, Lord, are thine.

THOMAS MOORE.

WHEN the soft dews of kindly sleep,
My wearied eye-lids gently steep,
Be my last thought, how sweet to rest
For ever on my Saviour's breast! KEBLE.

THE clouds that gather round the setting sun,
Do take a sober colouring from an eye
That hath kept watch o'er man's mortality.
WORDSWORTH.

BUT see where, in the clear, unclouded sky,
The crescent moon, with calm and sweet rebuke,
Doth charm away the spirit of complaint.
Her tender light falls on the snow-clad hills,
Like the pure thoughts that angels might bestow
Upon this world of beauty and of sin,
That mingle not with that wherein they rest;—
So should immortal spirits dwell below.
There is a holy influence in the moon,
And in the countless hosts of silent stars,
The heart cannot resist: its passions sleep,
And all is still; save that which shall awake
When all the vast and fair creation sleeps.
MRS. FOLLEN.

WHEN the Almighty did on Horeb stand,
Thy shades enclosed the hallowed land;
In clouds of Night He was arrayed,
And venerable darkness His Pavilion made.

When He appeared, armed in His power and might,
He veiled the beatific light;
When terrible with majesty,
In tempests He gave laws, and clad Himself in Thee.
THOMAS YALDEN.

BEHOLD this midnight glory; worlds on worlds!
Amazing pomp! redouble this amaze;
Ten thousand add; and twice ten thousand more;
Then weigh the whole: one soul outweighs them all
YOUNG.

HOW is night's sable mantle laboured o'er!
How richly wrought with attributes divine!
What wisdom shines! what love! This midnight pomp,
This gorgeous arch, with golden worlds inlaid!
Built with Divine ambition! nought to thee;
For others this profusion. YOUNG.

DARKNESS the curtain drops o'er life's dull scene:
'Tis the kind hand of Providence stretched out
'Twixt man and vanity; 'tis reason's reign,
And virtue's too. YOUNG.

NIGHT is the good man's friend and guardian too;
It no less rescues virtue than inspires. YOUNG.

BY night, an atheist half believes a God. YOUNG.

(*See also* SLEEP.)

EXAMPLE—INTERCOURSE.

EVIL communications corrupt good manners. I. CORINTHIANS, XV, 33.

Iron sharpeneth iron; so a man sharpeneth the countenance of his friend. PROVERBS xxvii, 17.

None of us liveth to himself, and no man dieth to himself. ROMANS, xiv, 7.

It is good neither to eat flesh, nor to drink wine, nor anything whereby thy brother stumbleth, or is offended, or is made weak. ROMANS, xiv, 21.

MEN safelier trust to Heaven than to themselves
When least themselves, in the mad whirl of crowds,
Where folly is contagious, and, too oft,
Even wise men leave their better sense at home,
To chide and wonder at them when returned.

COLERIDGE.

ONE drunkard loves another of the name.

SHAKSPEARE

AMBITION fires ambition; love of gain
Strikes like a pestilence from breast to breast;
Riot, pride, perfidy, blue vapours breathe;
And inhumanity is caught from man,
From smiling man. YOUNG.

If men of good lives,
Who, by their virtuous actions, stir up others
To noble and religious imitation,
Receive the greater glory after death,
As sin must needs confess; what may they feel
In height of torment, and in weight of vengeance,
Not only they themselves not doing well,
But set a light up to show men to hell?

MIDDLETON.

Blessed is the man who hath not walked astray
In counsel of the wicked; and i' the way
Of sinners hath not stood, and in the seat
Of scorners hath not sat. Milton.

FAITH.

Now Faith is the substance of things hoped for, the evidence of things not seen. Hebrews, xi, 1.

But without Faith it is impossible to please Him, for he that cometh to God must believe that He is, and that He is the rewarder of them that diligently seek Him. Hebrews, xi, 6.

Faith cometh by hearing, and hearing by the word of God. Romans, x, 17.

For as the body without the spirit is dead, so faith without works is dead also. James, ii, 26.

By grace are ye saved through faith. Ephesians, ii, 8.

The shield of faith, wherewith ye shall be able to quench all the fiery darts of the wicked. Ephesians, vi, 16.

For therein is the righteousness of God revealed from faith to faith: as it is written the just shall live by faith. Romans, i, 17.

However deep be the mysterious word,
However dark, she disbelieves it not:
Where Reason would examine, Faith obeys,
And "It is written" answers every doubt.

As evening's pale and solitary star
But brightens while the darkness gathers round;
So Faith, unmoved amid surrounding storms,
Is fairest seen in darkness most profound.

Caroline Fry.

To reason less is to imagine more;
They most aspire, who, meekly, most adore —
Therefore the God-like Comforter's decree —
"His sins be loosened who hath faith in me."

Sir E. B. Lytton.

Lo, when dangers closer threaten,
  And thy soul draws near to death;
When assaulted sore by Satan,
  Then present the Shield of Faith:
Fiery darts of fierce temptations,
  Intercepted by thy God,
Then shall lose their force in patience,
  Sheathed in love, and quenched in blood. HART.

WHAT though a cloud o'ershade my sight,
    Big with affliction's tear;
Yet Faith, amid the drops that fall,
    Discerns a rainbow there. LEIGH RICHMOND.

REDEEMED from fear, and washed from lustful blot,
By Faith we then might rise above our lot;
And like Thy chosen few, restored within,
By hearts, as morning pure, might conquer sin.
JOHN STERLING.

THOU ask'st why Christ, so lenient to the *deed*,
So sternly claims the ***Faith*** which founds the creed;
Because, reposed in Faith, the soul has calm;
The hope a haven, and the wound a balm;
Because the light, dim seen in Reason's dream,
On all alike, through faith alone, could stream.
God willed support to weakness, joy to grief,
And so descended from his throne, BELIEF!
SIR E. B. LYTTON.

DEATH's terror is the mountain Faith removes;
'Tis Faith disarms destruction. YOUNG.

REASON, pursued, is Faith; and unpursued,
Where Proof invites, 'tis Reason then no more.
YOUNG.

LADY, there is one star, and one alone,
That tells the future. It's interpreter
Is in man's heart, and is called Conscience:
The star, True Faith; the future that it shows
Is beyond human life. G. P. R. JAMES.

FOR bitter were our sojourn here,
  In this dark wilderness of sorrow,
Did not that rainbow beam appear,
  The herald of a brighter morrow;
A friendly beacon from on high,
To guide us to eternity. A. WATTS.

ALAS! a deeper test of Faith
  Than prison cell, or martyr's stake,
The self-abasing watchfulness
  Of silent prayer may make. J. G. WHITTIER.

FAITH, Hope, and Love, together work in gloom;
What Faith believes, Hope shapes in form and bloom,
And Love sends forth to daylight from the tomb.
JOHN STERLING.

    THE steps of Faith
Fall on the seeming void, and find
    The Rock beneath. J. G. WHITTIER.

BELIEVE, and show the reason of a man;
Believe, and task the pleasure of a God;
Believe, and look with triumph on the tomb.
YOUNG.

FROM purer manners to sublimer faith,
Is nature's unavoidable ascent;
An honest deist, where the gospel shines,
Matured to nobler, in the Christian ends. YOUNG.

E. Finden, sculp.

Faith.

If bliss had lien in art or strength,
None but the wise and strong had gained it;
Where now, by faith, all arms are of a length;
One size doth all conditions fit.

A peasant may believe as much
As a great clerk, and reach the highest stature;
Thus dost thou make proud knowledge bend and crouch,
While grace fills up uneven nature.

GEORGE HERBERT.

O, THOU that rearest with celestial aim
Thy future seraph in my mortal frame,
Thrice holy Faith! whatever thorns I meet,
As on I totter with unpractised feet,
Still let me stretch my arms, and cling to thee,
Meek muse of souls, through thine long infancy!

COLERIDGE.

O THOU of little faith, lift up thine eyes!
Are the ten thousand glorious stars of night
But a vain dream, because thy feeble sight
May not behold them in the noon-day skies?

MARY HOWITT.

For want of faith,
Down the steep precipice of wrong he slides;
There's nothing to support him in the right.
Faith, in the future wanting, is, at least
In embryo, every weakness, every guilt;
And strong temptation ripens it to birth.

YOUNG.

FAITH makes me any thing, or all
That I believe is in the sacred story;
And when sin placeth me in Adam's fall,
Faith sets me higher in his glory.

GEORGE HERBERT.

If weak thy faith, why choose the harder side?
We nothing know but what is marvellous;
Yet what is marvellous we can't believe.
So weak our reason, and so great our God,
What most surprises in the sacred page,
Or full as strange, or stranger, must be true.
Faith is not reason's labour, but repose. YOUNG.

FEAR—COWARDICE.

The fear of man bringeth a snare, but whoso putteth his trust in the Lord shall be safe. PROVERBS, xxix, 25.

For God hath not given us the spirit of fear, but of power, and of love, and of a sound mind. I. TIMOTHY, i, 7.

The fear of the wicked it shall come upon him; but the desire of the righteous shall be granted. PROVERBS, x, 24.

PERSUADE them then,
Fearless to be resolved to die like men;
For, want of such a resolution stings,
At point of death, and dreadful horror brings
Ev'n to the soul; 'cause, wanting preparation,
She dies, despairing of her own salvation.
Yea, and moreover this full well know I,
He that's at any time afraid to die,
Is in weak case, and, whatsoe'er he saith,
Hath but a wavering and a feeble faith.
GEORGE WITHER.

FEAR on guilt attends, and deeds of darkness;
The virtuous breast ne'er knows it. HAVARD.

WHO would lose,
For fear of pain, this intellectual being? MILTON.

GUILT is a timorous thing, ere perpetration:
Despair alone makes guilty men be bold.
COLERIDGE.

GOD'S altar grasping with an eager hand,
Fear, the wild-visaged, pale, eye-starting wretch,
Sure-refuged, hears his hot-pursuing fiends
Yell at vain distance. Soon refreshed from Heaven,
He calms the throb and tempest of his heart.
His countenance settles; a soft solemn bliss
Swims in his eye — his swimming eye upraised:
And faith's whole armour glitters on his limbs!
And thus transfigured with a dreadless awe,
A solemn hush of soul, meek he beholds
All things of terrible seeming. COLERIDGE.

FLOWERS.

CONSIDER the lilies how they grow: they toil not, they spin not; and yet I say unto you, That Solomon in all his glory was not arrayed like one of these.

If then God so clothe the grass, which to-day is, and to-morrow is cast into the oven, shall he not much more clothe you, O, ye of little faith? LUKE, xii, 27, 28.

For all flesh is as grass, and all the glory of man as the flower of the grass. The grass withereth, and the flower thereof falleth away: But the word of the Lord endureth for ever. I. PETER, i, 25.

As in the mighty arch which spans the world
God's power is manifest, in the gentle flowers
We read His mercy. And the wreath Eve twined
Of buds spontaneous, was a frontlet more
Expressive of calm love and innocence,
Of native and unsullied majesty,
Than her descendants may inscribe in words,
Or wear in gemm'd and sparkling coronet.
H. H. WELD.

The daisy with its petals, crimson-fringed,
Speaks of humility, disclaiming praise,
And fairer by abasement. Fiery zeal,
Stern, battling with calamity, and prompt
To seal its witness e'en with blood, shines out
Emblazoned in the poppy: and the slight
And sapphire-tinted cyanus gives note
Of faith, which, ever gazing on the skies,
Imbibes from thence her fair and peaceful hue.

J. F. Hollings.

The moss-clad violet, fragrant and concealed
Like hidden charity. J. F. Hollings.

To me the meanest flower that blows, can give
Thoughts that do often lie too deep for tears.

Wordsworth.

The enlivening sap,
Obedient to Thy laws, through fitted tubes
Ascends fermenting, and, at length matured,
Breaks forth in gems, and germinates in leaves.
By Thee each family of flowers is clothed
In one unvarying dress, and breathes the same
Transmitted essences; and though the loom
No virgin fingers ply to swell her pride,
The lily shines, more gorgeously arrayed
Than monarchs, where the East, with hand profuse,
Showers on their pomp barbaric, pearl and gold.

Smart.

Observe the rising lily's snowy grace,
Observe the various vegetable race;
They neither toil, nor spin, but careless grow,
Yet see, how warm they blush! how bright they glow

What regal vestments can with them compare!
What king so shining! or what queen so fair!
If ceaseless thus the fowls of heaven He feeds,
If o'er the earth such lucid robes He spreads;
Will He not care for you, ye faithless, say?
Is He unwise? or, are ye less than they?

THOMSON.

YES,—flowers have tones—God gave to each
A language of its own;
And bade the simple blossom teach
Where'er its seeds are sown;
His voice is on the mountain's height,
And by the river's side,
Where flowers blush in glowing light,
In lowliness, or pride;
We feel, all o'er the blooming sod,
It is the language of our God. MRS. ESLING.

FOSTER the good, and thou shalt tend the flower
Already sown on earth;—
Foster the beautiful, and every hour,
Thou call'st new flowers to birth. SCHILLER.

THE plants look up to Heaven, from whence
They have their nourishment. SHAKSPEARE.

PALE winter flowers! The clouds aloft
The sunless skies deform,—
How can ye spread your blossoms soft
To face the pelting storm?
Ye have a root beneath,
Defying stormy hours;—
Ye are like fearless faith,
O, precious winter flowers. MISS M. A. BROWNE.

FOR even like those drooping flowers
Fast hastening to the silent tomb,
A few short days — a few short hours —
And all things lose their transient bloom;
The friends who read this strain, and I,
Must follow, like a passing sigh.

ANNA PEYRE DINNIES.

HATH not God strown our weary way with flowers;
And clothed, with robes of many a hue,
The fragrant meadows, and the woodland bowers,
Feeding their beauty with his dew,
Making them glad, with sunshine and with showers?
Is it not written that He knew
Himself a joy divine,
Amidst young Eden's holy trees, when, walking
There, His children sought His love?
And the pure spirit still may hear Him talking
Such words as drew rapt Enoch's soul above.
So ask Him to draw thine:
Seek Him, for He is near thee;
Sing to Him, He will hear thee. BETHUNE.

YE are the scriptures of the earth,
Sweet flowers fair and frail;
A sermon speaks in every bud
That woos the Summer gale. ANONYMOUS.

THERE is a lesson in each flower,
A story in each stream and bower;
On every herb on which you tread
Are written words, which, rightly read,
Will lead you from earth's fragrant sod,
To hope, and holiness, and God.

ALLAN CUNNINGHAM.

Posthumous glories! Angel-like collection!
  Upraised from seed or bulb interred in earth,
Ye are to me a type of resurrection,
    A second birth.

Were I, O God, in churchless lands remaining,
  Far from the voice of teachers or divines,
My soul would find, in flowers of thy ordaining,
    Priests, sermons, shrines!

Horace Smith.

          The sickliest leaf,
The feeblest efflorescence of the moss,
That drinks thy dew reproves our unbelief.
The frail field-lily, which no florist's eye
Regards, doth win a garniture from thee
To kings denied. So while to dust we bow,
Needy and poor, O bid us learn the lore
Graved on the lily's leaf, as fair and clear
As on yon disk of fire — to trust in Thee.

Mrs. Sigourney.

FRAILTY.

For the good that I would I do not, but the evil which I would not, that I do. Romans, vii, 19.

Wherefore let him that thinketh he standeth, take heed lest he fall. I. Corinthians x, 12.

All have sinned, and come short of the glory of God. Romans, iii, 23.

          Adam's foul revolt
From the primeval law, on all his sons,
Through every age, the sad inheritance
Of sin and death entailed.

Samuel Hayes.

ALAS! — the evil that we fain would shun
We do, and leave the wished-for good undone:
Our strength to-day
Is but to-morrow's weakness, prone to fall;
Poor, blind, unprofitable servants, all,
Are we alway.
J. G. WHITTIER.

BUT man with frailty is allied by birth.
BP. LOWTH.

HOW weak is man! how frail his best resolves!
But frailest those which owe their hasty birth
To fear; how short, how transient is their life.
Hardly obtained, they shine but as the sparks
Struck from the flint, which scarce outlive the blow.
CHARLES JENNER.

POOR race of men! said the pitying Spirit,
Dearly ye pay for your primal Fall —
Some flowerets of Eden ye still inherit,
But the trail of the serpent is over them all!
THOMAS MOORE.

FEW bring back at eve,
Immaculate, the manners of the morn.
Something we thought is blotted; we resolved,
Is shaken; we renounced, returns again.
YOUNG.

BY nature peccable and frail are we,
Easily beguiled; to vice, to error prone;
But apt for virtue too. Humanity
Is not a field where tares and thorns alone
Are left to spring; good seed hath there been sown
With no unsparing hand. Sometimes the shoot
Is choked with weeds, or withers on a stone;
But in a kindly soil it strikes its root,
And flourisheth, and bringeth forth abundant fruit.
SOUTHEY.

(*See also* GUILT, SIN, THE FALL.)

FREEDOM—FREE WILL.

WHERE the spirit of the Lord is, there is liberty. II. CORINTHIANS, iii, 17.

So speak ye, and so do, as they that shall be judged by the law of liberty. JAMES ii, 12.

For so is the will of God, that with well-doing ye may put to silence the ignorance of foolish men:

As free, and not using your liberty as a cloak of maliciousness, but as the servants of God. I. PETER, ii, 15, 16.

And ye shall know the truth, and the truth shall make you free. JOHN, viii, 32.

f the Son therefore shall make you free, ye shall be free indeed. JOHN, viii, 36.

TRUE Liberty was Christian; sanctified,
Baptized and found in Christian hearts alone.
First-born of Virtue, daughter of the skies,
Nursling of truth divine; sister of all
The graces, meekness, holiness, and love:
Giving to God, and man, and all below
That symptom showed of sensible existence,
Their due, unasked. POLLOK.

THOUGHTS uncontrolled and unimpressed, the births
Of pure election, arbitrary range,
Not to the limits of one world confined. YOUNG.

RELIGION, richest favour of the skies,
Stands most revealed before the freeman's eyes.
No shades of superstition blot the day,
Liberty chases all that gloom away;
The soul, emancipated, unoppressed,
Free to prove all things, and hold fast the best,
Learns much, and to a thousand listening minds
Communicates with joy the good she finds.
COWPER.

MAN (ingenious to contrive his woe,
And rob himself of all that makes this vale
Of tears bloom comfort) cries, If God foresees
Our future actings, then the objects known
Must be determined, or the knowledge fail:
Thus liberty's destroyed, and all we do
Or suffer, by a fatal thread is spun.
Say, fool, with too much subtilty misled,
Who reasonest but to err, does Prescience change
The property of things? Is aught thou seest
Caused by thy vision, not thy vision caused
By forms that previously exist? To God
This mode of seeing future deeds extends,
And freedom with foreknowledge may exist.

GEORGE BALLY

PLACED for his trial on this bustling stage,
From thoughtless youth to ruminating age,
Free in his will to choose or to refuse,
Man may improve the crisis, or abuse;
Else, on the fatalist's unrighteous plan,
Say to what bar amenable were man?
With naught in charge, he could betray no trust;
And if he fell, would fall because he must;
If Love reward him, or if Vengeance strike,
His recompense in both unjust alike. COWPER

GRACE leads the right way: if you choose the wrong,
Take it and perish, but restrain your tongue;
Charge not, with light sufficient, and left free,
Your wilful suicide on God's decree. COWPER.

YET gave me in this dark estate
To see the good from ill,
And, binding Nature fast in fate,
Left free the human will. POPE.

Heaven made us agents, free to good or ill,
And forced it not, though He foresaw the will;
Freedom was first bestowed on human race,
And Prescience only held the second place.
Dryden.

Freely we serve,
Because we freely love, as in our will
To love or not: in this we stand or fall. Milton.

True freedom is where no restraint is known
That scripture, justice, and good sense disown,
Where only vice and injury are tied,
And all from shore to shore is free beside. Cowper.

But there is yet a liberty, unsung
By poets, and by senators unpraised,
Which monarchs cannot grant, nor all the powers
Of earth and hell confederate, take away:
A liberty which persecution, fraud,
Oppression, prisons, have no power to bind;
Which whoso tastes can be enslaved no more.
'Tis liberty of heart, derived from Heaven,
Bought with His blood, who gave it to mankind,
And sealed with the same token. Cowper.

He is the freeman whom the truth makes free,
And all are slaves besides. Cowper.

For what is freedom, but the unfettered use
Of all the powers which God for use had given?
But chiefly this, Him first, Him last to view
Through meaner powers and secondary things
Effulgent, as through clouds that veil his blaze.
Coleridge.

WHERE had been
The test of Faith, if the expanded arm
Of Heaven in glory, and in power displayed,
Had curbed the freedom of the human will,
Nor left the scope of choice? SAMUEL HAYES.

GETHSEMANE.

AND when He was at the place, He said unto them, Pray that ye enter not into temptation.

And He was withdrawn from them about a stone's cast, and kneeled down and prayed,

Saying, Father, if Thou be willing, remove this cup from me: nevertheless, not my will, but thine, be done.

And there appeared an angel unto Him from Heaven, strengthening Him.

And, being in agony, He prayed more earnestly: and His sweat was, as it were great drops of blood falling down to the ground. LUKE, xxii, 40—44.

BRING the thrilling scene
Home to thine inmost soul: — the sufferer's cry,
"Father, if it be possible, this cup
Take thou away.—Yet not my will, but Thine:"
The sleeping friends who could not watch one hour,
The torch, the flashing sword, the traitor's kiss,
The astonished angel, with the tear of Heaven
Upon His cheek, still striving to assuage
Those fearful pangs that bowed the Son of God
Like a bruised reed. Thou who hast power to look
Thus at Gethsemane, be still! be still!
What are thine insect-woes, compared to His
Who agonizeth there? Count thy brief pains
As the dust atom on life's chariot-wheels,
And in a Saviour's grief forget them all.

MRS. SIGOURNEY.

On His pale brow the drops are large and red
As victim's blood at votive altar shed—
  His hands are clasped, His eyes are raised in prayer—
  Alas, and is there strife he cannot bear,
Who calmed the tempest, and who raised the dead?
There is! there is! for now the powers of hell
  Are struggling for the mastery—'tis the hour
  When death exerts his last permitted power,
When the dread weight of sin, since Adam fell,
Is visited on Him who deigned to dwell—
  A man with men, that He might bear the stroke
  Of wrath divine, and break the captive's yoke—
But O, of that dread strife, what words can tell?
Those, only those which broke, with many a groan,
  From His full heart—"O, Father, take away
  The cup of vengeance I must drink to-day—
Yet, Father, not My will, but Thine, be done!"
It could not pass away—for He alone
  Was mighty to endure and strong to save;
  Nor would Jehovah leave Him in the grave,
Nor could corruption taint His Holy One. DALE.

'Tis midnight; and on Olive's brow
  The star is dimmed that lately shone;
'Tis midnight, in the garden, now,
  The suffering Saviour prays alone.

'Tis midnight; and from all removed,
  The Saviour wrestles lone, with fears;
E'en that disciple whom He loved
  Heeds not his Master's grief and tears.

'Tis midnight; and for others' guilt
  The Man of Sorrows weeps in blood;
Yet He that hath in anguish knelt,
  Is not forsaken by His God.

'Tis midnight; and from ether plains
  Is borne the song that angels know;
Unheard by mortals are the strains
  That sweetly soothe the Saviour's woe.

W. B. TAPPAN

NEXT, with strong cries and bitter tears,
  Thrice hallowed He that doleful ground,
Where, trembling with mysterious fears,
  His sweat like blood-drops fell around,
And being in an agony,
He prayèd yet more earnestly.

JAMES MONTGOMERY.

BUT now, see where He lies
On the cold ground, exposed to thick, dank air,
And all the fury of the madding skies!
See how each nerve and vein
Trembles and throbs with torture! how His eyes
Start from their seat with anguish and despair!
What drops of sanguine sweat roll down amain
From His fair limbs! "O Father, O remove,
If possible, this cup, yet not My will,
But thine be done!" O agonizing love!

JAMES SCOTT.

HERE He led
From the Last Supper, when the hymn was sung,
His few grieved followers out, in that drear night,
When, in the garden, on the mountain's slope,
His agony wrung forth the crimson drops!
While these sad pictures hang upon thy sides,
Thou consecrated height, dissolve the heart
In pious sorrow!

HANNAH F. GOULD.

THE GOSPEL.

For I am not ashamed of the gospel of Christ; for it is the power of God unto salvation to every one that believeth; to the Jew first, and also to the Gentile. ROMANS, i, 16.

If ye continue in the faith grounded and settled, and be not moved away from the hope of the gospel, which ye have heard, and which was preached to every creature under Heaven. COLOSSIANS, xv, 23.

The word of truth, the gospel of your salvation. EPHESIANS, i, 13

"LET there be light!" O'er heaven and earth,
The God who first the day-beam poured,
Uttered again his fiat forth,
And shed the Gospel's Light abroad.
And like the dawn, its cheering rays
On rich and poor were meant to fall,
Inspiring their Redeemer's praise,
In lowly cot and lordly hall. C. F. HOFFMAN.

GAZING ever on the Gospel light,
That endless source of evidence and truth,
Prove every doctrine by that golden rule,
And "try the spirits if they be of God."
MRS. SIGOURNEY.

THE Gospel's glorious hope,
Its rule of purity, its eye of prayer,
Its fort of firmness on temptation's steep,
Its bark that fails not, 'mid the storm of death,
He spread before them, and with gentlest tone,
Such as a brother to his sister breathes,
His little sister, simple and untaught,
Did urge them to the shelter of that ark
Which rides the wrathful deluge. MRS. SIGOURNEY

SOLEMN praise
And prayers devoutly breathed, the tears, the sighs
Of penitential grief, the broken heart,
Now formed the Gentile's purer sacrifice
To the true God. The philosophic lore
Of learned Athens, sunk ere long, eclipsed
By truth's resistless blaze. The vain parade
Of empty jargon, and unmeaning forms,
No longer won the prostituted praise
Of wondering Greece. The Stoic's fond pretence
Was urged no more; the boasted apathist
Confessèd the strength of nature, owned the power,
The use of passion, deigned to feel himself
And sympathize the miseries of man.

JOHN LETTICE.

THE silver trumpet's heavenly call
Sounds for the poor, but sounds alike for all;
Kings are invited, and, would kings obey,
No slaves on earth more welcome were than they;
But royalty, nobility, and state,
Are such a dead, preponderating weight,
That endless bliss, how strange soe'er it seem,
In counterpoise flies up, and kicks the beam.

COWPER.

(*See also* BIBLE, REVELATION.)

GRACE—MERCY—PARDON.

MERCY is seasonable in the time of affliction, as clouds of rain in the time of drought. ECCLESIASTICUS, xxxv, 20.

We have access by faith into this grace wherein we stand, and rejoice in hope of the glory of God. ROMANS, v, 2.

My grace is sufficient for thee, for my strength is made perfect in weakness. II. CORINTHIANS, xii, 9.

The grace of God that bringeth salvation hath appeared to all men. TITUS, ii, 11.

All the paths of the Lord are mercy and truth with such as keep His covenant and testimonies. PSALM xxv, 10.

The Lord is good to all; and His tender mercies are over all His works. PSALM cxlv, 9.

Be ye therefore merciful, as your Father also is merciful. LUKE, vi, 36.

MERCY, that wipes the penitential tear,
And dissipates the horrors of despair,
From righteous justice steals the 'vengeful hour,
Softens the dreadful attribute of power,
Disarms the wrath of an offended God,
And seals my pardon in a Saviour's blood!

MRS. CARTER.

THOUGH Nature her inverted course forego,
The day forget to rest, the time to flow,
Yet shall Jehovah's servants stand secure,
His Mercy, fixed, eternal shall endure;
On them her everlasting rays shall shine,
More mild and bright, and sure, O sun! than thine.

BP. LOWTH.

IN the course of justice, none of us
Should see salvation: we do pray for mercy,
And that same prayer doth teach us all to render
The deeds of mercy. SHAKSPEARE.

MANKIND are all pilgrims on life's weary road,
And many would wander astray
In seeking Eternity's silent abode,
Did Mercy not point out the way!

G. P. MORRIS.

THE quality of mercy is not strained;
It droppeth as the gentle rain from heaven
Upon the place beneath. It is twice blessed;
It blesseth him that gives, and him that takes.

SHAKSPEARE.

IT is an attribute of God himself,
And earthly power doth then show liker God's,
When mercy seasons justice. SHAKSPEARE.

THE flesh being proud, Desire doth fight with Grace,
And there it revels, and when that decays,
The guilty rebel for remission prays. SHAKSPEARE.

THAT word, Grace,
In an ungracious mouth, is but profane.

SHAKSPEARE.

BY all the tender mercy
God hath shown to human grief,
When fate, or man's perverseness,
Denied and barr'd relief,—
By the helpless woe which taught me
To look to Him alone,
From the vain appeals for justice
And wild efforts of my own,—
By thy light — thou unseen future,
And thy tears — thou bitter past,
I will hope — though all forsake me —
In His Mercy to the last! MRS. NORTON.

WHEN winter fortunes cloud the brows
  Of summer friends,—when eyes grow strange,—
When plighted faith forgets its vows,
  When earth and all things in it change,—
O Lord, thy mercies fail me never—
Where once thou lovest, thou lovest for ever!

JOHN QUARLES.

O GOD! how beautiful the thought,
  How merciful the bless'd decree,
That Grace can e'er be found, when sought,
  And naught shut out the soul from Thee.
The cell may cramp, the fetters gall,
  The flame may scorch, the rack may tear;
But torture, stake, or prison-wall,
  Can be endured with faith and prayer.

ELIZA COOK.

MERCY descends
From Heaven, and o'er the penitential heart,
Rent by the agonizing pangs of guilt,
Spreads the soft blessings of internal peace.

SAMUEL HAYES.

O, THOU bounteous Giver of all good,
Thou art of all Thy gifts, Thyself the crown;
Give what Thou canst, without Thee we are poor;
And with Thee rich, take what Thou wilt away!

COWPER.

IF Heaven
Did in the balance of strict justice weigh
The iniquity of men, who could abide
Its judgment? Did not Mercy temper wrath,
Eternal ruin would o'erwhelm mankind.

SAMUEL HAYES.

MERCY'S gentle attribute
Tempers the grief: He protects the poor
In needful hour of dearth, and from the dust
Raises the weeping penitent: His wrath
The blood of goats averts not, or the fat
Of costly hecatombs. Nor deigns He not
With pity's eye, the contrite heart to view
And troubled spirit: purest sacrifice
By Him accepted. THOMAS ZOUCH.

O, THOU, whose piercing thought
Doth note each secret path,
For mercy to Thy throne we fly,
From man's condemning wrath.

How fearless should our trust
In Thy compassion be,
When from our brother of the dust
We dare appeal to Thee! MRS. SIGOURNEY.

BUT grace, abused, brings forth the foulest deeds,
As richest soil, the most luxuriant weeds.
COWPER.

WHY, all the souls that were, were forfeit once;
And He that might the vantage best have took,
Found out the remedy. How would you be,
If He which is the top of judgment, should
But judge you, as you are? O, think on that!
And mercy then will breathe within your lips,
Like man new made. SHAKSPEARE.

IF, when you make your prayers,
God should be so obdurate as yourselves,
How would it fare with your departed souls?
SHAKSPEARE

MERCY is the highest reach of wit,
A safety unto them that save with it:
Born out of God, and unto human eyes,
Like God, not seen, till fleshly passion dies.
LORD BROOKS.

SHOULD e'er Thy wonder-working grace
  Triumph by our weak arm,
Let not our sinful fancy trace
  Aught human in the charm. KEBLE.

THE GRAVE.

WHATSOEVER thy hand findeth to do, do it with thy might, for there is no work, nor device, nor knowledge, nor wisdom, in the grave, whither thou goest. ECCLESIASTES ix, 10.

God will redeem my soul from the power of the grave, for He shall receive me. PSALM, xlix, 15.

The Lord killeth, and maketh alive; He bringeth down to the grave, and bringeth up. I. SAMUEL, ii, 6.

I will ransom them from the power of the grave; I will redeem them from death: O death, I will be thy plague: O grave, I will be thy destruction. HOSEA, xiii, 14.

O that they were wise, that they understood this, that they would consider their latter end! DEUTERONOMY, xxxii, 29.

OH! for a heart that seeks the sacred gloom
That hovers round the precincts of the tomb!
While fancy, musing there, sees visions bright,—
In death discovering life, in darkness, light.

What though the chilling blasts of Winter's day
Forbid the garden longer to be gay?
Of Winter yet I'll not refuse to sing,
Thus to be followed by eternal Spring.
LEIGH RICHMOND.

'Tis a solemn place:
For this dark purple loam, whereon I lie,
And this green mould, the mother of bright flowers,
Was bone and sinew once, now decomposed;
Perhaps has lived, breathed, walked, as proud as we,
And animate with all the faculties,
And finer senses of the human soul!
And now what are they? To their elements
Each has returned, dust crumbled back to dust,
The spirit gone to God.

William Thompson Bacon.

How loved, how valued once, avails thee not;
To whom related, or by whom begot;
A heap of dust alone remains of thee;
'Tis all thou art, and all the proud shall be!

Pope.

I pass, with melancholy state,
By all these solemn heaps of fate,
And think, as soft and sad I tread
Above the venerable dead,
"Time was, like me, they life possessed;
And time will be, when I shall rest." Parnell.

Here the lamented dead in dust shall lie,
Life's lingering languors o'er, its labors done;
Where waving boughs, between the earth and sky,
Admit the farewell radiance of the sun.

And here the impressive stone, engraved with words
Which grief sententious gives to marble pale,
Shall teach the heart; while waters, leaves and birds,
Make cheerful music in the passing gale.

Willis G. Clark.

AND side by side! (O, be it in the sky
As in the earth) the long-divided lie.
SIR E. B. LYTTON.

As flowers which night, when day is o'er, perfume,
Breathes the sweet memory from a good man's tomb.
SIR E. B. LYTTON.

THE voice of prayer at the sable bier!
A voice to sustain, to soothe, and to cheer.
It commends the spirit to God who gave;
It lifts the thoughts from the cold, dark grave;
It points to the glory where He shall reign
Who whispered, "Thy brother shall rise again!"
HENRY WARE, JR.

THROUGH these branched walks will contemplation wind,
And grave wise Nature's teachings on his mind;
As the white grave-stones glimmer to his eye,
A solemn voice will thrill him, "*Thou* must die!"
When Autumn's tints are glittering in the air,
That voice will whisper to his soul, "Prepare!"
When Winter's snows are spread o'er hill and dell,
"O, this is death!" that solemn voice will swell;
But when with Spring, streams leap, and blossoms wave,
"Hope, Christian, hope," 'twill say, "there's life beyond the grave."
ALFRED B. STREET.

THOU hast wept mournfully, O, human love!
E'en on this greensward; night hath heard thy cry,
Heart-stricken one! thy precious dust above,
Night, and the hills, which sent forth no reply
Unto thine agony!
But He who wept like thee, thy Lord, thy guide,
Christ, hath arisen, O love! thy tears shall all be dried.
MRS. HEMANS.

'Tis a blessing to live, but a greater to die,
And the best of the world, is its path to the sky,—
Be it gloomy or bright, for the life that He gave
Let us thank Him — but blessed be God for the grave!
'T is the end of our toil, 't is the crown of our bliss,
'T is the portal of happiness — aye, but for this,
How hopeless were sorrow, how narrow were love,
If they looked not from earth to the rapture above!

J. K. Mitchell.

What though the great,
With costly pomp, and aromatic sweets,
Embalmed his poor remains; or through the dome
A thousand tapers shed their gloomy light,
While solemn organs to his parting soul
Chaunted slow orisons; say, by what mark
Dost thou discern him from the lowly swain,
Whose mouldering bones beneath the thorn-bound turf
Long lay neglected? Glynn.

Hail, heavenly voice, once heard in Patmos! "Write,
Henceforth the dead who die in Christ are blest:
Yea, saith the Spirit, for they now shall rest
From all their labors!" But no dull, dark night
That rest o'ershadows: 't is the day-spring bright
Of bliss; the foretaste of a richer feast;
A sleep, if sleep it be, of lively zest,
Peopled with visions of intense delight.
And though the secrets of that resting-place
The soul embodied knows not; yet she knows
No sin is there God's likeness to deface,
To stint His love, no purgatorial woes;
Her dross is left behind, nor mixture base
Mars the pure stream of her serene repose.

Bp. Mant.

Come unto the churchyard near;
Where the gentle, whispering breeze
Softly rustleth through the trees;
Where the moonbeam pure and white,
Falls in floods of cloudless light,
Bathing many a turfy heap
Where the lowlier slumberers sleep;
And the graceful willow waves,
Banner-like, o'er nameless graves:
Here hath prayer arisen like dew,—
Here the earth is holy, too,
Lightly press each grassy mound:
Surely this is hallowed ground. M. A. Browne.

Art is long, and time is fleeting,
  And our hearts, though stout and brave,
Still, like muffled drums, are beating
  Funeral marches to the grave. Longfellow.

I like that ancient Saxon phrase which calls
  The burial-ground, God's Acre! It is just;
It consecrates each grave within its walls,
  And breathes a benison o'er the sleeping dust.

Into its furrows shall we all be cast,
  In the sure faith that we shall rise again
At the great harvest, when the Archangel's blast
  Shall winnow, like a fan, the chaff and grain.
Longfellow

(*See also* Death, The Departed.)

HEARING—THE EAR.

The ear that heareth the reproof of life abideth among the wise. Proverbs, xv, 31.

They are like the deaf adder that stoppeth her ear; which will not hearken to the voice of charmers, charming never so wisely. Psalm lviii, 4, 5.

The hearing ear, and the seeing eye, the Lord hath made even both of them. Proverbs, xx, 12.

For where there is no ear to be abused,
  None will be found that dare to inform a wrong:
The insolent depraver stands confused;
  The impious atheist seems to want a tongue.

Daniel.

This is the slowest, yet the daintiest sense;
  For even the ears of such as have no skill,
Perceive a discord, and conceive offence;
  And knowing not what 's good, yet find the ill.
And though this sense first gentle music sound,
  Her proper object is the speech of men;
But that speech, chiefly, which God's heralds sound,
  When their tongues utter what His spirit did pen.

Sir John Davies.

As Thou hast touched our ears, and taught
  Our tongues to speak Thy praises plain,
Quell Thou each thankless, godless thought
  That would make fast our bonds again.
From worldly strife, from mirth unblest,
Drowning Thy music in the breast,
From foul reproach, from thrilling fears,
Preserve, good Lord, Thy servants' ears.

From idle words that restless throng,
And haunt our hearts when we would pray,
From pride's false chime, and jarring wrong,
Seal Thou my lips, and guard the way:
For Thou hast sworn that every ear,
Willing, or loth, Thy trump shall hear,
And every tongue unchained be,
To own no hope, O God, but Thee. KEBLE.

IN time of service, seal up both thine eyes,
And send them to thy heart; that, spying sin,
They may weep out the stains by them did rise,
Those doors being shut, all by the ear comes in.
GEORGE HERBERT.

THE HEART—THE NEW HEART.

THE heart knoweth his own bitterness, and a stranger intermeddleth not with his joy. PROVERBS, xiv, 10.

The hypocrites in heart, heap up wrath. JOB, xxxvi, 13.

The heart is deceitful above all things, and desperately wicked; who can know it? JEREMIAH, xvii, 9.

A good man, out of the good treasure of his heart, bringeth forth that which is good; and an evil man, out of the evil treasure of his heart, bringeth forth that which is evil: for of the abundance of the heart his mouth speaketh. LUKE, vi, 45.

With the heart, man believeth unto righteousness. ROMANS, x, 10.

Blessed are the pure in heart, for they shall see God. MATTHEW, v, 8.

A new heart also will I give you, and a new spirit will I put within you: and I will take away the stony heart out of your flesh, and I will give you a heart of flesh EZEKIEL, xxxvi, 26.

Hope maketh not ashamed, because the love of God is shed abroad in our hearts by the Holy Ghost, which is given unto us. ROMANS, v, 5.

That Christ may dwell in your hearts by faith. EPHESIANS, iii, 17.

THE heart unwarmed within,
Prayer is mere babbling, sanctity is sin.
JAMES SCOTT.

ALL our actions take
Their hues from the complexion of the heart,
As landscapes their variety from light.

WILLIAM THOMPSON BACON.

I CARE not, so my kernel relish well,
How slender be the substance of my shell;
My heart being virtuous, let my face be wan,
I *am* to God, I only *seem* to man.

FRANCIS QUARLES.

A TEMPLE of the Holy Ghost, and yet
Oft lodging fiends; the dwelling-place of all
The heavenly virtues — charity and truth,
Humility, and holiness, and love —
And yet the common haunt of anger, pride,
Hatred, revenge, and passions foul with lust;
Allied to Heaven, yet parleying oft with Hell.

POLLOK.

HEAVEN'S Sovereign saves all beings but Himself
That hideous sight — a naked, human heart.

YOUNG.

THE Almighty, from His throne, on earth surveys
Naught greater than an honest, humble heart;
An humble heart, His residence! pronounced
His second seat, and rival to the skies.

YOUNG.

WOULD'ST thou the life of souls discern?
Nor human wisdom nor divine
Helps thee by aught beside to learn;
Love is life's only sign.
The spring of the regenerate heart,
The pulse, the glow of every part,
Is the true love of Christ our Lord,
As man embraced, as God adored.

KEBLE.

CONSIDER well. The heart is a deceiver,
Or, paltering with it, in some double sense,
Thou 'st shunned, perhaps, the word that would condemn thee,
E'en while thy will was partner in the crime.

SCHILLER. (*Peters' Translation.*)

SO now the soul's sublimed, her sour desires
Are re-calcined in Heaven's well-tempered fires;
The heart restored, and purged from drossy nature,
Now finds the freedom of a new-born creature;
It lives another life, it breathes new breath,
It neither fears nor feels the sting of death.

FRANCIS QUARLES.

WALK in the light! and sin, abhorred,
Shall ne'er defile again;
The blood of Jesus Christ, the Lord,
Shall cleanse from every stain.
Walk in the light! and thou shalt find
Thy heart made truly His,
Who dwells in cloudless light enshrined,
In whom no darkness is.

BERNARD BARTON.

WASH, Lord, and purify my heart,
And make it clean in every part;
And when 'tis clean, Lord, keep it too,
For that is more than I can do.

THOMAS ELLWOOD.

THOU too, my heart, whom He, and He alone,
Who all things knows, can know, with love replete,
Regenerate and pure, pour all thyself
A living sacrifice before His throne!

CHRISTOPHER SMART.

(*See also* REGENERATION.)

HEAVEN—HEAVENLY RICHES.

EYE hath not seen, nor ear heard, neither have entered into the heart of man, the things which God hath prepared for them that love Him. I. CORINTHIANS, ii, 9.

They shall hunger no more, neither thirst any more; neither shall the sun light on them, nor any heat.

For the Lamb which is in the midst of the throne shall feed them, and shall lead them unto living fountains of waters: and God shall wipe away all tears from their eyes. REVELATIONS, vii, 16, 17.

In my Father's house are many mansions: if it were not so, I would have told you. I go to prepare a place for you. JOHN, xiv, 2.

An inheritance incorruptible and undefiled, and that fadeth not away, reserved in Heaven. I. PETER, i, 4.

Lay up for yourselves treasures in Heaven, where neither moth nor rust doth corrupt, and where thieves do not break through nor steal:

For where your treasure is, there will your heart be also. MATTHEW, vi, 20, 21.

For we know that if our earthly house of this tabernacle were dissolved, we have a building of God, a house not made with hands, eternal in the heavens. II. CORINTHIANS, v, 1.

THERE is a world above,
  Where sorrow is unknown;
A long eternity of love,
  Formed for the good alone;
And faith beholds the dying here,
Translated to that glorious sphere.

JAMES MONTGOMERY.

WHERE that innumerable throng
Of saints and angels mingle song;
Where, wrought with hands, no temples rise,
For God Himself their place supplies;
Nor priests are needed, in the abode
Where the whole hosts are priests to God:
Think what a Sabbath there shall be,
The Sabbath of Eternity.

THOMAS GRINFIELD.

THERE smiles the mother we have wept! there bloom
Again the buds asleep within the tomb;
There o'er bright gates, inscribed "No more to part,"
Soul springs to soul, and heart unites to heart!

SIR E. B. LYTTON.

DREAMS cannot picture a world so fair—
Sorrow and death may not enter there:
Time doth not breathe on its fadeless bloom,
For beyond the clouds, and beyond the tomb,
It is there, it is there, my child!

MRS. HEMANS.

AS through the artist's intervening glass
Our eye observes the distant planets pass,
A little we discover, but allow
That more remains unseen than art can show:
So whilst our mind its knowledge would improve,
(Its feeble eye intent on things above,)
High as we may we lift our reason up,
By Faith directed, and confirmed by Hope:
Yet we are able only to survey
Dawnings of beams, and promises of day.
Heaven's fuller effluence mocks our dazzled sight;
Too great its swiftness, and too strong its light:
But soon the 'mediate clouds shall be dispelled;
The sun shall then be face to face beheld,
In all his robes, with all his glory on,
Seated sublime on his meridian throne. PRIOR.

THERE shall the good of earth be found at last,
Where dazzling streams and vernal fields expand;
Where love her crown attains—her trials past—
And, fill'd with rapture, hails the "better land!"

WILLIS G. CLARK

THRICE happy world, where gilded toys
No more disturb our thoughts, no more pollute our joys!
  There light or shade no more succeed by turns,
There reigns the eternal sun with an unclouded ray,
There all is calm as night, yet all immortal day,
  And truth for ever shines, and love for ever burns.

ISAAC WATTS.

IN having all things, and not Thee, what have I?
  Not having Thee, what have my labours got?
Let me enjoy but Thee, what further crave I?
  And having Thee alone, what have I not?
I wish not sea nor land; nor would I be
Possessed of Heaven, Heaven unpossessed of Thee.

FRANCIS QUARLES.

YET, far beyond the clouds outspread,
  Where soaring fancy oft hath been,
There is a land where Thou hast said
  The pure in heart shall enter in;
There, in those realms so calmly bright,
  How many a loved and gentle one
Bathe their soft plumes in living light,
  That sparkles from Thy radiant throne!
There, souls once soft and sad as ours,
Look up and sing 'mid fadeless flowers;
They dream no more of grief and care,
For Thou, the God of Peace, art there.

MRS. WELBY

O, WHEN a mother meets on high
The babe she lost in infancy,
Hath she not then for pains and fears,
The day of woe, the watchful night,
For all her sorrows, all her tears,
An over-payment of delight?

SOUTHEY.

THE ransomed shout to their glorious King,
Where no sorrow shades the soul as they sing;
But a sinless and joyous song they raise,
And their voice of prayer is eternal praise.

HENRY WARE, JR.

EYE hath not seen,
Ear hath not heard, nor can the human heart
Those joys conceive, which, blissful heritage,
Christ for His faithful votaries prepares.

SAMUEL HAYES.

To live in darkness — in despair to die —
Is this indeed the boon to mortals given?
Is there no port — no rock of refuge nigh?
There is—to those who fix their anchor-hope in Heaven

Turn then, O man! and cast all else aside;
Direct thy wandering thoughts to things above —
Low at the cross bow down — in *that* confide,
Till doubt be lost in faith, and bliss secured in love.

C. C. COLTON.

HERE, in our souls, we treasure up the wealth
Fraud cannot filch, nor waste destroy; — the more
'T is spent, the more we have; — the sweet affections —
The heart's religion,— the diviner instincts
Of what we shall be, when the world is dust.

SIR E. B. LYTTON.

WE live below the sky,
Yet we may lay up treasure even there;
Yea, life immortal — purity of heart —
Similitude to God, in that we bear
Our Saviour's image in our inward part.

THOS. MCKELLAR.

If God hath made the world so fair,
Where sin and death abound;
How beautiful beyond compare
Will Paradise be found! JAMES MONTGOMERY.

FRIENDS, even in Heaven, one happiness would miss,
Should they not know each other when in bliss.
BP. KEN.

SEEK well another world; who studies this,
Travels in clouds, seeks manna where none is.
HENRY VAUGHAN.

THE HOLY SPIRIT.

AND suddenly there came a sound from Heaven as of a rushing mighty wind, and it filled all the house where they were sitting.

And there appeared unto them cloven tongues like as of fire, and it sat upon each of them.

And they were all filled with the Holy Ghost, and began to speak with other tongues as the Spirit gave them utterance. ACTS, ii, 2, 3, 4.

If ye then, being evil, know how to give good gifts unto your children: how much more shall your Heavenly Father give the Holy Spirit to them that ask Him? LUKE, xi, 13.

The Comforter, which is the Holy Ghost, whom the Father will send in My name, he shall teach you all things. LUKE, XIV, 26.

Your body is the temple of the Holy Ghost. I. CORINTHIANS, vi, 19.

THE Spirit of God
From Heaven descending, dwells in domes of clay;
In mode far passing human thought, he guides,
Impels, instructs: intense pursuit of good
And cautious flight of evil he suggests,
But in such gentle murmurs, that to know
His heavenly voice, we must have done His will.
JOHN HEY.

THAT He, The Third
In the Eternal Essence, to the prayer
Sincere should come, should come as soon as asked,
Proceeding from the Father and the Son,
To give Faith and Repentance, such as God
Accepts. POLLOK.

HE to His own a Comforter will send,
The promise of the Father, who shall dwell
His Spirit within them, and the law of Faith
Working through love, upon their hearts shall write,
To guide them in all truth. MILTON.

ON your souls
The Spirit of God shall dart with inward ray,
And heavenly light in fullest streams be poured.
Then shall ye to remotest peoples, Jew
Or Gentile, bear Christ's name, and through the world
Proclaim forgiveness of repented sins.
THOMAS HUGHES.

IF yet the Holy Spirit deigns to dwell
In earthly domes, 'tis not in those defiled
With pride, with fraud, with rapine, or with lust;
'Midst the rough foliage of the thorny brake,
The clustering grape not blushes, and the fig
Decks not the prickly thistle's barren stalk;
Even thus shall all be measured by their fruits.
CHARLES JENNER.

DARKNESS profound
Covered the abyss; but on the watery calm
His brooding wings the Spirit of God outspread,
And vital virtue infused, and vital warmth,
Throughout the fluid mass. MILTON.

WHEN the Spirit of our God
  Came down, His flock to find,
A voice from Heaven was heard abroad—
  A rushing, mighty wind.

Nor doth the outward ear alone
  At that high warning start;
Conscience gives back th' appalling tone;
  'Tis echoed in the heart.

KEBLE.

HOME—PARENTS—FAMILY DEVOTION.

Lo children are a heritage of the Lord, and the fruit of the womb is His reward.

As arrows are in the hand of a mighty man, so are the children of the youth.

Happy is the man that hath his quiver full of them: they shall not be ashamed, but they shall speak with the enemies in the gate. PSALM cxxvii, 3, 4, 5.

Honour thy father and thy mother. EXODUS, xx, 12.

As for me and my house, we will serve the Lord. JOSHUA, xxiv, 15.

But if any provide not for his own, and specially for those of his own house, he hath denied the faith, and is worse than an infidel. I. TIMOTHY, v, 8

And these words which I command thee this day, shall be in thine heart,

And thou shalt teach them diligently unto thy children, and shalt talk of them when thou sittest in thine house, and when thou walkest by the way, and when thou liest down, and when thou risest up. DEUTERONOMY, vi, 6, 7.

To turn the hearts of the fathers to the children, and the disobedient to the wisdom of the just; to make ready a people prepared for the Lord. LUKE, i, 17.

A MOTHER'S love
  Is an undying feeling. Earth may chill
And sever other sympathies, and prove
  How weak all human bonds are—it may kill
Friendships, and crush hearts with them—but the thrill
  Of the maternal breast must ever move
In blest communion with her child, and fill
  Even Heaven itself with prayers and hymns of love.

S. D. PATTERSON.

AND say to mothers what a holy charge
Is theirs — with what a kingly power their love
Might rule the fountains of the new-born mind.
Warn them to wake at early dawn, and sow
Good seed before the world has sown its tares.

MRS. SIGOURNEY.

HONOUR thy parents to prolong thine end;
With them, though for a truth, do not contend;
Whoever makes his father's heart to bleed,
Shall have a son that will avenge the deed.

THOMAS RANDOLPH.

THE mother's love — there's none so pure,
So constant, and so kind,
Nor human passion doth endure
Like this within the mind.

MRS. HALL.

THE parent pair their secret homage pay,
And proffer up to Heaven the warm request,
That He who stills the raven's clamorous nest,
And decks the lily fair in flowery pride,
Would, in the way His wisdom sees the best,
For them and for their little ones provide,
But chiefly, in their hearts, with Grace Divine, preside.

BURNS.

FATHERS alone a father's heart can know;
What secret tides of sweet enjoyment flow
When brothers love! But if their hate succeeds,
They wage the war, but 'tis the father bleeds.

YOUNG.

LET parents be the same
To all their children; common in their care,
And in their love of them.

THOS. SOUTHERN.

O PROVIDENCE,
What is there like a father to a son?
A father, quick in love, wakeful in care,
Tenacious of his trust, proof in experience,
Severe in honour, perfect in example,
Stamped with authority! SHERIDAN KNOWLES.

A FATHER should to God pray, each new day at the latest,
"Lord, teach me how to use the power Thou delegatest!"
RUCKERT.

HER pious love excelled to all she bore;
New objects only multiplied it more;
And as the chosen found the pearly grain
As much as every vessel could contain;
As in the blissful vision, each shall share
As much of glory as his soul can bear,
So did she love, and so dispense her care.
DRYDEN.

LOOK! how he laughs and stretches out his arms,
And opens wide his blue eyes upon thine,
To hail his father; while his little form
Flutters as winged with joy. Talk not of pain!
The childless cherubs well might envy thee
The pleasures of a parent! BYRON.

IN all men sinful is it to be slow
To hope: in parents, sinful above all.
WORDSWORTH.

IF in the family thou art the best,
Pray oft, and be the mouth unto the rest;
Whom God hath made the heads of families,
He hath made priests to offer sacrifice.

Daily let part of Holy Writ be read,
Let as the body, so the soul have bread;
For look, how many souls in thy house be,
With just as many souls God trusteth thee.

ANONYMOUS. (1600.)

WHAT household thoughts around thee, as their shrine,
Cling reverently! — Of anxious looks beguiled,
My mother's eyes upon thy page divine,
Each day were bent; her accents, gravely mild,
Breathed out thy love: whilst I, a dreamy child,
Wandered on breeze-like fancies oft away,
To some lone tuft of gleaming spring-flowers wild,
Some fresh-discovered nook for woodland play,
Some secret nest: — yet would the solemn Word
At times, with kindlings of young wonder heard,
  Fall on my wakened spirit, there to be
A seed not lost; — for which in darker years,
O, book of Heaven! I pour, with grateful tears,
  Heart-blessings on the holy dead, and thee!

MRS. HEMANS.

AND silent stood his children by,
  Hushing their very breath,
Before the solemn sanctity
  Of thoughts o'er-sweeping death.
Silent — yet did not each young breast
  With love and reverence melt?
O, blest be those fair girls, and blest
  The home where God is felt! MRS. HEMANS.

FROM yon lowly roof, whose curling smoke
O'ermounts the mist, is heard at intervals
The voice of psalms — the simple song of praise.

GRAHAM

Lo! where yon cottage whitens through the green,
The loveliest feature of a matchless scene;
Beneath its shading elm, with pious fear,
An aged mother draws her children near;
While from the Holy Word, with earnest air,
She teaches them the privilege of prayer.
Look! How their infant eyes with rapture speak;
Mark the flushed lily on the dimpled cheek;
Their hearts are filled with gratitude and love,
Their hopes are centred in a world above,
Where, in a choir of angels, Faith portrays
The loved, departed, father of their days.

RUFUS DAWES.

THE private path, the secret acts of men,
If noble, far the noblest of our lives! YOUNG.

EXAMPLE strikes
All human hearts! A bad example more;
More still, a father's. YOUNG.

YET is He there: beneath our eaves
Each sound His wakeful ear receives;
Hush idle words, and thoughts of ill,
Your Lord is listening; peace, be still.
Christ watches by a Christian's hearth,
Be silent, vain, deluding mirth,
Till in thine altered voice be known,
Somewhat of Resignation's tone. KEBLE.

AROUND each pure, domestic shrine,
Bright flowers of Eden bloom and twine;
Our hearths are altars all:
The prayers of hungry souls and poor,
Like armed angels at the door,
Our unseen foes appal. EBLE

Sweet is the smile of home; the mutual look
  When hearts are of each other sure;
Sweet all the joys that crowd the household nook,
  The haunt of all affections pure;
Yet in the world even these abide, and we
  Above the world, our calling boast:
Once gain the mountain-top, and thou art free;
Till then, who rest, presume; who turn to look, are lost

Keble.

  So glorious let Thy pastors shine,
That, by their speaking lives, the world may learn
  First, filial duty, then divine;
That sons to parents, all to Thee may turn.

Keble.

Then, kneeling down, to Heaven's Eternal King
  The saint, the father, and the husband prays:
Hope "springs exulting on triumphant wing,"
  That thus they all shall meet in future days:
There ever bask in uncreated rays,
  No more to sigh, or shed the bitter tear;
Together hymning their Creator's praise,
  In such society yet still more dear,
When circling time moves round, in an eternal sphere.

Burns.

HOPE.

If in this life only we have hope in Christ, we are of all men the most miserable. I. Corinthians, xv, 19.

The Lord is my portion, saith my soul, therefore will I hope in Him. Lamentations, iii, 24.

It is good that a man should both hope and patiently wait for the salvation of the Lord. Lamentations, iii, 26.

Happy is he that hath the God of Jacob for his help, whose hope is in the Lord his God. Psalm xlvi, 5.

Which hope we have as an anchor of the soul, both sure and steadfast, and which entereth into that within the veil. Hebrews, vi, 19.

Hope, eager hope, the assassin of our joy,
All present blessings treading under foot,
Is scarce a milder tyrant than despair.
With no past toils content, still planning new,
Hope turns us o'er to death alone for ease.
Possession why more tasteless than pursuit?
Why is a wish far dearer than a crown?
That wish accomplished, why the grave of bliss?
Because in the great future buried deep,
Beyond our plans of empire and renown,
Lies all that man with ardour should pursue;
And He who made him, bent him to the right.

Young.

Hope, with uplifted foot, set free from earth,
Pants for the place of her ethereal birth;
On steady wings, sails through the immense abyss,
Plucks amaranthine joys from bowers of bliss,
And crowns the soul, while yet a mourner here,
With wreaths like those triumphant spirits wear.
Hope, as an anchor, firm and sure, holds fast
The Christian vessel, and defies the blast. Cowper

RICH Hope of boundless bliss!
Bliss, past man's power to paint it; time's to close!
This Hope is earth's most estimable prize:
This is man's portion while no more than man:
Hope, of all passions, most befriends us here;
Passions of prouder name befriend us less.
Joy has her tears, and transport has her death;
Hope, like a cordial, innocent, though strong,
Man's heart at once inspirits and serenes;
Nor makes him pay his wisdom for his joys;
'T is all our present state can safely bear,
Health to the frame, and vigour to the mind!
A joy attempered! A chastised delight!
Like the fair summer evening, mild and sweet,
'T is man's full cup, his paradise below. YOUNG.

THE Night is mother of the Day,
The Winter of the Spring,
And ever, upon old Decay,
The greenest mosses cling.
Behind the cloud the star-light lurks,
Through showers the sunbeams fall;
For God, who loveth all His works,
Hath left His Hope with all. J. G. WHITTIER.

She lights our gloom — she soothes our care —
She bids our fears depart,
Transmutes to gems each grief-fraught tear,
And binds the broken heart!

She glances o'er us from above,
The brightest star that's given,
And guides us still, through faith and love,
To endless peace, in Heaven.
ANNA PEYRE DINNIES.

UPON her arm a silver anchor lay,
Whereon she leaned ever, as befell:
And ever up to Heaven as she did pray,
Her steadfast eyes were bent, nor swerved otherway.
SPENSER.

HUMILITY.

GOD resisteth the proud, but giveth grace unto the humble. JAMES, iv, 6.

Whosoever shall exalt himself shall be abased; and he that shall humble himself shal be exalted. MATTHEW, xxiii, 12.

A man's pride shall bring him low: but honour shall uphold the humble in spiri PROVERBS, xxix, 23.

Better is it to be of an humble spirit with the lowly, than to divide the spoil with th proud. PROVERBS, xxi, 19.

Take my yoke upon you, and learn of me; for I am meek and lowly in heart: an ye shall find rest unto your souls. MATTHEW, xi, 29.

Blessed are the poor in spirit; for theirs is the kingdom of Heaven. MATTHEW, v, 3

By humility, and the fear of the Lord, are riches, and honour, and life. PROVERBS xxii, 4

EASIER to smite with Peter's sword,
Than watch one hour in humbling prayer:
Life's great things, like the Syrian lord,
Our hearts can do and dare.

But O, we shrink from Jordan's side,
From waters which alone can save:
And murmur for Abana's banks,
And Pharpar's brighter wave. J. G. WHITTIER.

HUMBLE we must be, if to Heaven we go;
High is the roof there, but the gate is low:
Whene'er thou speak'st, look with a lowly eye—
Grace is increased by humility. ROBERT HERRICK.

HEAVEN-GATES are not so highly arched
As princes' palaces; they that enter there
Must go upon their knees. JOHN WEBSTER

HE that high growth on cedars did bestow,
Gave also lowly mushrooms leave to grow.
In Haman's pomp poor Mardocheus wept,
Yet God did turn his fate upon his foe:
The lazar pined while Dives' feast was kept,
Yet he to Heaven, to hell did Dives go.
We trample grass, and prize the flowers of May,
Yet grass is green when flowers do fade away.
ROBERT SOUTHWELL

HE that is down need fear no fall;
He that is low, no pride:
He that is humble ever shall
Have God to be his guide. BUNYAN.

THE cedar's shade like cloud may lie
Athwart the lily's brightness—
Yet why complain? it leaves no stain,
To mar the blossom's whiteness;
And darkly thus may pride and power
Appear to press the lowly—
Yet never may the shadow stay
Where Faith, like blossom holy,
Keeps white the heart: to such there will be given
A blest assurance of the love of Heaven.
MRS. HALE.

The deep, perennial source of purest bliss,
The proof of goodness, and the solid stamp
Of blessed piety; the hallowed base,
On which the Christian virtues love to rest.
CHARLES PHILPOT.

LET me be ignorant, and in nothing good,
But graciously to know I am no better.

SHAKSPEARE.

MORE will I do:
Though all that I can do is nothing worth;
Since that my penitence comes after all,
Imploring pardon. SHAKSPEARE.

HYPOCRISY.

SATAN himself is transformed into an angel of light. Therefore it is no great thing if his ministers also be transformed as the ministers of righteousness. II. CORINTHIANS, xi, 14, 15.

He that covereth his sins shall not prosper. PROVERBS, xxviii, 13.

Beware of false prophets, which come to you in sheep's clothing; but inwardly they are ravening wolves. MATTHEW, vii, 15.

The triumphing of the wicked is short, and the joy of the hypocrite but for a moment. JOB, xx, 5.

Thou shalt not be as the hypocrites are; for they love to pray standing in the synagogues and in the corners of the streets, that they may be seen of men. Verily I say unto you, they have their reward. MATTHEW, vi, 5.

So smooth he daubed his life with show of virtue,
He lived from all attainder of suspect.

SHAKSPEARE

I DO the wrong, and first begin to brawl.
The secret mischiefs that I set abroach,
I lay unto the grievous charge of others.
But then I sigh, and with a piece of scripture
Tell them — that God bids us do good for evil.
And thus I clothe my naked villany,
With old, odd ends, stol'n forth of Holy Writ.

SHAKSPEARE.

THE devil can cite scripture for his purpose.
An evil soul producing holy witness,
Is like a villain with a smiling cheek;
A goodly apple, rotten at the heart;
O, what a goodly outside falsehood hath!

SHAKSPEARE

TIME shall unfold what plated cunning hides;
Who cover faults, at last them shame derides.

SHAKSPEARE.

No man's condition is so base as his;
None more accursed than he: for man esteems
Him hateful 'cause he seems not what he is:
God hates him 'cause he is not what he seems;
What grief is absent, or what mischief can
Be added to the hate of God and man?

FRANCIS QUARLES.

LIKE the detested tribe
Of ancient Pharisees, beneath the mask
Of clamorous piety, what numbers veil
Contaminated, vicious hearts! How many
In the devoted temple of their God,
With hypocritic eye, from which the tear
Of penitential anguish seems to flow,
Pour forth their vows, and by affected zeal
Prëeminent devotion boast; while vice
Within the guilty breast, rankles unseen.

SAMUEL HAYES.

THESE are they
That prey upon the widow, and devour
The orphan's portion, mocking Heaven with prayers
Ceaseless, and fasts, which will but more incense
His anger, and bring down worse chastisement.

CHARLES PEERS.

SEEMS he a dove? his feathers are but borrowed,
For he's disposed as the hateful raven.
Is he a lamb? his skin is surely lent him,
For he's inclined as are the ravenous wolves.
Who cannot steal a shape, that means deceit?

SHAKSPEARE

OFT, beneath
The saintly veil, the votary of sin
May lurk unseen, and to that eye alone
Which penetrates the inmost heart, revealed.

GEORGE BALLY.

GOD beholds thee, wretch, though wrapt in prayer,
A wolf disguised, a painted sepulchre;
Regards no more thy cant, and godly whine,
Than yon dumb statue, on the marble shrine,
Whose hands are seen, in holy rapture closed
And steadfast eyes, to Heaven alone disposed,
Prayer's senseless image, where no soul within
Speaks through the form, and animates the mien.

JAMES SCOTT.

HYPOCRISY, detest her as we may
(And no man's hatred ever wronged her yet)
May claim this merit still, that she admits
The worth of what she mimics with such care,
And thus gives virtue indirect applause. COWPER.

OUR better mind
Is as a Sunday's garment, then put on
When we have naught to do; but at our work,
We wear a worse, for thrift! CROWE.

NEITHER man nor angel can discern
Hypocrisy, the only evil that walks
Invisible, except to God alone. MILTON.

IDOLATRY.

COVETOUSNESS, which is idolatry. COLOSSIANS, iii, 5.

What agreement hath the temple of God with idols? II. CORINTHIANS, vi, 16.

Rebellion is as the sin of witchcraft, and stubbornness is as iniquity and idolatry. I. SAMUEL, xv, 23.

Thou shalt have no other gods before me. EXODUS, xx, 3.

Who changed the truth of God into a lie, and worshipped and served the creature more than the Creator, who is blessed for ever. ROMANS, i, 25.

HEAR, Father! hear and aid!
If I have loved too well, if I have shed,
In my vain fondness, o'er a mortal head
Gifts, on Thy shrine, my God, more fitly laid;
If I have sought to live
But in one light, and made a mortal eye
The lonely star of my idolatry,
Thou that art Love, oh! pity and forgive!

MRS. HEMANS.

BEFORE the idol-monster was the blood
Of man poured out by man. No mother there
Blessed the fair skies which smiled upon her babe,
But hastened rather, with unnatural hand,
To crush the unfolding life, and turn aside
The dark inheritance of woe and pain,
Ere yet the unconscious victim owned its doom.

A. ALEXANDER.

WHATEVER passes as a cloud between
The mental eye of faith, and things unseen,
Causing that brighter world to disappear,
Or seem less lovely, and its hopes less dear:
This is our world, our idol, though it bear
Affection's impress, or devotion's air! ANONYMOUS.

And still from Him we turn away,
  And fill our hearts with worthless things;
The fires of avarice melt the clay,
  And forth the idol springs!
Ambition's flame, and passion's heat,
  By wondrous alchemy transmute
  Earth's dross, to raise some gilded brute
To fill Jehovah's seat. J. H. CLINCH.

THIS deity, whose altars reek with blood,
Though millions bend the prostituted knee
Before the radiant shrine, though millions own
His power vindictive just, and call him Honour,
All cannot sanctify what public good,
What nature's moral dictates disavow,
And Heaven's almighty mandate impious deems.
SAMUEL HAYES.

IF, when the Lord of Glory was in sight,
  Thou turn thy back upon that fountain clear,
To bow before the "little drop of light"
  Which dim-eyed men call praise and glory here:
What dost thou, but adore the sun, and scorn
Him at whose only word both sun and stars were born?

If while around thee gales from Eden breathe,
  Thou hide thine eyes, to make thy peevish moan
Over some broken reed of earth beneath,
  Some darling of blind fancy, dead and gone,
As wisely might'st thou in Jehovah's fane
Offer thy love and tears to Thammuz slain.

Turn thee from these, or dare not to enquire
  Of Him whose Name is Jealous, lest in wrath,
He hear and answer thine unblest desire:
  Far better we should cross His lightning's path,
Than be according to our idols heard,
And God should take us at our own vain word.
KEBLE.

INGRATITUDE.

THE ox knoweth his owner, and the ass his master's crib; but Israel doth not know my people doth not consider. Isaiah, i, 5.

BRUTES leave ingratitude to man. COTTON.

A THANKFUL heart hath earned one favor twice,
But he that is ungrateful, wants no vice.
FRANCIS QUARLES.

THOSE "common blessings!" In this chequered scene,
How little gratitude ascends to God!
Is it, in truth, a privilege so mean
To wander with free footsteps o'er the sod,
See various blossoms paint the valley-clod,
And all things into teeming beauty burst?—
A miracle as great as Aaron's rod,
But that our senses, into dulness nurst,
Recurring custom still with apathy hath curst.
MRS. NORTON.

THE stall-fed ox, that is grown fat, will know
His careful feeder, and acknowledge too;
The generous spaniel loves his master's eye,
And licks his fingers, though no meat be by:
But man, ungrateful man, that's born and bred
By Heaven's immediate power; maintained and fed
By His providing hand; observed, attended
By His indulgent grace; preserved, defended
By His prevailing arm: this man, I say,
Is more ungrateful, more obdure than they.
FRANCIS QUARLES.

MAN, O, most ungrateful man, can ever
Enjoy Thy gift, but never mind the Giver;
And like the swine, though pampered with enough,
His eyes are never higher than the trough.

FRANCIS QUARLES.

HE that's ungrateful has no guilt but one;
All other crimes may pass for virtues in him.

YOUNG.

INSTRUCTION—EDUCATION.

TRAIN up a child in the way he should go; and when he is old, he will not depart from it. PROVERBS, xxii, 6.

The fear of the Lord is the beginning of knowledge, but fools despise wisdom and instruction. PROVERBS, i, 7.

LORD, grant our hearts be so inclined,
  Thy work to seek, Thy will to do;
And while we teach the youthful mind,
  Our own be taught Thy lessons too.

MISS LANDON.

WAS not our Lord a little child,
  Taught by degrees to pray,
By father dear, and mother mild,
  Instructed day by day?

And loved He not of Heaven to talk,
  With children in His sight,
To meet them in His daily walk,
  And to His arms invite?

KEBLE.

Break oblivion's sleep,
  And toil with florist's art,
To plant the gems of virtue deep
  In childhood's fruitful heart.
To thee the babe is given,
  Fair from its glorious Sire,
Go, nurse it for the King of Heaven,
  And He will pay the hire. Mrs. Sigourney.

(*See also* Children.)

JEWS—JERUSALEM—JUDEA.

[Sa]lvation is of the Jews. John, iv, 22.

[W]hat advantage then hath the Jew, or what profit is there of circumcision? Much, every way: chiefly, because that unto them were committed the oracles of God. Romans, iii, 1, 2.

Jerusalem shall be trodden down of the Gentiles, until the time of the Gentiles be fulfilled. Luke, xxi, 24.

The Lord shall establish thee as a holy people unto himself, as He hath sworn unto thee, if thou shalt keep the commandments of the Lord thy God, and walk in His ways.

And all the people of the earth shall see that thou art called by the name of the Lord and they shall be afraid of thee. Deuteronomy, xxviii, 9, 10.

But it shall come to pass, if thou wilt not hearken unto the voice of the Lord thy God, to observe to do all his commandments and his statutes, * * * thou shalt become an astonishment, a proverb, and a by-word, among all the nations whither the Lord shall lead thee. Deuteronomy, xxviii, 15, 37.

For yet the tenfold film shall fall
  O, Judah, from thy sight,
And every eye be purged to read
  Thy testimonies right,
When thou, with all Messiah's signs
  In Christ distinctly seen,
Shall, by Jehovah's nameless name,
  Invoke the Nazarene. William Crosswell.

O, 'TIS a land of kings — of poets, seers,
Wise men and holy, priests and prophets sage,
And the best home of heavenly poesy,
Since here the poet was the monarch too.

ARTHUR C. COXE.

O, THOU, the Shepherd of Thy flock,
  Who led'st Thy people through the wave,
And gav'st them water from the rock,
  And bar'dst thine arm in might to save:—
Hear Thou the strain our hearts prolong—
  List — list the suppliant captive's cry—
O, when shall cease the mournful song,
  O, when shall Judah's tears be dry?

C. W. EVEREST.

JERUSALEM! alas! alas! of old,
Deaf to whate'er prophetic seers foretold,
Assailing all, whom Heaven, in mercy sent,
And murdering those that warned thee to repent!
Thou, the world's Saviour who suspendedst high,
His works reviled, and mocked His agony,
How oft hath God, still gracious, striven to bring
Thy devious brood beneath His sheltering wing,
To save thee from the hovering eagle's power,
And shield the unequalled misery of this hour!
But no! thou would'st not! thence this signal fate!
Thence art thou fallen! deserted! desolate!

WILLIAM GIBSON.

THRICE happy nation! Favourite of Heaven!
Selected from the kingdoms of the earth
To be His chosen race, ordained to spread
His glory through remotest realms, and teach
The Gentile world Jehovah's awful name.

WILLIAM HODSON

Sion, the glory of whose refulgent fame
Gave earnest of an everlasting name,
Is now become an undigested mass,
And ruin is, where that brave glory was.

Francis Quarles.

Christian, behold the typic shade
  Of that dim path prepared for thee—
Behold, in Jordan's tide displayed,
  Death's overflowing sea.
But if thou still hast kept the Ark
Of God before thee as a mark,
Fear not the troubled waters dark,
  Howe'er they rage, and chafe, and roar;
On that mysterious voyage embark,
  And God will guide thee o'er. J. H. Clinch.

That people once
So famed, whom God Himself vouchsafed to call
His chosen race, and with a guardian hand
Deigned to protect, from Palestine exiled,
Are doomed to wander; although scattered thus
Through all the globe, there is no clime which they
Can call their own, no country where their laws
Hold sovereign rule. Irrefragable proof,
That every oracle of Holy Writ
Was given by Heaven itself! Samuel Hayes.

Whilst Pharaoh's pride withstood,
His pools turned poison, and his Nile ran blood,
From whose corrupting channel, moist and warm,
Leaped forth the frogs, a foul, offensive swarm;
No place was sheltered from their loathsome tread,
The festive banquet, nor the bridal bed.
Anon, destructive, sweeps the burning hail,
His trees stand branchless, and his furrows fail;

Whilst, from the East, devouring locusts ri
To spoil the pittance spared him by the sk
But why on each peculiar token dwell
Of God's deep wrath, or all His judgments tell?
Enough to add, that Israel's thraldom ceased,
From Pharaoh's stubborn hand, by Him released.

WILLIAM GIBSON

THEY, and they only, amongst all mankind,
Received the transcript of the Eternal Mind;
Were trusted with His own engraven laws,
And constituted guardians of His cause;
Theirs were the prophets, theirs the priestly call,
And theirs, by birth, the Saviour of us all.

COWPER.

THEIR glory faded, and their race dispersed,
The last of nations now, though once the first;
They warn and teach the proudest, would they learn,
Keep wisdom, or meet vengeance in your turn;
If we escaped not, if Heaven spared not us,
Peeled, scattered, and exterminated thus;
If vice received her retribution due,
When we were visited, what hope for you?

COWPER.

WHERE youthful Jacob slept,
Angels their bright watch kept,
And visions to his soul were given
That led him to the gate of Heaven.
Exiled pilgrim! many a morrow,
When thine earthly schemes were crossed,
Mourning o'er thy loved and lost,
Thou didst sigh, with holy sorrow,
For that blessed hour of prayer,
And exclaim, God met me there!

MRS. M'CARTEE.

"BURY me with my fathers, in the cave
The Patriarch purchased of the sons of Heth.
Where Abraham slumbers, and where Isaac rests,
Where Sarah and Rebekah wait the dawn
Of the last morning,—and where Leah sleeps,
Leah the tender-eyed, there let me lie—
I buried her in Hebron."—
Did the thought
That Rachel slept at Bethlehem, in that hour
Come to the dying man? He gathered up
His limbs in decent calmness; and his spirit,
Careful no longer where the body tarried,
Was gathered to his fathers. H. H. WELD.

GLORIOUS is the blending
Of light affections, climbing or descending
Along a scale of light and life, with cares
Alternate carrying holy thoughts and prayers
Up to the sovereign seat of the Most High;
Descending to the worm in charity;
Like those good angels, whom a dream of night
Gave, in the field of Luz, to Jacob's sight;
All, while he slept, treading the pendent stairs
Earthward or heavenward, radiant messengers,
That, with a perfect will, in one accord
Of strict obedience served the Almighty Lord;
And with untired humility, forbore
To speed their errand with the wings they wore.
WORDSWORTH.

JOY—HAPPINESS—PEACE.

PEACE I leave with you, my peace I give unto you; not as the world giveth, give I unto you. Let not your heart be troubled, neither let it be afraid. JOHN, XIV, 27.

The peace of God, which passeth all understanding, shall keep your hearts and minds, through Jesus Christ. PHILIPPIANS, iv, 7.

The fruit of the Spirit is love, joy, peace. GALATIANS, v, 22.

Happy is the man that findeth wisdom, and the man that getteth understanding * * * Her ways are ways of pleasantness, and all her paths are peace. PROVERBS, iii, 13, 17.

WHAT nothing earthly gives, or can destroy,
The soul's calm sunshine, and the heartfelt joy.
POPE.

POOR worldling! stay thy vain pursuit of peace
In empty vanities: no good can live
In all the gilded charms that mock thee: cease
Thy hold on these; loose every cord, and hear
The voice of God: "Come ye that weary are!
Ye heavy-laden, come, and I will give
You rest." O, heed that call! in holy fear,
In deep humility, bow down: the star
Of hope shall rise, and joy shall speak thy soul's release
ISAAC F. SHEPARD.

How long, ye miserably blind,
Shall idle dreams engage your mind;
How long the passions make their flight
At empty shadows of delight?
No more in paths of error stray,
The Lord, thy Jesus, is the Way,
The Spring of happiness, and where
Should men seek happiness, but there? PARNELL.

Return, my senses, range no more abroad,
He only finds his bliss, who seeks for God.
Parnell.

Go! hie thee to God's altar,—kneeling there,
List to the mingled voice of fervent prayer
  That swells around thee in the sacred fane;
Or catch the solemn organ's pealing note
When grateful praises on the still air float,
  And the freed soul forgets earth's heavy chain;
There learn that Peace, sweet Peace, is ever found
In her eternal home, on holy ground.
Mrs. Embury.

In active health or sad disease,
  O, ne'er forget that precious word—
"He shall be kept in perfect peace,
  Whose soul is stayed on God." G. B. Cheever.

"Save, Lord, we perish!" was their fearful cry,
While glancing upwards to the angry sky;
It was enough:—the Saviour gently rose,
And kindly bade his followers calm their woes:—
"Peace, peace, be still!" The rolling waves were stayed—
The storms were over, and the winds allayed.
Peace, troubled soul! The Saviour bids thee rest,
And calm the tumult raging in thy breast;
Into thy heart let His sweet smile descend,
For He will be thy Brother, and thy Friend."
J. L. Chester.

In His favour, life is found;
All bliss beside, a shadow, or a sound. Cowper.

The weak have remedies, the wise have joys:
Superior wisdom is superior bliss Young

CHRIST had His joys — but they were not
  The joys the son of pleasure boasts —
O, no! 't was when His Spirit sought
  Thy Will, Thy glory, God of hosts!
Christ had His joys — and so hath he,
  Who feels His Spirit in his heart;
Who yields, O God, his all to Thee,
  And loves Thy name, for what Thou art!

ANONYMOUS.

"PEACE" was the word our Saviour breathed,
  When from our world His steps withdrew;
The gift He to His friends bequeathed,
  With Calvary and the Cross in view:—
Redeemer! With adoring love
  Our spirits take Thy rich bequest,
The watchword of the host above,
  The passport to their realm of rest.

MRS. SIGOURNEY.

A DEITY believed, is joy begun;
A Deity adored, is joy advanced;
A Deity beloved, is joy matured.
Each branch of piety delight inspires.

YOUNG.

HE is the happy man whose life, e'en now,
Shows somewhat of that happier life to come;
Who, doomed to an obscure, but tranquil state,
Is pleased with it, and, were he free to choose,
Would make his fate his choice; whom peace, the fruit
Of virtue, and whom virtue, fruit of faith,
Prepare for happiness; bespeak him one
Content indeed to sojourn while he must
Below the skies, but having there his home.

COWPER.

On piety humanity is built;
And, on humanity, much happiness;
And yet still more, on piety itself. YOUNG.

Object of my first desire,
  Jesus, crucified for me!
All to happiness aspire,
  Only to be found in thee;
Thee to praise, and Thee to know,
Constitute our bliss below!
Thee to see, and Thee to love,
Constitute our bliss above. TOPLADY.

Happiness depends, as Nature shows,
Less on exterior things than most suppose.
Vigilant over all that He has made,
Kind Providence attends with gracious aid;
Bids equity throughout His works prevail,
And weighs the nations in an even scale. COWPER.

Religion does not censure, or exclude
Unnumbered pleasures, harmlessly pursued.
COWPER.

Pour forth thy fervours for a healthful mind,
Obedient passions, and a will resigned;
For love, which scarce collective man can fill;
For patience, sovereign o'er transmuted ill;
For faith, that, panting for a happier seat,
Counts death kind nature's signal of retreat;
These goods for man, the laws of Heaven ordain,
These goods He grants, who grants the power to gain;
With these, celestial wisdom calms the mind,
And makes the happiness she does not find.
DR. JOHNSON.

THE JUDGMENT.

AND He shall send His angels with a great sound of a trumpet, and they shall gather together His elect from the four winds, from one end of Heaven to the other. MATTHEW, xxiv, 31.

Then shall the King say unto them on His right hand, Come, ye blessed of My Father, inherit the kingdom prepared for you from the foundation of the world. MATTHEW xxv, 35.

Then shall He also say unto them on the left hand, Depart from me, ye cursed, into everlasting fire, prepared for the devil and his angels. MATTHEW, xxv, 41.

And these shall go away into everlasting punishment, but the righteous into life eternal. MATTHEW, xxv, 46.

We shall all stand before the judgment-seat of Christ. ROMANS, xiv, 10.

I DO believe myself the creature,
Subject and soldier, if I so may speak,
Of an Almighty Father, King and Lord;
Before whose presence, when my soul shall be
Of flesh and blood disrobed, I shall appear,
There to remain with all the great and good
That e'er have lived on earth; yea, and with spirits,
Higher than earth e'er owned, in such pure bliss
As human hearts conceive not,—if my life,
With its imperfect virtue, find acceptance
From pard'ning love and mercy; but if otherwise,—
That I shall pass into a state of misery,
With souls of wicked men and wrathful demons.

JOANNA BAILLIE.

THE sinner's doom,—the sinner's doom,—
How dark the agony
That haunts transgression to the tomb,
Then prays on endlessness to come,
Whose worm may never die.

From "CAPRICES."

GREAT day of dread, decision, and despair!
At thought of thee, each sublunary wish
Lets go its eager grasp, and quits the world.
YOUNG.

I'LL tell thee what is hell — thy memory
Still mountained up with records of the past,
Heap over heap, all accents and all forms,
Telling the tale of joy and innocence,
And hope, and peace, and love; recording, too,
With stern fidelity, the thousand wrongs
Worked upon weakness and defencelessness;
The blest occasions trifled o'er or spurned;
All that hath been that ought not to have been,
That might have been so different, that now
Cannot but be irrevocably past!
Thy gangrened heart,
Stripped of its self-worn mask, and spread at last
Bare, in its horrible anatomy,
Before thine own excruciated gaze! D. P. STARKEY.

IF you confess humanity, believe
There is a God, to punish or reward
Our doings here. THOMAS SOUTHERN.

THE judgment! the judgment! the thrones are all set,
Where the Lamb and the white-vested Elders are met!
All flesh is at once in the sight of the Lord,
And the doom of Eternity hangs on His word!

O mercy! O mercy! look down from above,
Creator! on us thy sad children, with love!
When beneath, to their darkness, the wicked are driven,
May our sanctified souls find a mansion in Heaven!
H. H. MILMAN.

THE soul once dying,
Dies ever, ever, no re-purifying;
No earnest sighs or groans, no intercession,
No cares, no penance, no too late confession
Can move the ear of justice, if it doom
A soul past cure, to an infernal tomb.

"The Queen." ANON. 1653

FROM Adam to his youngest heir,
Not one shall 'scape that muster-roll;
Each, as if he alone were there,
Shall stand, and win, or lose his soul:
These, from the Judge's presence, go
Down into everlasting woe;
Vengeance hath barred the gates of hell—
The scenes within, no tongue can tell.

But lo! far off, the righteous pass
To glory; from the King's right hand,
In silence, on the sea of glass,
Heaven's numbers without number stand,
While He, who bore the cross, lays down
His priestly robe and victor crown;
The mediatorial reign complete,
All things are put beneath His feet.

JAMES MONTGOMERY.

THEY who, through life,
By conscience and religion's warning voice
Unmoved, their prostituted hearts resigned
To sin, with the keen horrors of remorse
And anguish rent, call on the lofty hills
To cover their apostate heads. Alas!
Too late contrition comes: the doom is past.

SAMUEL HAYES.

'Tis done: again the conquering Chief appears,
In the dread vision of dissolving years;
His vesture dipped in blood, His eyes of flame,
The Word of God His everlasting name;
Throned in mid-heaven, with clouds of glory spread,
He sits in judgment on the quick and dead:
Strong to deliver; saints! your songs prepare;
Rush from your tombs to meet Him in the air:
But terrible in vengeance; sinners! bow
Your haughty heads, the grave protects not now;
He who alone in mortal conflict trod
The mighty wine-press of the wrath of God,
Shall fill the cup of trembling to His foes,
The unmingled cup of inexhausted woes;
The proud shall drink it in that dreadful day,
While earth dissolves, and Heaven is rolled away.

James Montgomery.

The day
Will come, when virtue from the cloud shall burst,
That long obscured her beams; when sin shall fly
Back to her native hell; there sink eclipsed
In penal darkness, where nor star shall rise,
Nor ever sunshine pierce the impervious gloom.

Glynn.

Every bashful grace that bloomed unseen,
Too delicate to bear the ruffling breath
Of worldly praise, is brought to light, before
Its best applauders — Angels, and their Lord.
The Judge, with accents mild, cries, Come, ye blessed,
Share the unfading pleasures of my realm,
Co-heirs of bliss, my Sire's adopted sons.
Straight at that word, the pious, like a flock
Of harmless doves are rapt, with ardent wing,
To meet their dear Redeemer.

George Bally.

The day of Christ; the last, the dreadful day;
  When thou and I, and all the world, shall come
  Before His judgment-seat, to hear their doom
For ever and for ever; and when they
Who loved not God, far, far from Him away
  Shall go; — but whither banished? and with whom?—
  And they who loved Him shall be welcomed home
To God, and Christ, and Heaven, and Heaven's array,
Angels and saints made perfect — may the scene
  Of that dread day be always present *here* —
Here in my heart! That every day between,
  Which brings my passage to the goal more near,
May find me fitter, by His love made clean,
  Before His throne of justice to appear.

Bp. Mant.

Every act
Which shunned the trifling plaudit of mankind,
Shall here to wondering millions be displayed,
A monument of grace.

C. P. Layard.

The day of wrath, that dreadful day,
When Heaven and earth shall pass away!—
What power shall be the sinner's stay?
How shall he meet that dreadful day?

When, shrivelling like a parched scroll,
The flaming heavens together roll,
And louder yet, and yet more dread,
Swells the high trump that wakes the dead?

O, on that day, that wrathful day,
When man to judgment wakes from clay,
Be Thou, O Christ! the sinner's stay,
Though Heaven and earth shall pass away.

Sir Walter Scott.

Then, all Thy saints assembled, Thou shalt judge
Bad men and angels; they, arraigned, shall sink
Beneath Thy sentence: Hell, her numbers full,
Thenceforth shall be for ever shut. Meanwhile
The world shall burn, and from her ashes spring
New Heaven and Earth, wherein the just shall dwell,
And after all their tribulations long
See golden days, fruitful of golden deeds,
With joy and love triumphing, and fair truth.
Then Thou Thy regal sceptre shalt lay by,
For regal sceptre thee no more shall need,
God shall be All in All. Milton.

The Book is opened, and the seal removed;
The adamantine Book; where every thought,
Though dawning on the heart, then sunk again
In the corrupted mass, each act obscure,
In characters indelible remain.
How vain thy boast, vile caitiff, to have 'scaped
An earthly forum; now, thy crimson stains
Glare on a congregated world; thy Judge
Omniscience, and Omnipotence thy scourge!
Thy mask hypocrisy, how useless here,
When, by a beam shot from the Fount of light,
The varnished saint starts up a ghastly fiend!

George Bally.

JUSTICE—DIVINE JUSTICE.

Shall not the Judge of all the earth do right? Genesis, xviii, 25.

Shall mortal man be more just than God? Shall a man be more pure than his Maker Job, iv, 17.

Justice and judgment are the habitation of Thy throne. Psalm lxxxix, 14.

So sure the fall of greatness raised on crimes!
So fixed the justice of all-conscious Heaven!
When haughty guilt exalts with impious joy,
Mistake shall blast, or accident destroy;
Weak man, with erring rage, may throw the dart,
But Heaven shall guide it to the guilty heart.

Dr. Johnson.

The words of Heaven, on whom it will, it will;
On whom it will not, so; yet still 'tis just.

Shakspeare.

Though with tardy step
Celestial Justice come, that step is sure.
Unerring is her bolt, and where it falls,
Eternal will the ruin be.

Samuel Hayes

The Sun of Justice may withdraw his beams
Awhile from earthly ken, and sit concealed
In dark recess, pavilioned round with clouds:
Yet let not guilt presumptuous rear her crest,
Nor virtue droop despondent: soon these clouds,
Seeming eclipse, will brighten into day,
And in majestic splendour He will rise,
With healing and with terror on His wings.

George Bally.

HUMAN LIFE.

Behold, Thou hast made my days as a hand-breadth, and mine age is as nothing before thee: verily every man at his best state is altogether vanity. Psalm xxxix, 5.

For what is your life? It is even a vapour, that appeareth for a little time, and then vanisheth away. James, iv, 14.

In God we live, and move, and have our being. Acts, xvii, 28.

A man's life consisteth not in the abundance of the things which he possesseth. Luke, xii, 15.

So teach us to number our days, that we may apply our hearts unto wisdom. Psalm xc, 12.

Between two breaths, what crowded mysteries lie,—
The first short gasp, the last and long-drawn sigh!
Like phantoms painted on the magic slide,
Forth from the darkness of the past we glide,
As living shadows for a moment seen
In airy pageant on the eternal screen,
Traced by a ray from one unchanging flame,
Then seek the dust and stillness, whence we came.

O. W. Holmes.

An aged Christian went tottering by,
And white was his hair, and dim was his eye;
And his broken spirit seemed ready to fly,
As he said, with faltering breath:
"It is life, to move from the heart's first throes,
Through youth and manhood, to age's snows,
In a ceaseless circle of joys and woes:—
It is life to prepare for death."

Charles D. Drake.

All look for happiness beneath the sun,
And each expects what God has given to none.

Mrs. Norton.

LIVE while you live, the epicure would say,
And seize the pleasures of the present day!
Live while you live, the sacred preacher cries,
And give to God each moment as it flies!
Lord, in my views let both united be—
I live in pleasure, when I live to Thee!

DODDRIDGE.

YET this is life! To mark from day to day,
Youth, in the freshness of its morning prime,
Pass, like the anthem of a breeze, away,
Sinking in waves of death, ere chilled by time!
Ere yet dark years on the warm cheek had shed
Autumnal mildew on the roses red!

WILLIS G. CLARK.

TRANSIENT, fickle, light, and gay,
Flattering only to betray;
What, alas! can life contain!
Life like all its circles,—vain! THOMAS MOORE.

So, in the passing of a day, doth pass
The bud and blossom of the life of man,
Nor e'er doth flourish more, but like the grass
Cut down, becometh withered, pale and wan.

TASSO.

HOW short is human life! the very breath,
Which frames my words, accelerates my death.

HANNAH MORE.

WE live in deeds, not years; in thoughts, not breaths;
In feelings, not in figures on a dial.
We should count time by heart-throbs. He most lives
Who thinks most; feels the noblest, acts the best.

J. P. BAILEY.

MAN'S life 's a book of history;
  The leaves thereof are days;
The letters, mercies closely joined;
  The title is God's praise. JOHN MASON

LIFE is most enjoyed
When courted least; most worth when disesteemed;
Then 't is the seat of comfort, rich in peace,
In prospect richer far; important, awful,
Not to be mentioned, but with shouts of praise!
Not to be thought on, but with tides of joy!
The mighty basis of eternal bliss! YOUNG

IN the same brook, none ever bathed him twice:
To the same life, none ever twice awoke.
We call the brook the same; the same we think
Our life, though still more rapid in its flow;
Nor mark the much, irrevocably lapsed,
And mingled with the sea. YOUNG.

OPENING the map of God's expansive plan,
We find a little isle, this life of man;
Eternity's unknown expanse appears
Circling around, and limiting his years.
The busy race examine and explore
Each creek and cavern of the dangerous shore,
With care collect what in their eyes excels,
Some shining pebbles, and some weeds and shells,
Thus laden, dream that they are rich and great,
And happiest he that groans beneath his weight.
The waves o'ertake them in their serious play,
And every hour sweeps multitudes away;
They shriek and sink — survivors start and weep,
Pursue their sport, and follow to the deep.
COWPER

I LIVE on earth upon a stage of sorrow;
Lord, if Thou pleasest, end the play to-morrow.
I live on earth, as in a dream of pleasure;
Awake me when Thou wilt, I wait Thy leisure.
I live on earth, but as of life bereaven;
My life's with Thee, for, Lord, Thou art in Heaven

FRANCIS QUARLES.

THY life's a warfare, thou a soldier art,
Satan's thy foeman, and a faithful heart
Thy two-edged weapon, patience thy shield,
Heaven is thy chieftain, and the world thy field.
To be afraid to die, or wish for death,
Are words and passions of despairing breath:
Who doth the first, the day doth faintly yield;
And who the second, basely flies the field.

FRANCIS QUARLES.

WHILE man is growing, life is in decrease;
And cradles rock us nearer to the tomb.
Our birth is nothing but our death begun;
As tapers waste that instant they take fire.

YOUNG.

HE sins against this life, who slights the next.

YOUNG.

THE LORD'S SUPPER—THE COMMUNION OF SAINTS.

THE Lord Jesus, the same night in which He was betrayed, took bread:

And when He had given thanks, He brake it, and said, Take, eat; this is my body, which is broken for you: this do in remembrance of me.

After the same manner also He took the cup, when He had supped, saying, This cup is the New Testament in my blood: this do ye, as oft as ye drink it, in remembrance of me.

For as often as ye eat this bread, and drink this cup, ye do show the Lord's death till He come. I. CORINTHIANS, xi, 23—26.

Whoso eateth my flesh, and drinketh my blood, hath eternal life; and I will raise him up at the last day.

For my flesh is meat indeed, and my blood is drink indeed. JOHN, vi, 54, 55.

That they all may be one; as Thou, Father, art in me, and I in them, that they also may be one in us: * * * I in them, and Thou in me, that they may be made perfect in one. JOHN, xvii, 21—23.

I LOVE to mingle there
In sympathy of praise and prayer,
And listen to that Living Word,
Which breathes the Spirit of the Lord:
Or, at the mystic table placed,
Those eloquent mementoes taste
Of Thee, Thou suffering Lamb divine,
Thy soul-refreshing bread and wine;
Sweet viands, given us to assuage
The faintness of the pilgrimage.

THOMAS GRINFIELD.

AND oft your willing steps renew, around the sacred board,
And break the bread, and pour the wine, in memory of your Lord:
To drink with me the grape's first juice, to you shall yet be given,
Fresh from the deathless vine that blooms in blest abodes of Heaven.

THOMAS DALE.

Him first to love, great right and reason is,
Who first to us our life and being gave,
And after, when we fared had amiss,
Us wretches from the second death did save;
And last, the Food of Life, which now we have,
Even He Himself, in His dear Sacrament,
To feed our hungry souls, unto us lent.
Then next to love our brethren, that were made
Of that self-mould, and that self-Maker's hand.

Spenser.

Bread of Heaven, on Thee we feed,
For Thy flesh is meat indeed;
Ever let our souls be fed
With this true and Living Bread.

Vine of Heaven, Thy blood supplies
This blest cup of sacrifice;
Lord, Thy wounds our healing give;
To Thy cross we look and live.

Day by day, with strength supplied,
Through the life of Him who died,
Lord of life, O, let us be
Rooted, grafted, built on Thee! Conder.

Bow thee to earth, and from thee cast
All stubbornness of human will;
Then dare to drink the Sacred Cup
Thy God and Saviour died to fill.

Come with thy guilt new-washed in tears,
Thy spirit raised in faith above;
Then drink, and so thy soul shall live,
Thy Saviour's blood,—thy Saviour's love.

Miss Landon.

BREAK to us each, this day, our daily bread,
  Nor let earth's fading food alone be given;
Feed us upon THY WORD,—in Christ our Head,
  To find Thy Peace, the Living Bread from Heaven.

H. H. WELD.

AND in the Comforter, the Holy Ghost;
  And in the Church, the purchase of Thy blood,
In blest communion bound, a saintly host,
  The living here, who taste Thy heavenly food,
The found in Heaven, who on earth are lost—
  All one in Thee:—in Thy uniting love,
  Lord, I believe! Mine unbelief remove!

H. H. WELD

So is it with true Christian hearts;
  Their mutual share in Jesus' blood
An everlasting bond imparts
  Of holiest brotherhood:
Oh! might we all our lineage prove,
Give and forgive, do good and love,
By soft endearments in kind strife
Lightening the load of daily life!

KEBLE.

FOR say, can fancy, fond to weave the tale
Of bliss ideal, feign more genuine joy
Than thine, Believer, when the man of God
Gives to thy hand the consecrated cup,
Blessed memorial of a Saviour's love!
Glowing with zeal, the humble penitent
Approacheth: Faith her fostering radiance points
Full on his contrite heart: Hope cheers his steps,
And Charity, the fairest in the train
Of Christian virtues, swells his heaving breast
With love unbounded.

THOMAS ZOUCH.

They knelt them side by side; the hoary man
Whose memory was an age, and she whose cheek
Gleamed like that velvet, which the young moss-rose
Puts blushing forth, from its scarce-severed sheath.
There was the sage,—whose eye of science spans
The comet in his path of fire,—and she
Whose household duty was her sole delight,
And highest study. On the chancel clasped,
In meek devotion, were those bounteous hands
That scatter thousands at the call of Christ,
And his, whose labor wins the scanty bread
For his young children. There the man of might
On bended knee, fast by his servant's side,
Sought the same Master,—brethren in the faith,
And fellow-pilgrims. Mrs. Sigourney

Thou who didst taste
Of man's infirmities, yet bar his sins
From thine unspotted soul, forsake us not,
In our temptations, but so guide our feet,
That our Last Supper in this world may lead
To that immortal banquet by thy side,
Where there is no betrayer. Mrs. Sigourney.

O, then the glory and the bliss,
When all that pained, and seemed amiss,
Shall melt, with earth and sin, away.
When saints beneath their Saviour's eye,
Fill'd with each other's company,
Shall spend in love the eternal day! Keble

By chain yet stronger must the soul be tied:
One duty more, last stage of this ascent,
Brings to thy food, memorial Sacrament,
The offspring, haply at the parents' side;
But not till they, with all that do abide

In Heaven, have lifted up their hearts to laud
And magnify the glorious name of God,
Fountain of Grace, whose Son for sinners died.
Here must my song in timid reverence pause:
But shrink not, ye, whom to the saving rite
The Altar calls; come early, under laws
That can secure for you a path of light
Through gloomiest shade; put on, nor dread its weight,
Armour divine, and conquer in your cause.

WORDSWORTH.

LOVE—DIVINE LOVE.

THIS is my commandment, that ye love one another, as I have loved you.
Greater love hath no man than this, that a man lay down his life for his friends.
Ye are my friends, if ye do whatsoever I command you. JOHN, xv, 12—14.

Beloved, let us love one another: for love is of God; and every one that loveth is born of God, and knoweth God.

He that loveth not, knoweth not God, for God is love. I. JOHN, iv, 7, 8.

Hereby perceived we the love of God, because He laid down His life for us: and we ought to lay down our lives for the brethren. I. JOHN, iii, 16.

The Lord preserveth all them that love Him. PSALM cxlv, 20.

Love your enemies, bless them that curse you. MATTHEW, v, 44.

THEY sin, who tell us love can die. SOUTHEY.

HE prayeth best, who loveth best
All things, both great and small;
For the dear God who loveth us,
He made and loveth all. COLERIDGE.

I MUST love on, O God!
This bosom must love on! but let thy breath
Touch and make pure the flame that knows not death,
Bearing it up to Heaven, Love's own abode.

MRS. HEMANS.

WEAK though we are, to love is no hard task,
And love for love is all that Heaven does ask.

WALLER.

'TIS with our minds as with a fertile ground;
Wanting this love, they must with weeds abound;
Unruly passions, whose effects are worse
Than thorns and briars, springing from the curse.

WALLER.

LEGIONS of angels, which He might have used,
For us resolved to perish, He refused;
While they stood ready to prevent His loss,
Love took Him up, and nailed Him to the cross.
Immortal love! which in His bowels reigned,
That we might be by such high love constrained
To make return of love; upon this pole
Our duty does, and our religion roll.
To love is to believe, to hope, to know;
'Tis an essay, a taste of Heaven below.
He to proud potentates would not be known;
Of those who loved Him, He was hid from none.

WALLER

BEFORE the sparkling lamps on high
Were kindled up, and hung around the sky:
Before the sun led on the circling hours,
Or vital seeds produced their active powers;
Before the first intelligences strung
Their golden harps, and soft preludiums sung
To Love, the mighty cause whence their existence sprung,
Th' ineffable Divinity
His own resemblance meets in thee.
By this thy glorious lineage, thou dost prove
Thy high descent — for God Himself is Love.

MRS. ROWE.

TRUE, there is better love, whose balance just
Mingles soul's instinct with our grosser dust;
And leaves affection, strengthening day by day,
Firm to assault, impervious to decay.

MRS. NORTON.

O, HE is good, He is immensely good
Who all things formed, and formed them all for man;
Who marked the climates, varied every zone,
Dispensing all His blessings for the best,
In order and in beauty.

SMART.

ETERNAL Love doth keep,
In His complacent arms, the earth, the air, the deep.

WM. C. BRYANT.

ALL things that are on earth, shall wholly pass away,
Except the Love of God, which shall live and last for aye.

* * * * *

Anon the great globe itself (so the holy writings tell,)
With the rolling firmament, where the starry armies dwell,
Shall melt with fervent heat — they shall all pass away,
Except the Love of God, which shall live and last for aye.

WM. C. BRYANT.

GOD is Love, saith the Evangel;
And our world of woe and sin
Is made light and happy only,
When a love is shining in.

J. G. WHITTIER

O LOVE! thy essence is thy purity!
Breathe one unhallowed breath upon thy flame,
And it is gone for ever, and but leaves
A sullied vase — its pure light lost in shame.

MISS LANDON.

HUMBLE love,
And not proud science, keeps the door of Heaven;
Love finds admission where proud science fails.

YOUNG.

THEY err, who deem love's brightest hour in blooming youth is known:
Its purest, tenderest, holiest power in after life is known,
When passions chastened and subdued, to riper years are given,
And earth, and earthly things, are viewed in light that breaks from Heaven.

BERNARD BARTON.

THERE is, in life, no blessing like affection:
It soothes, it hallows, elevates, subdues,
And bringeth down to earth its native Heaven.

MISS LANDON.

LOVE celestial! wondrous heat!
O, beyond expression great!
What resistless charms were thine,
In thy good, thy best design!
When God was hated, sin obeyed,
And man undone, without thy aid,
From the seats of endless peace
They brought the Son, the Lord of Grace;
They taught Him to receive a birth,
To clothe in flesh, to live on earth,
And after, lifted Him on high,
And taught Him on the cross to die.

PARNELL.

MALICE—ENVY.

WRATH is cruel, and anger is outrageous; but who is able to stand before envy? PROVERBS, xxvii, 4.

For where envying and strife is, there is confusion and every evil work. JAMES, iii, 16.

Brethren, be not children in understanding: howbeit in malice be ye children, but in understanding be men. I. CORINTHIANS, xiv, 20.

MEN that make
Envy and crooked malice nourishment,
Do bite the best. SHAKSPEARE.

FOR it is hard indeed that mere suspicion,
Hating all good and charitable deeds,
Should take from men the glorious names they win
By constant virtues and a life of toil.
ISAAC C. PRAY

WHO made the heart, 'tis He alone
Decidedly can try us;
He knows each chord—its various tone,
Each spring—its various bias:
Then at the balance let's be mute,
We never can adjust it;
What's *done* we partly may compute,
But never what's *resisted*. BURNS.

HE hated all good works and virtuous deeds,
And him no less that any like did use;
And who with gracious bread the hungry feeds,
His alms, for want of faith, he doth accuse.
SPENSER.

MAMMON.

No man can serve two masters: for either he will hate the one, and love the other; or else he will cleave to the one, and despise the other. Ye cannot serve God and mammon. MATTHEW, vi, 24.

If therefore ye have not been faithful in the unrighteous mammon, who will commit to your trust the true riches? LUKE, xvi, 11.

How hardly shall they that have riches enter into the kingdom of God! MARK, x, 23.

PERCHANCE he gives his thousands to the poor—
He well may give what he can use no more.
What willing charity! gives, dares he say?
He gives, but not till Heaven has snatched away.

THOMAS WARD.

MAY not a golden lading, too profound,
Risk the soul's bark to starry haven bound?

THOMAS WARD.

HIGH-BUILT abundance, heap on heap! for what?
To breed new wants, and beggar us the more;
Then make a richer scramble for the throng,
Soon as this feeble pulse, which leaps so long,
Almost by miracle, is tired of play. YOUNG.

NOR riches boast intrinsic worth,
Their charms at best superior earth:
These oft the heaven-born mind enslave,
And make an honest man a knave.
"Wealth cures my wants," the miser cries.
Be not deceived — the miser lies:
One want he has, with all his store,
That worst of wants — the want of more.

COTTON.

Zucchi. Sartain.

The Love of Gold.

WIDE-WASTING pest! that rages unconfined,
And crowds with crimes the records of mankind;
For gold, his sword the hireling ruffian draws;
For gold, the hireling judge distorts the laws;
Wealth heaped on wealth, nor truth nor safety buys,
The dangers gather as the treasures rise.

DR. JOHNSON.

ALL flesh is grass, and all its glory fades
Like the fair flower, dishevelled in the wind;
Riches have wings, and grandeur is a dream.

COWPER.

SAY, what is wealth? A gilded pain:
  And what is power? A weakness hid:
And what is life? A shadow vain:
  And joy? A phantom, still forbid:
Shall then proud man his grandeur ward
By toys which God doth not regard?

H. H. WELD.

(*See also* AVARICE, EARTH.)

MAN.

IN the day that God created man, in the likeness of God created He him.

Male and female created He them; and blessed them, and called their name Adam, in the day when they were created. GENESIS, v, 1, 2.

Man's goings are of the Lord; how can a man, then, understand his own way? PROVERBS, xx, 24.

Man shall not live by bread alone, but by every word that proceedeth out of the mouth of God. MATTHEW, iv, 4.

When I consider Thy heavens, the work of Thy fingers, the moon and the stars which Thou hast ordained,

What is man that Thou art mindful of him, and the son of man that Thou visitest him?

For Thou hast made him a little lower than the angels, and crowned him with glory and honour. PSALM viii, 3, 4, 5.

Behold, even to the moon, and it shineth not; yea, the stars are not pure in His sight:

How much less man, that is a worm? and the son of man, which is a worm? JOB, xxv, 5, 6.

ALAS! that man
Must prove the direst enemy of man—
His boasted reason wielded to contrive
Dark systems of despair—his vaunted skill,
To forge the fetters which enthral the soul.

A. ALEXANDER.

A BEAM ethereal, sullied and absorpt!
Though sullied and dishonoured, still divine;
Dim miniature of greatness absolute!
An heir of glory! a frail child of dust!
Helpless immortal! insect infinite!
A worm! a god! I tremble at myself,
And in myself am lost. At home a stranger,
Thought wanders up and down, surprised, aghast,
And wondering at her own. How reason reels!
Oh! what a miracle to man is man!

YOUNG.

Whate'er of earth is formed, to earth returns
Dissolved: the various objects we behold—
Plants, animals, this whole material mass—
Are ever changing, ever new. The soul
Of man alone, that particle divine,
Escapes the wreck of worlds, when all things fail:
Hence the great distance 'twixt the beasts that perish,
And God's bright image, man's immortal race.

Somerville.

How poor, how rich, how abject, how august,
How complicate, how wonderful is man!
How passing wonder He who made him such,
Who centred in our make such strange extremes!

Young.

Where were flown
Our hopes, if man were left to man's decree alone?

Mrs. Hemans.

So fair is man, that death (a parting blast,)
Blasts his fair flower, and makes him earth at last;
So strong is man, that with a gasping breath
He totters, and bequeaths his strength to death;
So wise is man, that if with death he strive,
His wisdom cannot teach him how to live;
So rich is man, that (all his debts being paid,)
His wealth's the winding-sheet wherein he's laid;
So young is man, that (broke with care and sorrow,)
He's old enough to-day to die to-morrow.

Francis Quarles.

O, what is man, great Maker of mankind!
That Thou to him so great respect dost bear;
That Thou adornest him with so bright a mind,
Mak'st him a king, and even an angel's peer?

O, what a lively life, what heavenly power,
  What spreading virtue, what a sparkling fire,
How great, how plentiful, how rich a dower
  Dost Thou within the dying flesh inspire!

Thou leav'st Thy print in other works of Thine,
  But Thy whole image Thou in man hast writ;
There cannot be a creature more divine,
  Except, like Thee, it should be infinite.

But it exceeds man's thoughts, to think how high
  God hath raised man, since God a man became;
The angels do admire this mystery,
  And are astonished when they view the same:

Nor hath He given these blessings for a day,
  Nor made them on the body's life depend;
The soul, though made in time, survives for aye;
  And though it hath beginning, sees no end.

Sir John Davies.

Man's not a lawful steersman of his days,
His bootless wish nor hastens, nor delays;
We are God's hired workmen; He discharges
Some late at night, and (when He list) enlarges
Others at noon, and in the morning some:
None may relieve himself, till He bid, Come.

Francis Quarles.

And what is man? In outward guise
  Let him be prince, or peer, or slave,
Or poor and weak, or great and wise—
  A mortal, tending to the grave:
Such are all men—from earth we came,
Earth doth her own poor dust reclaim.

H. H. Weld.

But, if Thy works, through sea and land,
Or the wide fields of ether wending,
In man Thy noblest thoughts are blending;
Man is the glory of Thy hand; —
Man, modelled in a form of grace,
Where every beauty has its place;
A gentleness and glory sharing
His spirit, where we may behold
A higher aim, a nobler daring:
'Tis Thine immortal mould.

Jacob Bellamy.

MARRIAGE.

Therefore shall a man leave his father and his mother, and shall cleave unto his wife: and they shall be one flesh. Genesis, ii, 24.

Marriage is honourable in all. Hebrews, xiii, 4.

Save the love we pay
To Heaven, none purer, holier than that
A virtuous woman feels, for him she'd cleave
Thro' life to. Sisters part from sisters — brothers
From brothers — children from their parents — but
Such woman from the husband of her choice,
Never!

Sheridan Knowles.

There are smiles and tears in that gathering band,
Where the heart is pledged with the trembling hand.
What trying thoughts in the bosom swell,
As the bride bids parents and home farewell!
Kneel down by the side of the tearful fair,
And strengthen the perilous hour with prayer.

Henry Ware, Jr.

NOT for herself was woman first create,
Nor yet to be man's idol, but his mate.

MRS. NORTON.

LOOK down, O Thou
Who wast at Cana! Bless the rite that's past!
Help me to put a wedding-garment on
For the great marriage supper; and to wear
Thy choice of ornaments, while I await
The coming of the Bridegroom.

HANNAH F. GOULD.

JOY, serious and sublime,
Such as doth nerve the energies of prayer,
Should swell the bosom, when a maiden's hand,
Filled with life's dewy flowerets, girdeth on
That harness which the ministry of death
Alone unlooseth, but whose fearful power
May stamp the sentence of Eternity.

MRS. SIGOURNEY.

MARTYRDOM.

And others had trial of cruel mockings and scourgings, yea, moreover of bonds and imprisonment:

They were stoned, they were sawn asunder, were tempted, were slain with the sword: they wandered about in sheep-skins and goat-skins; being destitute, afflicted, tormented;

(Of whom the world was not worthy;) they wandered in deserts and in mountains, and in dens and caves of the earth. Hebrews, xi, 36—38.

In Rama was there a voice heard, lamentation, and weeping, and great mourning. Rachel mourning for her children, and would not be comforted, because they are not. Matthew, ii, 18.

I saw the souls of them that were beheaded for the witness of Jesus, and for the Word of God. Revelations, xx, 4.

In rendering to the Lord what is the Lord's,
  Doth not the thought of violence bring shame?
Think ye, He gave the branching forest-tree
  To furnish fagots for the funeral pyre,
Or bid His sunrise light the world, to see
  Pale, tortured victims perish there by fire?

Mrs. Norton.

The Sacred Book, its value understood,
Received the seal of martyrdom in blood.
Those holy men, so full of truth and grace,
Seem, to reflection, of a different race;
Meek, modest, venerable, wise, sincere,
In such a cause they could not dare to fear;
They could not purchase earth with such a price,
Or spare a life too short to reach the skies.
From them to thee conveyed along the tide,
Their streaming hearts poured freely when they died;
Those truths which neither use nor years impair,
Invite thee, woo thee, to the bliss they share.

Cowper.

WHEN persecution's torrent blaze
  Wraps the unshrinking martyr's head,
When fade all earthly flowers and bays,
  When summer friends are gone and fled,
Is he alone in that dark hour,
Who owns the Lord of love and power?

Or waves there not around his brow,
  A wand no human arm may wield,
Fraught with a spell no angels know,
  His steps to guide, his soul to shield?
Thou, Saviour, art his Charmed Bower,
His Magic Ring, his Rock, his Tower. KEBLE.

THY children, even as martyrs perished:
  Those first-loved fruits that sprang from thee,
From which thy heart was doomed to sever,
In praise of God, shall bloom for ever,
  Unhurt, untouched, by tyranny. VONDEL.

    IN vain the Roman lord
    Waved the relentless sword,
And spread the terrors of the circling flame;
    In vain the heathen sought,
    If chance some lurking spot,
Might mar the lustre of the Christian name:
The Eternal Spirit, by His fruits confessed,
In life secured from stains, and steel'd in death, the breast.
BP. MANT.

AND when religious sects ran mad,
  He held, in spite of all his learning,
That if a man's belief is bad,
  It will not be improved by burning. PRAED.

THE lion's feet, the lion's lips, are dyed with crimson gore,—
A look of faith, an unbreathed prayer, the martyr's pangs are o'er.
Proud princes and grave senators gazed on that fearful sight,
And even woman seemed to share the savage crowd's delight;
But what the guilt, that on the dead a fate so fearful drew?
A blameless faith, was all the crime the Christian martyr knew:
And where the crimson current flowed, upon that barren sand,
Up sprung a tree, whose vigorous boughs soon over-spread the land;
O'er distant isles its shadow fell, nor knew its roots decay,
E'en when the Roman Cæsar's throne and empire passed away.

HAMILTON BUCHANAN.

THE fatal pile
Would be to me a car of joyful triumph,
Mounted more gladly than the laurelled hero
Vaults to his envied seat.

JOANNA BAILLIE.

I AM so pleased to die, and am so honoured
In dying for the pure and holy truth,
That nature's instinct seems in me extinguished.

JOANNA BAILLIE.

MIRACLES.

JESUS of Nazareth, a man approved of God among you, by wonders, and miracles, and signs. ACTS, ii, 22.

God also bearing them witness, both with signs and wonders, and divers miracles HEBREWS, ii, 4.

O, WHAT a scale of miracles is here—
Its lowest round high planted in the skies;
Its towering summit lost, beyond the thought
Of man or angel! YOUNG.

WHEN God came down from Heaven, the Living God,
What signs and wonders marked his stately way?
Brake out the winds in music where he trode?
Shone o'er the heavens a brighter, softer day?

The dumb began to speak, the blind to see,
And the lame leaped, and pain and darkness fled;
The mourner's sunken eye grew bright with glee,
And from the tomb awoke the wondering dead.
H. H. MILMAN.

THE Lord of Hosts hath walked
This world of man; the one Almighty sent
His everlasting Son to wear the flesh,
And glorify this mortal human shape;
And the blind eyes unclosed to see the Lord,
And the dumb tongues broke out in songs of praise,
And the grave cast forth its wondering dead,
And trembling devils murmured sullen homage.
H. H. MILMAN.

"COME forth!" He cries, "thou dead!"
  O God, what means that strange and sudden sound,
That murmurs from the tomb? That ghastly head,
  With funeral fillets bound?
It is a living form—
  The loved, the lost, the won,
Won from the grave, corruption, and the worm—
  "And is not this the Son
Of God?" they whispered, while the sisters poured
Their gratitude in tears, for they had known the Lord.

DALE.

SEE, from the yawning tomb,
Bound in the solemn vestments of the grave,
Comes forth the living Lazarus! Ah! see
Upon his pallid cheek returning life
Breathe roseate hues, and his unclosing eye
Beam with new radiance. Hail! thou mystic type
Of that great day, when, with the thunder's voice,
The King of kings to earth's remotest climes
Shall speak His will; when the unpeopled graves
Shall render up their dead, and all shall stand,
Like Lazarus, before a judging God.

WILLIAM BOLLAND.

AT His command fled fever, thirsty fiend,
Whose parching fire dries up the wholesome blood:
And madness wild, whose moon-struck eye-balls glare,
With steady gaze, on vacancy: His touch,
With healing virtue, from the withered limbs
Drove nerveless palsy, that with fatal stroke
'Numbs every fibre, grafting death on life—
Unnatural union! Scaly leprosy,
At His appearance, vanished: dropsy, swol'n,
Withdrew his bloated form, and each confessed
A present God.

WILLIAM BOLLAND.

WHEN raging winds
Rushed from their caverns, and resistless swept
The foaming waves, when hideous roared the storm,
As if the wild contending elements
Had strove for mastery, at His command
The tempest ceased, the towering billows sunk
In undulations calm, and zephyrs played
Upon the bosom of the peaceful deep.

WILLIAM BOLLAND.

A MIRACLE, with miracles enclosed,
Is man; and starts his faith at what is strange?
What less than wonders from the Wonderful;
What less than miracles, from God can flow?
Admit a God — that mystery supreme,
That Cause uncaused, all other wonders cease.

YOUNG.

WHO! O, who shall tell
His acts miraculous? When His own decrees
Repeals He, or suspends; when by the hand
Of Moses or of Joshua, or the mouths
Of His prophetic seers, such deeds He wrought,
Before the astonished sun's all-seeing eye,
That faith was scarce a virtue. Need I sing
The fate of Pharaoh, and his numerous band,
Lost in the reflux of the watery walls,
That melted to their fluid state again?
Need I recount how Sampson's warlike arm
With more than mortal nerves was strung, to o'erthrow
Idolatrous Philistia? Shall I tell
How David triumphed, and what Job sustained?
—But, O supreme, unutterable mercy!
O love unequalled, mystery immense,
Which angels long to unfold! 'Tis man's redemption
That crowns Thy glory, and Thy power confirms.

SMART.

MISSIONARIES.

How beautiful are the feet of them that preach the gospel of peace, and bring glad tidings of good things! ROMANS, x, 15.

They are the messengers of the churches, and the glory of Christ. II. CORINTHIANS, iii, 23.

This gospel of the kingdom shall be preached in all the world for a witness unto all nations; and then shall the end come. MATTHEW, xxiv. 14.

WHERE is your heathen brother?—From his grave
 Near thy own gates, or 'neath a foreign sky,
From the thronged depths of ocean's mourning wave,
 His answering blood reproachfully doth cry,
Blood of the soul!—Can all earth's fountains make
Thy dark stain disappear?—Stewards of God, awake!

MRS. SIGOURNEY.

BY Heaven directed, by the world reviled,
Amidst the wilderness they sought a home,
Where beasts of prey and men of murder roam,
And untamed Nature holds her revels wild.
There on their pious toil their Master smiled,
And prospered them, unknown or scorned of men,
Till, in the satyr's haunt, and dragon's den,
A garden bloomed, and savage hordes grew mild.
So, in the guilty heart, when heavenly grace
Enters, it ceaseth not till it uproot
All evil passions from each hidden cell;
Planting again an Eden in their place,
Which yields to men and angels pleasant fruit,
And God Himself delighteth there to dwell.

PRINGLE.

LIGHT for the darkened earth!
  Ye blessed its beams who shed;
Shrink not, till the day-spring hath its birth,
  Till, wherever the footstep of man doth tread,
Salvation's banner spread broadly forth,
  Shall gild the dream of the cradle-bed,
      And clear the tomb
      From its lingering gloom,
  For the aged to rest his weary head.

MRS. SIGOURNEY.

O, BLESS the pious zeal
And crown with glad success the labouring sons
Of that best charity, whose annual mite
Sends forth Thy gospel to the distant isles!
So shall the nations, rescued myriads, hear,
And own Thy mercy over all Thy works!
So, from each corner of the enlightened earth,
Incessant peals of universal joy
Shall hail Thee, heavenly Father, God of all!

MADAN.

THUS saith the Lord,—My Church, to thee,
  Peace, like a river, I will send;
The Gentiles in a stream shall see
  My mercy, flowing without end.

The isles that never heard my fame,
  Nor knew the glory of my might,
They shall be taught to fear my name
  —Called out of darkness into light.

And it shall come to pass, that vows
  From Sabbath unto Sabbath day,
From moon to moon, in mine own house,
  All nations, tribes, and tongues, shall pay.

JAMES MONTGOMERY.

He goes to speak the words of life
  To souls by error tossed;
And bear the Gospel's joyful sound
  To lands in darkness lost—
To speak his Master's glorious works,
  His grace and power proclaim,
And teach untutored savages
  To breathe Messiah's name.

And O, the rich reward that waits
  A work of grace like this!
A life of love, a death of peace,
  A Heaven of endless bliss!
Earth's proudest, noblest honours, fall
  Far, far below the prize
He gains, who claims this work his own—
  His glory never dies! S. D. Patterson.

Blessings be on their pathway, and increase!
  These are the moral conquerors, and belong
  To them the palm-branch and triumphal song—
Conquerors,—and yet the harbingers of peace!
Miss Landon.

Strange scenes, strange men, untold, untried distress;
Pain, hardships, famine, cold and nakedness,
Diseases; death, in every hideous form,
On shore, at sea, by fire, by flood, by storm;
Wild beasts, and wilder men:—unmoved with fear,
Health, comfort, safety, life they count not dear,
May they but hope a Saviour's love to show,
And warn one spirit from eternal woe:
Nor will they faint, nor can they strive in vain,
Since thus—to live is Christ, to die is gain.
James Montgomery.

OUR prayers be with them — we who know
  The value of a soul to save,
Must pray for those who seek to show
  The heathen, hope beyond the grave.

MISS LANDON.

MORNING—DAY—LIGHT.

MY voice shalt Thou hear in the morning, O Lord; in the morning will I direct my prayer unto Thee, and will look up. PSALM v, 3.

Seek Him that maketh the seven stars and Orion, and turneth the shadow of death into the morning, and maketh day dark with night. AMOS, v, 8.

Every one that doeth evil, hateth the light; neither cometh to the light, lest his deeds should be reproved. JOHN, iii, 20.

The day-spring from on high hath visited us, to give light to them that sit in darkness, and in the shadow of death, to guide our feet in the way of peace. LUKE, i, 78, 79.

THE morning breaks,
And earth in her Maker's smile awakes;
His light is on all, below and above,
The light of gladness, and life, and love.
O, then, on the breath of this early air,
Send up the incense of grateful prayer!

HENRY WARE, JR

SEE, the time for sleep has run,
Rise before, or with the sun:
Lift thy hands, and humbly pray
The Fountain of eternal day,
That, as the light, serenely fair,
Illustrates all the tracts of air;
The Sacred Spirit so may rest,
With quickening beams, upon thy breast. PARNELL.

WHEN first thy eyes unveil, give thy soul leave
  To do the like; our bodies but forerun
The spirit's duty; true hearts spread and heave
  Unto their God, as flowers do to the sun:
Give Him thy first thoughts then, so shalt thou keep
Him company all day, and in Him sleep.
Yet never sleep the sun up; prayer should
  Dawn with the day, there are set awful hours
'Twixt Heaven and us; the manna was not good
  After sun-rising, for day sullies flowers.

HENRY VAUGHAN.

NEW, every morning, is the love
Our wakening and uprising prove;
Through sleep and darkness safely brought,
Restored to life, and power, and thought.

New mercies each returning day,
Hover around us while we pray;
New perils past, new sins forgiven,
New thoughts of God, new hopes of Heaven.

KEBLE.

MORN is the time to think,
  While thoughts are fresh and free,
Of life, just balanced on the brink
  Of vast eternity!
To ask our souls if they are meet
To stand before the judgment-seat.

MISS GRAY.

THE waking cock, that early crows
  To wear the night away,
Puts in my mind the trump that blows
  Before the latter day;
And as I rise up lustily,
  When sluggish sleep is past,
So hope I to rise joyfully
  To judgment, at the last.

GEORGE GASCOIGNE.

AND heavenly day, now night is past,
  Doth show his pleasant face,
So must we hope to see God's face,
  At last, in Heaven on high,
When we have changed this mortal place
  For immortality. GEORGE GASCOIGNE.

THE day that only springeth from on high,
That high day-light wherein the heavens do live;
The life that loves but to behold that eye
Which doth the glory of all brightness give,
And from the enlightened doth all darkness drive:
  Where saints do see, and angels know to see
  A brighter light than saints or angels see.

In this light's love, O, let me ever live!
And let my soul have never other love
But all the pleasures of the world to give,
The smallest spark of such a joy to prove,
And ever pray unto my God above,
  To grant my humble soul good Simeon's grace,
  In love to see my Saviour in the face.
NICHOLAS BRETON.

PRIME cheerer, Light!
Of all material beings, first and best!
Efflux divine! Nature's resplendent robe!
Without whose vesting beauty, all were wrapt
In unessential gloom! and thou, O Sun!
Soul of surrounding worlds, in whom, best seen,
Shines out thy Maker! THOMSON.

HEARD as each morn relumes the eastern cloud,
Thy voice of holiest comfort cries aloud,
Bidding us rise, the night-like past above,
And soar on morning's wing to thoughts of light and love!
ANONYMOUS.

MOSES.

By faith Moses, when he was come to years, refused to be called the son of Pharaoh's daughter;

Choosing rather to suffer affliction with the people of God, than to enjoy the pleasures of sin for a season;

Esteeming the reproach of Christ greater riches than the treasures in Egypt: for he had respect unto the recompense of the reward. HEBREWS, xi, 24—26.

So Moses, the servant of the Lord, died there in the land of Moab, according to the word of the Lord.

And He buried him in a valley in the land of Moab, over against Baal-peor: but no man knoweth of his sepulchre unto this day. DEUTERONOMY, xxxiv, 5, 6.

On the Mount
Of Sinai, whose foundations shook, whose top
Was lost in smoke and fire, while seraphim
At distance gazed, full forty days and nights,
Guest of terrestrial mould, did he sojourn,
Within the dread pavilion, and the veil
Of cloud and tempest; there as face to face,
In visions of beatitude rejoice
Past utterance, till his countenance imbibed
Transcendant splendours. CHARLES HOYLE.

In his hand
The rod which blasted, with strange plagues, the realm
Of Mizraim, and from its time-worn channels
Upturned the Arabian Sea. Fair was his broad
High front, and forth from his soul-piercing eye,
Did legislation look. HILLHOUSE.

Moses, the patriot fierce, became
The meekest man on earth,
To show us how love's quickening flame
Can give our souls new birth.

Moses, the man of meekest heart,
  Lost Canaan by self-will,
To show, where Grace has done its part,
  How sin defiles us still.

LYRA APOSTOLICA.

WHAT lofty obsequies were rendered
  That hour, when darkness held the pall:
What pomp, when stood, in clouds pavilioned,
  The silent, present Lord of all!
How blest the man whose dust Jehovah
  Hid in a grave that's yet untrod!
Thrice blessed he, that soul most happy,
  Whose life is hid, with Christ, in God.

W. B. TAPPAN

GOD made his grave, to men unknown,
  Where Moab's rocks a vale infold;
And laid the aged seer alone,
  To slumber while the world grows old.
Thus still, where'er the good and just
  Close the dim eye on life and pain,
Heaven watches o'er their sleeping dust,
  Till the pure spirit comes again.

WM. C. BRYANT.

THE son of Amram spurns the regal prize,
From the rich scene the zealous hero flies,
And dwells 'mongst Israel's sons. Resigned he bears
The servile yoke, and every burden shares;
Rather than violate Jehovah's trust,
And live the pampered slave of sordid lust,
He quits the Egyptian court, and, undismayed,
Seeks poverty's inhospitable shade.

SAMUEL HAYES.

MURDER—CAIN.

THE voice of thy brother's blood crieth unto me from the ground. GENESIS, iv 10.

Whoso sheddeth man's blood, by man shall his blood be shed: for in the image of God made He man. GENESIS, ix, 6.

Thou shalt not kill. EXODUS, xx, 13.

Whosoever hateth his brother, is a murderer; and ye know that no murderer hath eternal love abiding in him. I. JOHN, iii, 15.

THE voice of blood
Passes Heaven's gates, ev'n ere the crimson flood
Sinks through the greensward! MRS. HEMANS.

FIRST Envy, eldest born of Hell, imbrued
Her hands in blood, and taught the sons of men
To make a death which Nature never made,
And God abhorred; with violence rude to break
The thread of life ere half its length was run,
And rob a wretched brother of his being.
BP. PORTEUS

OTHER sins only speak; murder shrieks out.
The element of water moistens the earth,
But blood mounts upwards. JOHN WEBSTER.

THE earliest death a son of Adam died
Was murder, and that murder fratricide.
JAMES MONTGOMERY.

HE told how murderers walked the earth
Beneath the curse of Cain;
With crimson clouds before their eyes,
And flames about their brain:
For blood has left upon their souls
Its everlasting stain! THOMAS HOOD.

SILENTLY, swiftly as the lightning's blast,
A hand of fire across his temples passed;
He ran, as in the terror of a dream,
To quench his burning anguish in the stream;
But, bending o'er the brink, the swelling wave
Back to his eye the branded visage gave;
As soon on murdered Abel durst he look;
Yet power to fly his palsied limbs forsook;
There turned to stone, for his presumptuous crime,
A monument of wrath to latest time,
Might Cain have stood; but mercy raised his head
In prayer for help,—his strength returned, he fled.

JAMES MONTGOMERY.

O THOU,
Whose ruthless sword each lovely scene laid waste,
Who through the husband's bosom stabbed the wife,
Say, can the phantom Honour, can the pride
Of conquest, or the transport of revenge—
Say, can the vain applause of those whose praise
Stamps thee unworthy of the name of man,
Can these lull conscience in eternal sleep,
Or bribe reflection to withhold her stings?

C. P. LAYARD.

EARTH shudders with secret awe;
There is blood on its bright and flowery sod,
And it feels the frown of an angry God.
The first of human gore
On the blushing earth has been shed;
It held of human kind but four;
Now one is cold and dead;
And one, with a fierce and bloodshot eye,
And crimson club, is standing by,
A sered and blasted man.

ANONYMOUS.

Lo, on the everlasting stone engraved,
"No murder shalt thou do." From God to man
The solemn law came down: by specious gloss
Of subtle learning, seek not to evade
The great command. SAMUEL HAYES.

TALK not of fame! What fame enjoyed that wretch
That slew his brother? he who could not brook
Rejection from his God, with anger fired,
With envy stung, the ties of nature burst,
And sacrificed the guiltless to revenge.
C. P. LAYARD.

MUSIC.

Is any merry? Let him sing psalms. JAMES, v,

And when they had sung a hymn, they went out into the Mount of Olives. MARK, xiv, 26.

Praise Him with the sound of the trumpet: praise Him with the psaltery and harp PSALM cl, 3.

Sing unto Him a new song, play skilfully, with a loud noise. PSALM xxxiii, 3.

O, SURELY melody from Heaven was sent
To cheer the soul, when tired with human strife,
To soothe the wayward heart by sorrow rent,
And soften down the rugged road of life.
KIRKE WHITE.

THERE'S music ever in the kindly soul;
For every deed of goodness done, is like
A chord set in the heart, and joy doth strike
Upon it, oft as memory doth unroll
The immortal page whereon good deeds are writ.
THOMAS MCKELLAR.

Look, how the floor of Heaven
Is thick inlaid with patines of bright gold;
There's not the smallest orb that thou beholdest
But in his motion like an angel sings,
Still choiring to the young-eyed cherubim;
Such harmony is in immortal souls;
But while the muddy vesture of decay
Doth grossly close it in, we cannot hear it.

Shakspeare

O, what a gentle ministrant is music
To piety — to mild, to penitent piety!
O, it gives plumage to the tardy prayer
That lingers in our lazy, earthly air,
And melts with it to Heaven. H. H. Milman.

Music, the tender child of rudest times,
The gentle native of all lands and climes;
Who hymns alike man's cradle and his grave,
Lulls the low cot, or peals along the nave.

Mrs. Norton.

'Tis He that taught the lark, from earth upspringing,
To warble forth his matin strain;
And the pure stream, in liquid gushes singing,
Gladly to bless the thirsty plain;
And from the laden bee, when homeward winging
Its tuneful flight, doth not disdain
To hear the song of praise.
There's not a voice in Nature, but is telling
(If we will hear that voice aright,)
How much, when human hearts with love are swelling,
His blessed bosom hath delight
In our rejoicing lays.
His love, that never slumbers,
Taught thee those tuneful numbers. Bethune.

THERE let the pealing organ blow,
To the full-voiced choir below,
In service high, and anthems clear,
As may with sweetness through mine ear,
Dissolve me into ecstacies,
And bring all Heaven before mine eyes. MILTON.

THE church triumphant, and the church below,
In songs of praise their present union show;
Their joys are full, our expectation long,
In life we differ, but we join the song.
Angels and we, assisted by this art,
May sing together, though we dwell apart.
WALLER.

BORNE on the swelling notes, our souls aspire,
While solemn airs improve the sacred fire,
And angels lean from Heaven to hear. POPE.

How sour sweet music is
When time is broke, and no proportion kept!
So is it in the music of men's lives. SHAKSPEARE.

THE solemn hymn to ancient music set,
In many a heart response of memory met.
To me, it seemed departed Sabbaths hung
Upon those notes, which gave the past a tongue
To speak again in voices from the dead,
And wake an echo from their silent bed.
ELIZABETH BOGART.

THE song of Zion is a tasteless thing,
Unless, when, rising on a joyful wing,
The soul can mix with the celestial bands,
And give the strain the compass it demands.
COWPER.

BUT O, her richest, dearest notes to man,
In strains aerial over Bethlehem poured,
When He, whose brightness is the light of Heaven,
To earth descending, for a mortal's form,
Laid by His glory, save one radiant mark,
That moved through space, and o'er the infant hung.
He summoned Music to attend Him here,
Announcing peace below!
He called her, too,
To sweeten that sad Supper, and to twine
Her mantles round Him and His few grieved friends,
To join their mournful spirits with the hymn,
Ere to the Mount of Olives He went out
So sorrowful.
And now, His blessed word,
A sacred pledge, is left to dying man,
That at His second coming, in His power,
Music shall still be with Him, and her voice
Sound through the tombs, and wake the dead to life.
HANNAH F. GOULD

HARK! The organs blow
Their swelling notes 'round the cathedral's dome,
And grace the harmonious choir, celestial feast
To pious ears, and med'cine of the mind!
The thrilling trebles, and the manly base,
Join in accordance meet, and with one voice
All to the sacred subject suit their song;
While in each breast sweet melancholy reigns,
Angelically pensive, till the joy
Improves and purifies. SMART.

SHOULD the well-meant songs I leave behind,
With Jesus' lovers an acceptance find,
'T will heighten even the joys of Heaven, to know
That in my verse the saints hymn God below.
BP. KEN.

MUTABILITY.

AND the world passeth away, and the lust thereof: but he that doeth the will of God abideth for ever. I. JOHN, ii, 17.

The grass withereth, the flower fadeth; but the word of our God shall stand for ever. ISAIAH, xl, 8.

I returned, and saw under the sun, that the race is not to the swift, nor the battle to the strong, neither yet bread to the wise, nor yet riches to men of understanding, nor yet favour to men of skill; but time and chance happeneth to them all. ECCLESIASTES, ix, 11.

WHAT ground, alas, has any man
  To set his heart on things below,
Which, when they seem most like to stand,
  Fly, like the arrow from the bow!
Who's now atop, ere long shall feel
The circling motion of the wheel!

THOMAS ELLWOOD.

HOW fading are the joys we dote upon,
Like apparitions, seen and gone;
  But those who soonest take their flight,
Are the most exquisite and strong,
  Like angels' visits, short and bright;
Mortality's too weak to bear them long.

NORRIS, of *Bemerton.*

THE flower that smiles to-day,
  To-morrow dies;
All that we wish to stay,
  Tempts, and then flies:
What is this world's delight?
Lightning, that mocks the night,
Brief even, as bright.

SHELLEY.

22

WHEN the mother bids her son farewell,
With tears and bodings none but she can tell;
And, long, corroding, care-worn years gone round,
They meet again upon that holy ground,
Fair flaxen curls now locks of silver grey,
And promise, pride, and manhood fled away,
No glad remembrance beams in either face,
But kindly instinct locks the long embrace.

From CAPRICES.

LIKE crowded forest trees we stand,
And some are marked to fall:
The axe shall smite, at God's command,
And soon shall smite us all.

Green as the bay tree, ever green,
With its new foliage on,
The gay, the thoughtless have I seen;
I passed, and they were gone.

COWPER.

ALL earthly things must pass away,
And leave a ruined shrine;
But there *are* those which ne'er decay—
The Holy, the Divine.

ANNA PEYRE DINNIES.

HEAR a brief fable. One, with heedless tread,
Came o'er the wild, fair grass that ne'er was mown.
Then said the grass,—"Your heel is on my head;
And, where in harmless freedom I have grown,
Sorely your iron foot hath tramped me down;
But God, who to my veins such freshness gave,
Shall heal me, with a healing of His own,
Till I, perchance, may lift my head, to wave
Above the marble tomb, that presses down your grave."

MRS. NORTON.

'Tis well to learn that sunny hours
May quickly change to mournful shade;
'Tis well to prize life's scattered flowers,
Yet be prepared to see them fade.
I thank Thee, God, for weal and woe;
And, whatsoe'er the trial be,
'Twill serve to wean me from below,
And bring my spirit nigher Thee! ELIZA COOK.

THE NATIVITY.

FOR unto us a Child is born, unto us a Son is given: and the government shall be upon His shoulder: and His name shall be called Wonderful, Counsellor, The Mighty God, The Everlasting Father, The Prince of Peace.

Of the increase of His government and peace there shall be no end, upon the throne of David, and upon His kingdom, to order it, and to establish it with judgment and with justice, from henceforth, even for ever. ISAIAH, ix, 6, 7.

Behold, a Virgin shall conceive, and bear a Son, and shall call His name Immanuel. ISAIAH, vii, 14.

And the angel said unto them, Fear not: for, behold, I bring you good tidings of great joy, which shall be to all people.

For unto you is born this day, in the city of David, a Saviour, which is Christ the Lord.

And this shall be a sign unto you; Ye shall find the babe wrapped in swaddling clothes, lying in a manger.

And suddenly there was with the angel a multitude of the heavenly host, praising God, and saying,

Glory to God in the highest, and on earth, peace, good will to men. LUKE, 10—14.

SOME say, that ever, 'gainst that season comes
Wherein our Saviour's birth is celebrate,
The bird of dawning singeth all night long;
And then, they say, no spirit walks abroad;
The nights are wholesome, then no planets strike;
No fairy tales, no witch hath power to charm;
So hallowed and so gracious is the time.

SHAKSPEARE.

AND now, at length, the fated term of years
The world's desire have brought, and lo, the God appears.
The Heavenly Babe the Virgin Mother bears,
And her fond looks confess the parent's cares;
The pleasing burden on her breast she lays,
Hangs o'er His charms, and with a smile surveys;
The Infant smiles, to her warm bosom pressed,
And wantons, sportive, on the Mother's breast.
A radiant glory speaks Him all Divine,
And in the Child the beams of Godhead shine.

BP. LOWTH

WHEREFORE, from His throne exalted,
Came He on this earth to dwell;
All His pomp, an humble manger—
All His court, a narrow cell?
"From that world to bring to this,
Peace, which of all earthly blisses
Is the brightest, purest bliss." VIOLANTE DI CEO.

THIS is the time when the grey old man
Leaps back to the days of youth;
When brows and eyes bear no disguise,
But flush and gleam with truth.
O, then is the time when the soul exalts,
And seems right heavenward turning;
When we love and bless the hands we press,
When the Christmas log is burning.

ELIZA COOK.

JESSE'S son,
From 'midst the folds, to the exalted throne
Of sovereignty was called; the throne from whence
The blessings of salvation should descend.
How fitting, then, that the auspicious birth
Of Christ, benignant Shepherd of the soul,
Should thus be published. SAMUEL HAYES.

WHEN man in darkness lay, and death forlorn,
  The Heavenly Love, which did at first create,
Caused on death's shadow a new light to dawn.
  Once more the Spirit over chaos sate:
The Son of God was of the Virgin born—
  Emmanuel, Saviour! Thy Incarnate Love,
  Lord, I believe! Mine unbelief remove!

H. H. WELD.

Lo, where the Magi, from the Eastern clime,
Led by the shining star, their choicest gifts,
Propitiatory odours, suppliant bring;
And meekly at the Infant's blessed feet,
With adoration, and with hymns of praise,
Arabia's tributary honours lay.
With them, let us, before the throne of grace
Low bending, the appointed tribute bring,
The accepted incense of the grateful heart.

SAMUEL HAYES.

BRIGHT emanation of that hallowed fire
Circling celestial Majesty, which God
So oft has chosen to impart His will,
Thou messenger of bliss, how this exceeds
Thy former missions! When to Abraham sent,
Thy flame consumed the parted sacrifice;
Or from the burning bush on Horeb's top
Beamed forth divine commands, or from the rock
In Jezreel's vale on Gideon's doubting mind
Conviction flashed, then was Thy partial aid
Exerted to defend the single tribe
Of wandering Israel; but when o'er the plains
Of Bethlehem thy conducting lustre shone,
A guardian Saviour smiled amid thy beams,
His promise, Heaven's rewards; a world, His care.

WILLIAM BOLLAND.

No earthquake shock
Shivered the everlasting rock;
No trumpet-blast nor thunder-peal
Made earth through all her regions reel;
And but for the mysterious voicing
Of that unearthly choir rejoicing;
And but for that strange herald gem,
The star which burned o'er Bethlehem,
The shepherds on His natal morn
Had known not that their Lord was born.
There were no terrors, for the song
Of peace rose from the seraph throng;
On wings of love He came, to save—
To pluck pale terror from the grave. CARRINGTON.

THE tidings which that infant brings,
Are not for conquerors, or for kings:
Not for the sceptre or the brand,
For crowned head, or red right hand.
But to the contrite and the meek,
The sinful, sorrowful, and weak:
Or those who, with a hope sublime,
Are waiting for the Lord's good time.
Only for those the angels sing,
"All glory to our new-born King,
And peace and good will unto men,
Hosanna to our God! Amen!" MISS LANDON.

No war or battle's sound
Was heard the world around:
The idle spear and shield were high up hung,
The hooked chariot stood
Unstained with hostile blood,
The trumpet spake not to the armed throng;
And kings sat still, with awe-full eye
As if they surely knew their sovereign Lord was by

But peaceful was the night
Wherein the Prince of Light
  His reign of peace upon the earth began:
The winds, with wonder whist,
Smoothly the waters kissed,
  Whispering new joys to the mild ocean,
Who now hath quite forgot to rave,
While birds of calm sat brooding on the charmed wave.

MILTON.

At His birth, a star,
Unseen before in Heaven, proclaims Him come,
And guides the Eastern sages, who inquire
His place, to offer incense, myrrh, and gold.
His place of birth, a solemn angel tells
To simple shepherds, keeping watch by night:
They gladly thither haste, and by a choir
Of squadroned angels, hear His carol sung:
A Virgin is His Mother, but His Sire,
The Power of the Most High.

MILTON.

NATURE.

For the invisible things of Him from the creation of the world are clearly seen, being understood by the things that are made, even His eternal power and Godhead. Romans, i, 20.

I am the First, I also am the Last.

My hand also hath laid the foundation of the earth, and my right hand hath spanned the heavens: when I call unto them, they stand up together. Isaiah, xlviii, 12, 13.

He looks abroad into the varied field
Of Nature; and though poor, perhaps, compared
With those whose mansions glitter in his sight,
Calls the delightful scenery all his own.
His are the mountains, and the valleys his,
And the resplendent rivers; his to enjoy
With a propriety that none can feel,
But who, with filial confidence inspired,
Can lift to Heaven an unpresumptuous eye,
And smiling say, "My Father made them all!"

Cowper.

In light before my pathway spread,
In darkness round my peaceful bed,
In sunshine o'er the dewy glade,
In coolness through the warbling shade,
In every scene, at every hour,
I feel Thy love, I bless Thy power. Wm. Peter.

One Spirit, His
Who wore the plaited thorns, with bleeding brows,
Rules universal Nature! Not a flower
But shows some touch, in freckle, streak, or stain,
Of His unrivalled pencil! Cowper.

ALMIGHTY Father! such the lesson is
That in these cool and venerable woods,
I con to-day; and firmer in my breast,
By every syllable, these truths are fixed
That Thou art the Beginning and the End
Of all this glorious work, and that Thy love
Pervades the universe; and that Thy smile
Seeketh all hearts, to sun them; and that Thou,
In every glorious thing we here behold,
Declarest and reveal'st Thyself to be
The Majesty Supreme — Eternal God.
WM. D. GALLAGHER.

FROM Nature's constant or eccentric laws,
The thoughtful soul this general inference draws —
That an effect must pre-suppose a cause. PRIOR.

BY swift degrees the love of Nature works,
And warms the bosom; till, at last sublimed
To rapture and enthusiastic heat,
We feel the present Deity, and taste
The joy of God to see a happy world. THOMSON.

LIVE thou with God in Nature: never falter
In thy communings with Him. Be
Like those blest birds we read of in the Psalter,
Who found a home from peril free
In God's own house, and nestled near His altar,
Making it ring with melody.
That temple stands no more,
But Nature standeth still; God's holy presence
Abideth with us, and the offering
Of thankful joy to Him whose perfect essence
Is perfect love, our glowing lips may bring,
Till this brief life is o'er;
And in a brighter, better,
Our spirits know no fetter. BETHUNE.

I READ His awful name emblazoned high,
With golden letters, on the illumined sky;
Nor less the mystic characters I see
Wrought in each flower, inscribed on every tree:
In every leaf that trembles to the breeze,
I hear the voice of God among the trees.

MRS. BARBAULD.

THOU art, O God, the life and light
  Of all this wondrous world we see;
Its glow by day, its smile by night,
  Are but reflections, caught from Thee;
Where'er we turn, Thy glories shine,
And all things fair and bright are Thine.

THOMAS MOORE.

READ Nature; Nature is a friend to truth:
Nature is Christian; preaches to mankind;
And bids dead matter aid us in our creed. YOUNG.

NATURE'S self, which is the breath of God,
Or His pure Word by miracle revealed.

WORDSWORTH.

THE simple flowers and streams
Are social and benevolent, and he
Who holdeth converse in their language pure,
Roaming among them at the cool of day,
Shall find, like him who Eden's garden dressed,
His Maker there to teach his listening heart.

MRS. SIGOURNEY.

NATURE, employed in her allotted place,
Is hand-maid to the purposes of Grace;
By good vouchsafed, makes known superior good,
And bliss not seen, by blessings understood.

COWPER.

THE stars are out in Heaven! How the soul
Expands, while gazing on their silver light!

DAVID BATES.

MY heart leaps up when I behold
  A rainbow in the sky!
So was it when my life began;
So is it now I am a man;
So let it be when I grow old,
  Or let me die.
The child is father of the man,
And I would wish my days to be
Bound each to each, by natural piety.

WORDSWORTH

GOD of the fair and open sky!
  How gloriously above us springs
The tented dome of heavenly blue,
  Suspended on the rainbow's rings!
Each brilliant star that sparkles through,
  Each gilded cloud that wanders free
In evening's purple radiance, gives
  The beauty of its praise to Thee!

W. B. O. PEABODY.

OMNIPOTENCE—OMNIPRESENCE—OMNISCIENCE.

WITH God all things are possible. MARK, x, 27.

Lo, these are part of His ways; but how little a portion is heard of Him! But the thunder of His power who can understand? JOB, xxvi, 14.

Whither shall I go from Thy Spirit? or whither shall I flee from Thy presence?

If I ascend up into Heaven, Thou art there: if I make my bed in hell, behold, Thou art there.

If I take the wings of the morning, and dwell in the uttermost parts of the sea;

Even then shall Thy hand lead me, and Thy right hand shall hold me. PSALM cxxxix, 7—10.

He ruleth by His power for ever; His eyes behold the nations. PSALM lxvi, 7.

Known unto God are all His works, from the beginning of the world. ACTS, xv, 18.

He that planted the ear, shall He not hear? He that formed the eye, shall He not see?

He that chastiseth the heathen, shall not He correct? He that teacheth men knowledge, shall not He know? PSALM xciv, 9, 10.

Thou God seest me. GENESIS, xvi, 13.

"TELL them, I am," Jehovah said
To Moses, while earth heard in dread,
And, smitten to the heart,
At once above, beneath, around,
All nature, without voice or sound,
Replied, "O Lord! Thou art." SMART.

THE Almighty King,
Not always in the splendid scene of pomp
Tremendous, on the sounding tempest rides,
Or sweeping whirlwind; nor in the awful peal
Of echoing thunder is He always heard,
Or seen in lightning's livid flames; but oft,
When every turbid element is hushed,
In the still voice of nature stands confest
The Lord Omnipotent. SAMUEL HAYES.

WHAT is too great if we the Cause survey?
Stupendous Architect! Thou, Thou art all!
My soul flies up and down in thoughts of Thee,
And finds herself but at the centre still!
I AM, Thy name! Existence, all Thine own!
Creation's nothing; flattered much, if styled
"The thin, the fleeting atmosphere of God."

YOUNG.

THOU beckonest, Almighty! from the tree
  The blossom's leaf doth fall;—
Thou beckonest, and in immensity
  Is quenched a solar ball!

MATHISSON.

IN all the immense, the strange, and old,
Thy presence careless men behold;
In all the little, weak, and mean,
By Faith be thou as clearly seen.

Thou teachest not a leaf can grow,
Till life from Thee within it flow;
That not a speck of dust can be,
O Fount of Being, save by Thee!

JOHN STERLING.

SOUL of the world, All-seeing Eye,
Where, where shall man Thy presence fly?
Say, would he climb the starry height?
All Heaven is instinct with Thy Light:—
Dwell in the darkness of the grave?
Yea, Thou art there to judge and save.

In vain on wings of Morn we soar,
In vain the realms of Space explore,
In vain retreat to shades of Night,—
For what can veil us from Thy sight?
Distance dissolves before Thy ray,
And darkness kindles into day.

WM. PETER.

WHEN up to nightly skies we gaze,
Where stars pursue their endless ways,
We think we see, from earth's low clod,
The wide and shining home of God.

'T is vain to dream those tracts of space,
With all their worlds, approach His face:
One glory fills each wheeling ball—
One love has shaped and moved them all.

This earth, with all its dust and tears,
Is no less His than yonder spheres;
And rain-drops weak, and grains of sand,
Are stamped by His immediate hand.

JOHN STERLING.

GOD hath a presence, and that ye may see
In the fold of the flower, the leaf of the tree,
In the sun of the noon-day, the star of the night,
In the storm-cloud of darkness, the rainbow of night,
In the waves of the ocean, the furrows of land,
In the mountain of granite, the atom of sand,
Turn where ye may, from the sky to the sod,
Where can ye gaze that ye see not God?

ELIZA COOK.

No secret cave,
Nor gloom of midnight, can from Him, whose eye
Through all creation instantaneous darts,
Veil the nefarious deed.

SAMUEL HAYES.

WHEN in my mother's womb concealed, I lay
A senseless embryo, then my soul Thou knewest,
Knewest all her future workings, every thought,
And every faint idea yet unformed.

SMART.

A THOUSAND nameless acts,
That lurk in lovely secresy, and die
Unnoticed, like the trodden flowers which fall
Beneath a proud man's foot, to Thee are known,
And written, with a sunbeam, in the Book
Of Life, where Mercy fills the brightest page.

ROBERT MONTGOMERY.

WE cannot think too oft
There is a never, never-sleeping eye
Which reads the heart, and registers our thoughts.

W. T. BACON.

THOUGH all the doors are sure, and all our servants
As sure bound with their sleeps; yet there is One
That wakes above, whose eye no sleep can bind;
He sees through doors, and darkness, and our thoughts!
And, therefore, as we should avoid with fear,
To think ourselves amiss before His search;
So should we be as curious to shun
All cause that others think not ill of us.

GEORGE CHAPMAN.

GOD nought foresees, but sees: for to His eyes
Nought is to come, or past: nor are you vile
Because that Heaven foresees, for God, not we,
Sees as things are; things are not as we see.

JOHN MARSTON.

THERE is an ear that hears the voice of prayer
Rising from lonely spots, where Christians meet,
Although it stir not more the sleeping air
Than the soft water-fall or forest breeze.

MRS. HALL.

PARTINGS.

SORROWING most of all for the words which he spake, that they should see his face no more. ACTS, xx, 38.

Entreat me not to leave thee, or to return from following after thee: for whither thou goest, I will go; and where thou lodgest, I will lodge: thy people shall be my people, and thy God my God:

Where thou diest will I die, and there will I be buried: the Lord do so to me, and more also, if aught but death part thee and me. RUTH, i, 16, 17.

And they sent away Rebekah their sister, and her nurse, and Abraham's servant, and his men.

And they blessed Rebekah, and said unto her, Thou art our sister. GENESIS, xxiv, 59, 60.

I NEVER spoke the word "Farewell,"
But with an utterance faint and broken;
And earth-sick longing for the time
When it shall never more be spoken.

MRS. SOUTHEY.

O, 'TIS one scene of parting here,
Love's watchword is farewell!
And almost starts the following tear,
Ere dried the last that fell!
'Tis but to feel that one most dear
Is needful to the heart,
And straight a voice is muttering near,
Imperious, Ye must part!

But happiest he, whose gifted eye
Above this world can see,
And those diviner realms descry,
Where partings cannot be;
Who, with One changeless Friend on high,
Life's various path has trod,
And soars to meet, beyond the sky,
The ransomed and their God.

TOWNSHEND

THOUGH warmly smile beam back to smile,
  And answering heart to heart,
They meet in gladness, who, too oft,
  Have only met to part.

Then bind not earthly ties too close,
  But hope let Heaven sustain;
There, and there only, mayest thou say,
  "We'll never part again!"

ANNA MARIA WELLS.

O, HEAVEN is where no secret dread
  May haunt love's meeting hour,
Where, from the past, no gloom is shed
  O'er the heart's chosen bower:
Where every severed wreath is bound—
  Where none have heard the knell
That smites the heart with that deep sound—
  Farewell— beloved,—*farewell!* MRS. HEMANS.

AND though scarce less than death it seem,
  When children from their home depart,
O, let not the beloved deem
  Heaven for no purpose rends the heart:
With Laban yield with meek accord;
"The thing proceedeth from the Lord."

Above are partings never known,
  But O, it is not thus below:
Rebekah could Heaven's mandate own,
  And say, submissive, "I will go!"
Losing her kindred's tender care,
But blessed in their fervent prayer. H. H. WELD.

THE PASSIONS—APPETITES.

For all that is in the world, the lust of the flesh, and the lust of the eyes, and the pride of life, is not of the Father, but is of the world. I. John, ii, 16.

All the labour of man is for his mouth, and yet the appetite is not filled. Ecclesiastes, vi, 7.

Now the works of the flesh are manifest, which are these: adultery, fornication, uncleanness, lasciviousness,

Idolatry, witchcraft, hatred, variance, emulations, wrath, strife, sedition, heresies,

Envyings, murders, drunkenness, revellings, and such like: of the which I tell you before, as I have also told you in time past, that they which do such things shall not inherit the kingdom of God. Galatians, v, 19—21.

While passions glow, the heart like heated steel
Takes each impression, and is worked at pleasure.
Young.

Govern well thy appetite; lest sin
Surprise thee, and her black attendant, death.
Milton.

Thou must chain thy passions down:
Well to serve, but ill to sway,
Like the fire, they must obey.
They are good, in subject state,
To strengthen, warm, and animate;
But if once we let them reign,
They sweep with desolating train,
'Till they but leave a hated name,
A ruined soul, and blackened fame. Eliza Cook.

Pleasure and revenge
Have ears more deaf than adders, to the voice
Of any true decision. Shakspeare.

PASSIONS, indulged beyond a certain bound,
Lead to a precipice, and plunge in woe
The heedless agent. GEORGE BALLY.

WHEN carnal passions reign,
And grosser acts of sin the heart distain,
Our souls all clotted by contagion grow,
And brood and grovel in the dust below:
Like lingering ghosts, that loth, as fables say,
To leave their body, haunt their kindred clay.
JAMES SCOTT.

SOME dream that they can silence, when they will,
The storm of Passion, and say "Peace, be still:"
But "Thus far, and no farther," when addressed
To the wild wave, or wilder human breast,
Implies authority that never can—
That never ought to be, the lot of man. COWPER.

MAN'S heart eats all things, and is hungry still
"More! more!" the glutton cries; for something new
So rages appetite, if man can't mount,
He will descend. YOUNG.

PASTORS—THE PULPIT.

How then shall they call on Him in whom they have not believed? and how shall they believe in Him of whom they have not heard? and how shall they hear without a preacher?

And how shall they preach, except they be sent? ROMANS, x, 14, 15.

For, after that in the wisdom of God, the world by wisdom knew not God, it pleased God by the foolishness of preaching to save them that believe. I. CORINTHIANS, i, 22.

Preach the word; be instant in season, out of season; reprove, rebuke, exhort, with all long-suffering and doctrine. II. TIMOTHY, iv, 2.

For though I preach the gospel, I have nothing to glory of: for necessity is laid upon me; yea, woe is unto me if I preach not the gospel. I. CORINTHIANS, ix, 16.

Woe be unto the pastors that destroy and scatter the sheep of my pasture, saith the Lord. JEREMIAH, xxiii, 1.

He which converteth a sinner from the error of his way, shall save a soul from death, and hide a multitude of sins. JAMES, v, 20.

Neglect not the gift that is in thee, which was given thee by prophecy, with the laying on of the hands of the Presbytery. I. TIMOTHY, iv, 14.

Let the elders that rule well be counted worthy of double honour, especially those who abour in the word and doctrine. I. TIMOTHY, v, 17.

TURN to the world — its curious dwellers view,
Like Paul's Athenians, seeking something new.
* * * * * *
Does Langdon preach? — (I veil his quiet name
Who serves his God, and cannot stoop to fame;) —
No; 'tis some reverend mime, the latest rage,
Who thumps the desk, that should have trod the stage;
Cant's veriest ranter crams a house, if new,
When Paul himself, oft heard, would hardly fill a pew

CHARLES SPRAGUE.

No studied eloquence was there displayed,
Nor poetry of language lent its aid;
But plain the words that from the preacher came;
A preacher young, and all unknown to fame;
While youth and age a listening ear inclined,
To learn the way the pearl of price to find.

ELIZABETH BOGART.

O, REST not now, but scatter wide the seeds
Of faithful words, and yet more faithful deeds;
So thou shalt rest above eternally,
When God the harvest fruit shall give to thee.

BETHUNE.

AT his approach, complaint grew mild,
  And when his hand unbarr'd the shutter,
The clammy lips of fever smiled
  The welcome which they could not utter. PRAED.

I SAW one man, armed simply with God's Word,
  Enter the souls of many fellow-men,
And pierce them sharply as a two-edged sword,
  While conscience echoed back his words again;
  Till, even as showers of fertilizing rain
Sink through the bosom of the valley clod,
  So their hearts opened to the wholesome pain,
And hundreds knelt upon the flowery sod,
One good man's earnest prayer, the link 'twixt them and
  God.

MRS. NORTON

HOW beauteous are the feet of those who bear
Mercy to man, glad tidings to despair!
Far from the mountain's top, they lovelier seem
Than moonlight dews, or morning's rosy beam;
Sweeter the voice than spell, or hymning sphere,
And listening angels hush their harps to hear.

C. H. JOHNSON

HIS ready smile a parent's warmth expressed;
Their welfare pleased him, and their cares distressed;
To them his heart, his love, his griefs were given,
But all his serious thoughts had rest in Heaven.

GOLDSMITH.

By weakest ministers, the Almighty thus
Makes known His sacred will, and shows His power:
By Him inspired, they speak with urgent tongue
Authoritative, whilst the illumined breast
Heaves with unwonted strength; high as their theme,
Their great conceptions rise in rapturous flow,
As quick the ready organs catch the thought,
And, in such strains as science could not teach,
Bear it, in all its radiance, to the heart;
The listening throng there feel its bless'd effect,
And deep conviction glows in every breast.

CHARLES JENNER.

He bore his great commission in his look,
But sweetly tempered awe, and softened all he spoke.
He preached the joys of Heaven, and pains of hell,
And warned the sinner with becoming zeal,
But on eternal mercy loved to dwell. DRYDEN

Of the deep learning in the schools of yore,
The reverend pastor hath a golden stock:
Yet, with a vain display of useless lore,
Or sapless doctrine, never will he mock
The better cravings of his simple flock;
But faithfully their humble shepherd guides
Where streams eternal gush from Calvary's rock;
For well he knows, not learning's purest tides
Can quench the immortal thirst that in the soul abides

MRS. LITTLE.

Nor did the pulpit's oratory fail
To achieve its higher triumph.—Not unfelt
Were its admonishments, nor lightly heard
The awful truths, delivered thence by tongues
Endowed with various power to search the soul.

WORDSWORTH.

YE to whom a prophet-voice is given,
  Stirring men, as by a trumpet's call,
Utter forth the oracles of Heaven!—
  Earth gives back the echoes as they fall:
Rouse the world's great heart, while yet the day
Breaks life's slumber with its blessed ray,—
    For the night cometh! MRS. EMBURY.

THOUGH meek and patient as a sheathed sword,
Though pride's least lurking thought appear a wrong
To human kind; though peace be on his tongue,
Gentleness in his heart,—can earth afford
Such genuine state, preëminence so free,
As when, arrayed in Christ's authority,
He from the pulpit lifts his awful hand;
Conjures, implores, and labours all he can
For re-subjecting to divine command
The stubborn spirit of rebellious man?

WORDSWORTH.

WITH eloquence innate his tongue was armed;
Though harsh the precept, yet the preacher charmed:
For, letting down the golden chain from high,
He drew his audience upward to the sky.

DRYDEN.

THE priestly brotherhood, devout, sincere,
From mean self-interest and ambition clear,
Their hope in Heaven, servility their scorn,
Prompt to persuade, expostulate, and warn,
Their wisdom pure, and given them from above,
Their usefulness ensured by zeal and love,
As meek as the man Moses, and withal
As bold as in Agrippa's presence, Paul,
Should fly the world's contaminating touch,
Holy and unpolluted. COWPER.

As your guide,
He in the heaven-ward path hath firmly walked,
Bearing your joys and sorrows in his breast,
And on his prayers. He at your household hearths
Hath spoke his Master's message, while your babes
Listening, imbibed, as blossoms drink the dew;
And when your dead were buried from your sight,
Was he not there? MRS. SIGOURNEY.

BUT chiefly ye should lift your gaze
Above the world's uncertain haze,
And look with calm, unwavering eye
On the bright fields beyond the sky,
Ye who your Lord's commission bear,
His way of mercy to prepare:
Angels He calls ye: be your strife
To lead, on earth, an angel's life. KEBLE.

THIS noble ensample to his flock he gave,
The first he wrought, and afterward he taught.
The word of life he from the Gospel caught,
And well this comment added he thereto —
If that gold rusteth, what should iron do?
And if the priest be foul in whom we trust,
What wonder if the unlettered layman lust?
And shame it were in him the flock should keep,
To see a sullied shepherd and clean sheep.
But sure a priest the sample ought to give,
By his own cleanness, how his flock should live.
CHAUCER.

AT church, with meek and unaffected grace,
His looks adorned the venerable place;
Truth from his lips prevailed with double sway,
And those who came to scoff, remained to pray.
GOLDSMITH.

Beside the bed where parting life was laid,
And sorrow, guilt, and pain by turns dismayed,
The reverend champion stood. At his control,
Despair and anguish fled the struggling soul;
Comfort came down, the trembling wretch to raise,
And his last faltering accents whispered praise.

Goldsmith.

Judge not the preacher, for he is thy judge:
If thou mislike him, thou conceivest him not.
God calleth preaching folly. Do not grudge
To pick out treasures from an earthen pot.
The worst speak something good: if all want sense,
God takes a text, and preacheth patience.

George Herbert.

Their's the high task to teach man's greatest good,
And turn his erring steps from evil ways;
Nor empty pomp, nor mad ambition, throw
Their dazzling lures along their peaceful course;
Content are they a virtuous life to show,
And Christian precepts meekly to enforce
In mournful dying scenes, and Sabbath-days' discourse.

McLellan

He who slumbereth not, nor sleepeth,
His ancient watch around us keepeth;
Still sent from His creating hand,
New witnesses for truth shall stand—
New instruments to sound abroad
The Gospel of a risen Lord;
To gather to the fold once more
The desolate and gone astray,
The scattered of a cloudy day,
And Zion's broken walls restore.

J. G. Whittier.

A TRUE, good man there was, of religion
Pious, and poor — the parson of a town.
But rich he was in holy thought and work;
And thereto a right learned man, a clerk
That Christ's pure Gospel would sincerely preach,
And his parishioners devoutly teach. CHAUCER.

THUS, to relieve the wretched was his pride,
And e'en his failings leaned to virtue's side;
But, in his duty prompt at every call,
He watched and wept, he prayed and felt for all;
And as a bird each fond endearment tries,
To tempt its new-fledged offspring to the skies,
He tried each art, reproved each dull delay,
Allured to brighter worlds, and led the way.
GOLDSMITH.

CLAD in the armour of the Living God,
Approach, unsheathe the Spirit's flaming sword;
Faith's shield, salvation's glory-compassed helm,
With fortitude assume, and o'er your heart
Fair truth's invulnerable breast-plate spread.
SMART.

THERE stands the messenger of truth; there stands
The legate of the skies: his theme divine,
His office sacred, his credentials clear.
By him the violated law speaks out
Its thunders; and by him, in strains as sweet
As angels use, the Gospel whispers peace.
He 'stablishes the strong, restores the weak,
Reclaims the wanderer, binds the broken heart,
And, armed himself in panoply complete
Of heavenly temper, furnishes with arms
Bright as his own; and trains, by every rule
Of holy discipline, to glorious war,
The sacramental host of God's elect. COWPER.

PATIENCE—RESIGNATION.

THE Lord gave, and the Lord hath taken away; blessed be the name of the Lord JOB, i, 21.

Take, my brethren, the prophets who have spoken in the name of the Lord, for an example of suffering affliction, and of patience.

Behold, we count them happy which endure. Ye have heard of the patience of Job and have seen the end of the Lord; that the Lord is very pitiful, and of tender mercy. JAMES, v, 10, 11.

In your patience possess ye your souls. LUKE, xxi, 19.

And not only so, but we glory in tribulations also; knowing that tribulation worketh patience;

And patience, experience; and experience, hope. ROMANS, v, 3.

Though He slay me, yet will I trust in Him. JOB, xiii, 15.

WHATE'ER thy lot, whoe'er thou be,
Confess thy folly,—kiss the rod;
And in thy chastening sorrow, see
The hand of God.

A bruised reed He will not break—
Afflictions all His children feel:
He wounds them for His mercy's sake—
He wounds to heal.

JAMES MONTGOMERY.

LEANING on Him, make with reverent meekness,
His own, thy will;
And with strength from Him shall thy utter weakness
Life's task fulfil;

And that cloud itself, which now before thee
Lies dark in view,
Shall, with beams of light, from the inner glory,
Be stricken through.

J. G. WHITTIER.

WHEN, in justice, He appals us
  By the threat of endless pain,
Sink not — soon His mercy calls us
  To His pardoning arms again.
Father! O, with patience bless us,
  Till each seeming ill be past:
Let whatever gloom oppress us,
  All must end in light at last. THOMAS WARD.

THOU Power Supreme, whose mighty scheme
  These woes of mine fulfil,
Here, firm, I rest, they must be best,
  Because they are Thy Will!
Then all I want, (O, do Thou grant
  This one request of mine,)
Since to *enjoy* Thou dost deny,
  Assist me to *resign*. BURNS.

"O FATHER! not my will, but Thine be done!"
    So spake the Son.
Be this our charm, mellowing earth's ruder noise
    Of griefs and joys —
That we may cling for ever to Thy breast,
    In perfect rest! KEBLE

GIVE me care,
By thankful patience, to prevent despair:
Fit me to bear whate'er Thou shalt assign;
I kiss the rod, because the rod is Thine.
FRANCIS QUARLES

LORD, I submit. Complete Thy gracious will,
For, if Thou slay me, I will trust Thee still.
O, be my will so swallowed up in Thine,
That I may do Thy will, in doing mine!
HANNAH MORE.

FAITH and hope
Will teach me how to bear my lot!
To think Almighty Wisdom best,
To bow my head, and murmur not.
The chast'ning hand of One above
Falls heavy, but I kiss the rod:
He gives the wound, and I must trust
Its healing to the self-same God.

ELIZA COOK.

O YE, whose hearts in secret bleed
O'er transient hope, like morning dew,
O'er friendship faithless in your need,
Or love to all its vows untrue,
Who shrink from persecution's rod,
Or slander's fang, or treachery's tone,
Look meekly to the Son of God,
And in His griefs forget your own.

Forsaken are ye?—so was He;
Reviled?—yet check the 'vengeful word;
Rejected?—should the servant be
Exalted o'er his suffering Lord?
Nor deem that Heaven's omniscient eye
Is e'er regardless of your lot,—
Deluded man from God may fly,
But when was man by God forgot?

MRS. SIGOURNEY.

LIKE some well-fashioned arch thy patience stood,
And purchased strength from each increasing load.

GOLDSMITH.

FOR God, who binds the broken heart,
And dries the mourner's tear,
If faith and patience be their part,
Will unto these be near.

Let such but say "Thy will be done!"
And He who Jesus raised,
Will qualify them, through His Son,
To say "Thy name be praised!"

BERNARD BARTON

GOD is much displeased
That you take with unthankfulness His doing;
In common, worldly things, 'tis called—ungrateful,
With dull unwillingness to repay a debt
Which with a bounteous hand was kindly lent;
Much more to be thus opposite with Heaven,
For it requires the debt it lent you. SHAKSPEARE

THERE is a secret in the ways of God
With His own children, which none others know,
That sweetens all He does: and if such peace
While under His afflicting hand we find,
What will it be to see Him as He is,
And past the reach of all that now disturbs
The tranquil soul's repose? SWAINE

IF, friendless, in a vale of tears I stray,
Where briers wound, and thorns perplex my way—
Still let my steady soul Thy goodness see,
And with strong confidence lay hold on Thee;
With equal eye my various lot receive,
Resigned to die, or resolute to live:
Prepared to kiss the sceptre or the rod,
While God is seen in all, and all in God.

MRS. BARBAULD

AND wilt thou not, coy wretch! drink one poor sup
Of bitter drink for Him that drank a cup
To sweeten thine? JOHN QUARLES.

WISDOM, the antidote of sad despair,
Makes sharp afflictions seem not as they are,
Through patient sufferance; and doth apprehend,
Not as they seeming are, but as they end.

FRANCIS QUARLES.

TAKE all, great God! I will not grieve,
But still will wish that I had still to give.

NORRIS, *of Bemerton.*

IN patience, then, possess thy soul,
Stand still!—for while the thunders roll,
Thy Saviour sees thee through the gloom,
And will to thy assistance come;
His love and mercy will be shown
To those who trust in Him alone.

WILLIAM ALLEN.

MY blest Redeemer lives.—In that last day
  When, like the baseless fabric of a dream,
Earth's unsubstantial glories pass away,
  He then shall stand, acknowledged Lord supreme.
My blest Redeemer lives.—Though death the head
  Consign, a victim to the silent tomb;
Though worms around my lifeless body spread,
  Though noisome worms these mouldering limbs consume,
Triumphant still o'er Satan's power I rise,
My God, my God appears, and wakes these languid eyes.

SAMUEL HAYES.

O, SHAME upon thee, listless heart,
  So sad a sigh to heave,
As if thy Saviour had no part
  In thoughts that make thee grieve.

KEBLE.

LOVE, born in hours of joy and mirth
With mirth and joy may perish;
That to which darker hours gave birth
Still more and more we cherish:
It looks beyond the clouds of time,
And through death's shadowy portal;
Made, by adversity, sublime,
By faith and hope, immortal. BERNARD BARTON.

HE who each bitter cup rejects,
No living spring shall quaff;
He whom Thy rod in love corrects,
Shall lean upon Thy staff:
Happy, thrice happy, then, is he,
Who knows the chastening is from Thee!
BERNARD BARTON.

COME, Resignation, spirit meek,
And let me kiss thy placid cheek,
And read in thy pale eye serene
Their blessing, who by faith can wean
Their hearts from sense, and learn to love
God only, and the joys above. KEBLE.

(*See also* CONSOLATION.)

PEDANTRY.

PROFESSING themselves to be wise, they became fools. ROMANS, i, 22.

Seest thou a wise man in his own conceit? There is more hope of a fool than of him. PROVERBS, xxvi, 12.

Is Christ the abler teacher, or the schools?
If Christ, then why resort, at every turn,
To Athens, or to Rome, for wisdom short
Of man's occasions, when in Him reside
Grace, knowledge, comfort, an unfathomed store!
How oft, when Paul has served us with a text,
Has Epictetus, Plato, Tully preached! COWPER.

AND when I weigh this seeming wisdom well,
And prove it in the infallible result
So hollow and so false — I feel my heart
Dissolve in pity, and account the learned,
If this be learning, most of all deceived.
Great crimes alarm the conscience, but it sleeps,
While thoughtful man is plausibly amused.
Defend me, therefore, common sense, say I,
From reveries so airy, from the toil
Of dropping buckets into empty wells,
And growing old in drawing nothing up! COWPER.

YOUR learning, like the lunar beam, affords
Light, but not heat; it leaves you undevout,
Frozen at heart, while speculation shines. YOUNG.

HOW empty learning, and how vain is art,
But as it mends the life, and guides the heart!
YOUNG.

PILGRIM—PILGRIMAGE.

THESE all died in faith, not having received the promises, but having seen them afar off, and were persuaded of them, and embraced them, and confessed that they were strangers and pilgrims on the earth.

For they that say such things, plainly declare that they seek a country. HEBREWS, xi, 13.

For here we have no continuing city, but we seek one to come. HEBREWS, xiii, 14.

Dearly beloved, I beseech you, as strangers and pilgrims, beware of fleshly lusts which war against the soul. I. PETER, ii, 11.

IT is a short and simple prayer,
But 'tis the Christian's stay
Through every varied scene of care,
Until his dying day.
As through the wilderness of life
Calmly he wanders on,
His prayer in every time of strife
Is still "Thy will be done!"

MARY ANNE BROWNE.

FROM darkness, here, and dreariness,
We ask not full repose;
Only be Thou at hand, to bless
Our trial hour of woes.
Is not the pilgrim's toil o'erpaid
By the clear rill and palmy shade?
And see we not, up earth's dark glade,
The gate of Heaven unclose?

KEBLE.

THERE is light on the hills, and the valley is past!
Ascend, happy pilgrim! thy labours are o'er!
The sunshine of Heaven around thee is cast,
And thy weak, doubting footsteps can falter no more

On, pilgrim! that hill richly circled with rays
  Is Zion! Lo, there is "the city of saints!"
And the beauties, the glories, that region displays,
  Inspiration's own language imperfectly paints.

MRS. OPIE.

WE journey through a vale of tears
  By many a cloud o'ercast;
And worldly cares, and worldly fears,
  Go with us to the last!
Not to the last—Thy word hath said,
  Could we but read aright;
Poor pilgrim! lift, in hope, thy head;
  At eve there shall be light. BERNARD BARTON.

HAPPY, O, happy he, who, not affecting
  The endless toils affecting worldly cares,
With mind reposed, all discontent rejecting,
  In silent pace his way to Heaven prepares,
Deeming his life a scene, the world a stage,
Whereon man acts his weary pilgrimage.

ANONYMOUS.

WHILE his staff the traveller handles
  In his weary journeying,
Thorns may tear his dusty sandals,
  Fangs his tender feet may sting;
But were life devoid of pain,
Bliss were proffered man in vain.

Look aloft, where light is breaking
  Through this doubt-enveloped sky—
Forward leap, the joy partaking,
  Of a higher destiny.
Lift thy staff, and move apace
In the pilgrim-thronging race. T. G. SPEAR.

Give me my scallop-shell of quiet,
My staff of faith to walk upon;
My scrip of joy, immortal diet;
My bottle of salvation;
My gown of glory (hope's true gage),
And thus I'll take my pilgrimage.
Blood must be my body's only balmer
Whilst my soul, like a quiet Palmer,
Travelleth towards the land of Heaven;
No other balm will there be given.

Sir Walter Raleigh.

Heaven is a great way off, and I shall be
Ten thousand years in travel; yet 'twere happy
If I may find a lodging there at last,
Though my poor soul get thither upon crutches.

Shirley.

PLEASURE.

He that loveth pleasure shall be a poor man: he that loveth wine and oil shall not be rich. Proverbs, xxi, 17.

When lust hath conceived, it bringeth forth sin; and sin, when it is finished, bringeth forth death. James, i, 15.

Delight thyself also in the Lord, and He shall give thee the desires of thy heart. Psalm xxxvii, 4.

Pleasure, admitted in undue degree,
Enslaves the will, nor leaves the judgment free.

Cowper.

Count all the advantage prosperous vice attains,
'T is but what virtue flies from, and disdains.

Pope.

In the embattled plain
Though Death exults and claps his raven wings,
Yet reigns he not, even there, so absolute,
So merciless, as in yon frantic scenes
Of midnight revel and tumultuous mirth,
Where, in the intoxicating draught concealed,
Or couched beneath the glance of lawless love,
He snares the simple youth, who, nought suspecting,
Means to be blest — but finds himself undone.

Bp. Porteus.

Peace follows virtue as its sure reward;
And pleasure brings as surely in her train
Remorse, and sorrow, and vindictive pain.

Cowper.

While music flows around,
Perfumes, and oils, and wine, and wanton hours;
Amid the roses, fierce repentance rears
Her snaky crest: a quick returning pang
Shoots through the conscious heart. Thomson.

A languid, leaden iteration reigns,
And ever must, o'er those whose joys are joys
Of sight, smell, taste; the cuckoo-seasons sing
The same dull note to such as nothing prize
But what those seasons, from the teeming earth,
To doating sense indulge. But nobler minds,
Which relish fruits unripened by the sun,
Make their days various. Young.

Pleasure is good, and man for pleasure made;
But pleasure full of glory as of joy;
Pleasure which neither blushes nor expires.

Young

DEATH treads in pleasure's footsteps round the world,
When pleasure treads the paths which reason shuns.
YOUNG.

IT is a shame, that man, that has the seeds
Of virtue in him springing unto glory,
Should make his soul degenerate with sin,
And slave to luxury; to drown his spirits
In lees of sloth; to yield up the weak day
To wine, to lust, and banquets. SHACKERLY.

PLEASURES are few, and fewer we enjoy;
Pleasure, like quicksilver, is bright and coy;
We strive to grasp it, with our utmost skill,
Still it eludes us, and it glitters still:
If seized at last, compute your mighty gains;
What is it but rank poison in your veins?
YOUNG.

THAT pleasure is of all
Most bountiful and kind,
That fades not straight, but leaves
A living joy behind. CAMPION.

PLEASURES, like wonders, quickly lose their price,
When reason or experience makes us wise.
BP. KING.

ALL these fond pleasures, if fond things
Deserve so good a name,
Should not seduce a noble mind
To stain itself with shame.
The time shall come when all these same,
Which seem so rich with joy,
Like tyrants, shall torment thy mind,
And vex thee with annoy. BRANDON.

MEMORY confused, and interrupted thought,
Death's harbingers, lie latent in the draught,
And, in the flowers that wreathe the sparkling bowl,
Fell adders hiss, and poisonous serpents roll.

PRIOR.

WOE unto those that with the morning sun
Rise to drink wine, and set till he have done
His weary course; not ceasing, until night
Have quenched their understanding with the light.

BP. KING.

ADMIRERS of false pleasures must sustain
The weight and sharpness of ensuing pain.

JOHN BEAUMONT.

FLY drunkenness, whose vile incontinence
Takes away both thy reason and thy sense,
Till with Circean cups, thy mind possessed,
Leaves to be man, and wholly turns to beast.

THOMAS RANDOLPH.

SHORT is the course of every lawless pleasure —
Grief, like a shade, on all its footsteps waits,
Scarce visible in joy's meridian height;
But, downwards as its blaze declining speeds,
The dwarfish shadow to a giant spreads.

MILTON.

HEALTH
Flies the luxurious glutton's rich repast,
And with the hermit, at his temperate board,
Sits a pleased guest. GEORGE BALLY.

POETRY.

MOREOVER, Hezekiah the king, and the princes, commanded the Levites to sing praise unto the Lord, with the words of David and of Asaph the seer. II. CHRONICLES, xxix, 30.

A word fitly spoken is like apples of gold in pictures of silver. PROVERBS, xxv, 11.

And the Lord said unto Moses, * * * Now therefore write ye this song for you, and put it in the mouths of the children of Israel, that this song may be a witness for me. DEUTERONOMY, xxxi, 16—19.

Speaking to yourselves in psalms and hymns, and spiritual songs, singing and making melody in your heart to the Lord. EPHESIANS, v, 19.

PITY Religion has so seldom found
A skilful guide into poetic ground!
The flowers would spring where'er she deigned to stray,
And every muse attend her in the way.
Virtue, indeed, meets many a rhyming friend,
And many a compliment politely penned;
But, unattired in that becoming vest
Religion weaves for her, and half undressed,
Stands in the desert, shivering and forlorn,
A wintry figure, like a withered thorn.
The shelves are full, all other themes are sped;
Hackneyed and worn to the last flimsy thread,
Satire has long since done his best, and curs'd;
And loathsome ribaldry has done his worst;
Fancy has sported all her powers away
In tales and trifles, and in children's play;
And 't is the sad complaint, and almost true,
Whate'er we write, we bring forth nothing new.
'T were new, indeed, to see a bard all fire,
Touched with a coal from Heaven, assume the lyre
And tell the world, still kindling as he sung,
With more than mortal music on his tongue,
That He who died below, and reigns above,
Inspires the song, and that His name is Love.

COWPER.

DEBASED to servile purposes of pride,
How are the powers of genius misapplied!
The gift, whose office is the Giver's praise,
To trace Him in His word, His work, His ways,
Then spread the rich discovery, and invite
Mankind to share in the divine delight;
Distorted from its use and just design,
To make the pitiful possessor shine,
To purchase at the fool-frequented fair
Of vanity, a wreath for self to wear,
Is profanation of the basest kind—
Proof of a trifling and a worthless mind. COWPER.

O GRACIOUS God! How far have we
Profaned Thy heavenly gift of poesy!
Made prostitute and profligate the muse,
Debased to each obscene and impious use,
Whose harmony was first ordained above
For tongues of angels, and for hymns of love!
DRYDEN.

How shall the harp of poesy regain
That old victorious tone of prophet-years—
A spell divine o'er guilt's perturbing fears,
And all the hovering shadows of the brain?
Dark, evil wings took flight before the strain,
And showers of holy quiet, with its fall,
Sank on the soul:—O, who may now recall
The mighty music's consecrated reign?—
Spirit of God! whose glory once o'erhung
A throne, the Ark's dread cherubim between,
So let Thy presence brood, though now unseen,
O'er those two powers by whom the harp is strung—
Feeling and thought!—till the rekindled chords
Give the long-buried tone back to immortal words.
MRS. HEMANS.

Poesy, thou sweet'st content
That e'er Heaven to mortals lent;
Though they as a trifle leave thee
Whose dull thoughts cannot conceive thee;
Though thou be to them a scorn
That to nought but earth are born;
Let my life no longer be
Than I am in love with thee!
Though our wise ones call it madness,
Let me never taste of gladness
If I love not thy maddest fits
Above all their greatest wits!
And though some, too seeming holy,
Do account thy raptures folly,
Thou dost teach me to contemn
What makes knaves and fools of them.

George Wither.

Hence learned the bard in lofty strains to tell
How patient virtue triumphed over hell;
And hence the chief, who led the chosen race
Through parting seas, derived his songs of praise:
She gave the rapturous ode whose ardent lay
Sings female force, and vanquished Sisera;
She tuned to pious notes the Psalmist's lyre,
And filled Isaiah's breast with more than Pindar's fire.

John Hughes.

Nor think the muse, whose sober voice ye hear,
  Contracts, with bigot frown, her sullen brow;
Casts round Religion's orb the mists of fear,
  Or shades with horrors what with smiles should glow

No; she would warn you, with seraphic fire,
  Heirs as ye are, of Heaven's eternal day;
Would bid you boldly to that Heaven aspire,
  Nor sink and slumber in your cells of clay.

William Mason.

POVERTY.

GIVE me neither poverty nor riches; feed me with food convenient for me:

Lest I be full, and deny Thee, and say, Who is the Lord? or lest I be poor, and steal, and take the name of my God in vain. PROVERBS, xxx, 8, 9.

In a great trial of affliction, the abundance of their joy, and their deep poverty abounded unto the riches of their liberality. II. CORINTHIANS, viii, 2.

The Lord maketh poor, and maketh rich: He bringeth low, and lifteth up. I SAMUEL, ii, 7.

Blessed be ye poor: for yours is the kingdom of God. LUKE, vi, 20.

No soil like poverty for growth divine,
As leanest land supplies the richest mine.
Earth gives too little, giving only bread,
To nourish pride, or turn the weakest head.

COWPER.

THINKS he me mad? 'cause I've no monies on earth,
That I'll go forfeit my estate in Heaven,
And live eternal beggar? He shall pardon me:
That's my soul's jointure; I'll starve ere I sell that.

MIDDLETON.

WANT is a bitter and a hateful good,
Because its virtues are not understood.
Yet many things, impossible to thought,
Have been, by need, to full perfection brought.
The daring of the soul proceeds from thence,
Sharpness of wit, and active diligence;
Prudence at once, and fortitude it gives,
And, if in patience taken, mends our lives;
For even that indigence that brings me low,
Makes me myself, and Him above, to know.

DRYDEN

IF poverty — a bitter medicine — cure
The soul's distempers, blessed are the poor;
Yea, if ye be Christ's poor, thrice blessed men are ye.
THOMAS MCKELLAR.

MAN is God's image, but a poor man is
Christ's stamp to boot; both images regard.
GEORGE HERBERT.

(*See also* CONTENT.)

POWER—PRINCES—KINGS.

IT is better to trust in the Lord than to put any confidence in princes. PSALM, cxviii, 9.

He that ruleth over men must be just, ruling in the fear of God. II. SAMUEL, xxiii, 3.

O, HOW wretched
Is that poor man that hangs on princes' favours!
There is, betwixt the smile we would aspire to,
That sweet aspect of princes, and their ruin,
More pangs and fears than wars or women have;
And when he falls, he falls like Lucifer,
Never to hope again! SHAKSPEARE.

I PITY kings, whom worship waits upon,
Obsequious, from the cradle to the throne;
Before whose infant eyes the flatterer bows,
And binds a wreath about their baby brows;
Whom education stiffens into state,
And death awakens from that dream too late.
COWPER.

A CROWN,
Golden in show, is but a wreath of thorns;
Brings dangers, troubles, cares and sleepless nights
To him who wears the regal diadem,
When on his shoulders each man's burden lies;
For therein stands the office of a king,
His honour, virtue, merit, and chief praise,
That for the public all this weight he bears.
MILTON.

(*See also* AMBITION.)

PRAYER—PRAISE.

YE ask and receive not, because ye ask amiss. JAMES, iv, 3.

I will, therefore, that men pray every where, lifting up holy hands, without wrath or doubting. I. TIMOTHY, ii, 8.

But thou, when thou prayest, enter into thy closet, and when thou hast shut thy door, pray to thy Father which is in secret; and thy Father, which seeth in secret, shall reward thee openly. MATTHEW, vi, 6.

Is any among you afflicted? Let him pray. JAMES, v, 13.

Ask, and it shall be given you: seek, and ye shall find; knock, and it shall be opened unto you. MATTHEW, vii, 7.

Hitherto have ye asked nothing in my name: ask, and ye shall receive, that your joy may be full. JOHN, xvi, 24.

Praise ye the Lord: for it is good to sing praises unto our God; for it is pleasant, and praise is comely. PSALM clxvii, 1.

If ye, then, being evil, know how to give good gifts unto your children, how much more shall your Father which is in Heaven give good things to them that ask Him? MATTHEW, vii, 11.

They that wait upon the Lord shall renew their strength; they shall mount up with wings, as eagles; they shall run, and not be weary; and they shall walk, and not faint. ISAIAH, xl, 31.

THOUGH to speak thou be not able,
Always pray and never rest:
Prayer 's a weapon for the feeble—
Weakest souls can wield it best. HART.

Man's plea to man is, that he never more
Will beg, and that he never begged before:
Man's plea to God is, that he did obtain
A former suit, and therefore sues again.
How good a God we serve, that, when we sue,
Makes his old gifts the examples of his new.

Quarles.

When we of helps or hopes are quite bereaven,
Our humble prayers have entrance into Heaven.

Ford.

Temporal blessings Heaven oft doth share
Unto the wicked, at the good man's prayer.

Quarles.

With boldness, therefore, at the throne
Let us make all our sorrows known;
And ask the aid of heavenly power
To help us in the evil hour.

Logan.

O, come, when in the orient first
  Flashes the signal-light for prayer;
Come with the earliest beams that burst
  From God's bright throne of glory there.
Come kneel to Him who through the night
  Hath watched above thy sleeping soul,
To Him whose mercies, like His light,
  Are shed abroad from pole to pole.

C. F. Hoffman.

First worship God; he that forgets to pray,
Bids not himself good-morrow nor good-day:
Let thy first labour be to purge thy sin,
And serve Him first, whence all things did begin.

Thomas Randolph.

GIVE me, O Lord, the spirit of prayer,
  Thy grace, thy mercy to implore;
Let not my wilful spirit dare
  To count secure, her present store.
The richer falls Thy dew of grace,
  The humbler let my head descend,
Till mercy's sun in boundless space
  Shall shed its bliss, time without end.

JOHN JAY ADAMS.

A LIFE of prayer is the life of Heaven.

HENRY WARE, JR.

OUR God is a Spirit, and they who, aright,
  Would perform the pure worship He loveth,
In the heart's holy temple will seek with delight,
  That spirit the Father approveth.

BERNARD BARTON.

BUT holiest rite or longest prayer
  That soul can yield, or wisdom frame,
What better import can it bear
  Than "Father, hallowed be Thy name!"

ELIZA COOK.

WE, ignorant of ourselves,
Beg often our own harms, which the wise powers
Deny us for our good; so find we profit,
By losing of our prayers.

SHAKSPEARE.

EVEN as Elias, mounting to the sky,
  Did cast his mantle to the earth behind,
So, when the heart presents the prayer on high,
  Exclude the world from traffic with the mind:
Lips near to God, and ranging heart within,
Is but vain babbling, and converts to sin.

ROBERT SOUTHWELL.

SHALL Heaven, which gave us ardour, and has shown
Her own for man so strongly, not disdain
What smooth emollients in theology,
Recumbent virtue's downy doctors preach,
That prose of piety, a lukewarm praise? YOUNG.

PETITIONS yet remain
Which Heaven may hear, nor deem Religion vain.
Still raise for good the supplicating voice,
But leave to Heaven the measures and the choice.
Safe in His power whose eyes discern afar,
The secret ambush of a specious prayer;
Implore His aid, in His decisions rest,
Secure whate'er He gives, He gives the best.
DR. JOHNSON.

PRAYER, surpassing human might;
Prayer, Heaven's holy portress;
Prayer, the saint's supreme delight,
Prayer, the sinner's fortress.
Prayer and faith can joy impart,
Joy beyond expressing,
And call down upon the heart
Israel's choicest blessing. BERNARD BARTON.

THE PRESENT—DELAY—THE FUTURE.

Go to now, ye that say, To-day or to-morrow we will go into such a city, and continue there a year, and buy and sell, and get gain:

Whereas ye know not what shall be on the morrow. JAMES, iv, 13, 14.

Thou fool! this night thy soul shall be required of thee: then whose shall those things be, which thou hast provided? LUKE, xii, 20.

To-day, if ye will hear His voice, harden not your heart. PSALM xcv, 7, 8.

Behold, now is the accepted time; behold, now is the day of salvation. II. CORINTHIANS, vi, 2.

Boast not thyself of to-morrow; for thou knowest not what a day may bring forth. PROVERBS, xxvii, 1.

UP, Christian! up! thy cares resign!
The Past, the Future are not thine!
Show forth to-day thy Saviour's praise,
Redeem the course of evil days;
Life's shadow, in its lengthening gloom,
Points daily nearer to the tomb! ANONYMOUS.

Too curious man, why dost thou seek to know
Events, which, good or ill, foreknown, are woe?
The All-seeing power which made thee mortal, gave
Thee every thing a mortal state should have.
Fore-knowledge only is enjoyed by Heaven,
And, for his peace of mind, to man forbidden.
Wretched were life, if he foreknew his doom;
Even joys foreseen give pleasing hope no room,
And griefs assured, are felt before they come.

DRYDEN.

CATCH, then, O catch the transient hour,
  Improve each moment as it flies;
Life's a short summer,—man a flower;
  He dies — alas! how soon he dies!

DR. JOHNSON.

LEARN that the present hour alone is man's.
DR. JOHNSON.

SHUN delays, they breed remorse;
Take thy time while time doth serve thee;
Creeping snails have weakest force,
Fly their fault lest thou repent thee:
Good is best, when soonest wrought,
Lingering labours come to nought.
ROBERT SOUTHWELL.

TO-MORROW!
That fatal mistress of the young, the lazy,
The coward and the fool, condemned to lose
An useless life in waiting for to-morrow,
Till interposing death destroys the prospect:
Strange! that this general fraud, from day to day,
Should fill the world with wretches undetected.
DR. JOHNSON.

TO-MORROW, and to-morrow, and to-morrow
Creeps in this petty pace, from day to day,
To the last syllable of recorded time;
And all our yesterdays have lighted fools
The way to dusty death. SHAKSPEARE.

TO-DAY is so like yesterday, it cheats;
We take the lying sister for the same. YOUNG.

EACH night we die,
Each day are born anew: each day, a life!
And shall we kill each day? YOUNG.

O, BLINDNESS to the future! kindly given,
That each may fill the circle marked by Heaven.
POPE.

To-DAY is yesterday returned; returned
Full-powered to cancel, expiate, raise, adorn,
And reinstate us on the rock of peace.
Let it not share its predecessors' fate;
Nor, like its elder sisters, die a fool. YOUNG.

PRIDE.

PRIDE goeth before destruction, and a haughty spirit before a fall. PROVERBS, xvi, 18.

Yea, all of you be subject one to another, and be clothed with humility; for God resisteth the proud, and giveth grace to the humble. I. PETER, v, 5.

Better is the end of a thing than the beginning thereof; and the patient in spirit is better than the proud in spirit. PROVERBS, vii, 8.

WHAT if his very virtues
Had pampered his swol'n heart, and made him proud?
And what if pride had duped him into guilt?
COLERIDGE.

PRIDE, self-adoring pride, was primal cause
Of all sin past, all pain, all woe to come. POLLOK.

HATE, unbelief, and blasphemy of God,
Envy and slander, malice and revenge,
And murder and deceit, and every birth
Of damned sort, were progeny of pride. POLLOK.

PRIDE blasted Eden, and the world has bowed
Beneath her sceptre, which to break in dust,
The God incarnate every meekness wore.
ROBERT MONTGOMERY.

SMALL things make base men proud. SHAKSPEARE.

THOUGH various foes against the truth combine,
Pride, above all, opposes her design;
Pride, of a growth superior to the rest,
The subtlest serpent, with the loftiest crest,
Swells at the thought, and, kindling into rage,
Would hiss the cherub Mercy from the stage.

COWPER.

PRIDE was not made for men; a conscious sense
Of guilt and folly, and their consequence,
Destroys the claim, and to beholders tells,
Here nothing but the shape of manhood dwells.

WALLER.

SPITE of all the fools that pride has made,
'T is not on man a useless burden laid;
Pride has ennobled some, and some disgraced;
It hurts not in itself, but as 't is placed;
When right, its view knows none but virtue's bound;
When wrong, it scarcely looks one inch around.

STILLINGFLEET.

PRISON—PRISONERS.

THE Lord looseth the prisoners. PSALM cxl, 6.

Let the sighing of the prisoner come before thee; according to the greatness of thy power, preserve thou those that are appointed to die. PSALM lxxix, 11.

I called upon the Lord in distress: the Lord answered me, and set me in a large place. PSALM cxviii, 5.

WE see no more in thy pure skies,
How soft, O God! the sunset dies:
How every coloured hill and wood
Seems melting in the golden flood:
Yet, by the precious memories won
From bright hours, now for ever gone,
Father, o'er all Thy works we know
Thou still art shedding beauty's glow;
Still touching every cloud and tree
With glory, eloquent of Thee;
Still feeding all Thy flowers with light,
Though man hath barred it from our sight.
We know Thou reignest, the unchanging One, All-just!
And bless Thee still, with free and boundless trust!

MRS. HEMANS.

THOUGH not a human voice he hears,
And not a human form appears
His solitude to share,
He is not all alone—the eye
Of Him who hears the prisoner's sigh
Is even on him there.

J. L. CHESTER.

THE captive welcomes even death's relief:
What then, to him, the frowning prison-walls,
The clanking chain, the tyrant's 'vengeful spite?
From the freed spirit every shackle falls,—
Earth's gloom is lost, in Heaven's glorious light.

H. H. WELD.

AND this place our fore-fathers made for man!
This is the process of our love and wisdom
To each poor brother who offends against us—
Most innocent, perhaps—and what if guilty?
Is this the only cure! Merciful God!
Each pore and natural outlet shrivelled up
By ignorance and parching poverty,
His energies roll back upon his heart,
And stagnate and corrupt, till, changed to poison,
They break on him like a loathsome plague-spot!

COLERIDGE.

PROPHECY—PROPHETS.

KNOWING this first, that no prophecy of the scripture is of any private interpretation. For the prophecy came not in the old time by the will of man: but holy men of God spake as they were moved by the Holy Ghost. I. PETER, i, 20, 21.

He spake by the mouth of His holy prophets, since the world began. LUKE, i, 70.

THE word of prophecy, those truths divine,
Which make that Heaven, if thou desire it, thine—
(Awful alternative! believed, beloved,
Thy glory—and thy shame if unimproved),
Are never long vouchsafed, if pushed aside
With cold disgust, or philosophic pride. COWPER.

THE gift
Of Prophecy was lost; O, proof beyond
A doubt, that every oracle of old
To the same centre tended, and that all
The promises to God's selected race
Through every age, received the stamp of truth
In the appearance of the blessed Seed.

SAMUEL HAYES.

THE world's a prophecy of worlds to come.

YOUNG.

YES!—what was earth to him, whose spirit passed
Time's utmost bounds?—on whose unshrinking sight
Ten thousand shapes of burning glory cast
Their full resplendence?—Majesty and might
Were in his dreams;—for him the veil of light
Shrouding Heaven's inmost sanctuary and throne,
The curtain of the unutterably bright,
Was raised!—to him, in fearful splendour shown,
Ancient of days! e'en Thou mad'st Thy dread presence known.

MRS. HEMANS.

PROSPERITY.

FOR I was envious at the foolish, when I saw the prosperity of the wicked;
Until I went into the sanctuary of God; then understood I their end.
Surely thou didst set them in slippery places; thou castedst them down into destruction. PSALM lxxiii, 3, 17, 18.
Incline my heart unto Thy testimonies, and not to covetousness.
Turn away mine eyes from beholding vanity; and quicken Thou me in Thy way PSALM cxix, 36, 37.

O, HOW portentous is prosperity!
How, comet-like, it threatens while it shines!

YOUNG.

THE swelling of an outward fortune can
Create a prosperous, not a happy man:
A peaceful conscience is the true content,
And wealth is but her golden ornament.

FRANCIS QUARLES

SOME, in foul seasons, perish through despair;
But more, through boldness, when the days are fair.

SIR JOHN BEAUMONT.

THAT opulence thou vainly gildest
With specious name of good, if scanned aright,
Is Heaven's sharp visitation to the fool.

GEORGE BALLY.

PROVIDENCE—ORDER.

UPHOLDING all things by the word of His power. HEBREWS, i, 3.

God is the King of all the earth. * * * God reigneth over the heathen: God sitteth upon the throne of His holiness. PSALM xlvii, 7, 8.

For my thoughts are not your thoughts, neither are your ways my ways, saith the Lord. ISAIAH, lv, 8.

I form the light, and create darkness; I make peace, and create evil. I the Lord do all these things. ISAIAH, xlv, 7.

It is He that sitteth upon the circle of the earth, and the inhabitants thereof are as grasshoppers; that stretcheth out the heavens as a curtain, and spreadeth them out as a tent to dwell in. ISAIAH, xl, 22.

O, ALL-PREPARING Providence divine!
In thy large book, what secrets are enrolled,
What sundry helps doth Thy great power assign,
To prop the course which Thou intend'st to hold!
What mortal sense is able to define
Thy mysteries, Thy councils manifold!
It is Thy wisdom strangely that extends
Obscure proceedings to apparent ends.

MICHAEL DRAYTON.

THERE is a Power
Unseen that rules the illimitable world,
That guides its motions, from the brightest star,
To the least dust of this sin-tainted mould;
While man, who madly deems himself the lord
Of all, is nought but weakness and dependence.

THOMSON.

ALL Nature is but art, unknown to thee;
All chance, direction which thou canst not see;
All discord, harmony not understood;
All partial evil, universal good.

POPE.

By scale and method works the Will Supreme,
Nor clouds, nor waves, without a limit stream;
And all the floods that daylight never saw,
The rayless tide of ruin, owns a law.

O'er all confusions marring earth and air,
O'er all the shuddering hours of man's despair,
Still reigns one fixed decree of peace and love,
And still, though dim below, 't is bright above.

JOHN STERLING.

WHAT if the foot, ordained the dust to tread,
Or hand, to toil, aspire to be the head?
What if the head, the eye, or ear repined
To serve, mere engines to the ruling mind?
Just as absurd for any part to claim
To be another in this general frame:
Just as absurd to mourn the task or pains
The great directing Mind of all ordains. POPE.

ORDER is Heaven's first law, and this confest,
Some are, and must be, greater than the rest,
More rich, more wise; but who infers from hence
That such are happier, shocks all common sense.

POPE.

ALL is best, though we oft doubt
What the unsearchable dispose
Of highest wisdom brings about;
And ever best found in the close. MILTON.

THAT things to mortals are mysterious,
Is not because the things themselves are dark,
But the perceptions through which they are viewed.

DAVID BATES.

Yet, since the effects of Providence, we find,
Are variously dispensed to human kind;
That Vice triumphs and Virtue suffers here,
A brand that sovereign justice cannot bear;
Our reason prompts us to a future state,
The last appeal from fortune and from fate:
Where God's all-righteous ways will be declared;
The bad meet punishment, the good reward.

Dryden.

His ways are dark, and deeply intricate—
When Heaven was kindest, innocence was lost,
And Paradise gave birth to misery.

Rufus Dawes.

Or that one half creation is to know
Luxurious joy, and others only woe,
And so go down into the common tomb
With none to question their unequal doom?
Shall we give credit to a thought so fond?
Ah! no—the world beyond—the world beyond!
There shall the desolate heart regain its own!
There the oppressed shall stand before God's throne!
There, when the tangled web is all explained,
Wrong suffered, pain inflicted, grief disdained,
Man's proud, mistaken judgments and false scorn
Shall melt, like mists before the uprising morn,
And holy truth stand forth, serenely bright,
In the rich flood of God's eternal light!

Mrs. Norton.

PRUDENCE—INDUSTRY.

A PRUDENT man foreseeth the evil, and hideth himself: but the simple pass on, and are punished. PROVERBS, xxii, 3.

I, Wisdom, dwell with prudence. PROVERBS, viii, 12.

The simple believeth every word: but the prudent man looketh well to his going. PROVERBS, xiv, 15.

Go to the ant, thou sluggard, consider her ways, and be wise. PROVERBS, vi, 6.

To doubtful matters do not headlong run,
What 's well, left off, were better not begun.
THOMAS RANDOLPH.

PRUDENCE protects and guides us, wit betrays;
A splendid source of ill, ten thousand ways;
A certain snare to miseries immense;
A gay prerogative from common sense;
Unless strong judgment the wild thing can tame,
And break to paths of virtue and of fame. YOUNG.

WHO buys a minute's mirth to wail a week?
Or sells eternity to get a toy?
For one sweet grape, who would a vine destroy?
SHAKSPEARE.

PRUDENCE, thou virtue of the mind, by which
We do consult of all that's good or evil
Conducing to felicity; direct
My thoughts and actions by the rule of reason:
Teach me contempt of all inferior vanities. NABB.

IF plants be cropt because their fruits are small,
Think you to thrive, that bear no fruit at all?
FRANCIS QUARLES.

HE that outlives Nestor, and appears
To have passed the date of grey Methusalem's years,
If he his life to sloth and sin doth give,
I say he only *was*, he did not *live*.

THOMAS RANDOLPH.

WHAT is a man,
If his chief good and market of his time,
Be but to sleep and feed?—a beast, no more.
Sure he who made us with such large discourse,
Looking before, and after, gave us not
That capability and godlike reason
To rust in us, unused.

SHAKSPEARE.

THE means that heaven yields must be embraced,
And not neglected; else, if Heaven would,
And we will not, Heaven's offer we refuse;
The proffered means of succour and redress.

SHAKSPEARE.

VIRTUE, though chained to earth, will still live free,
And hell itself must yield to industry.

BEN JONSON.

INDUSTRIOUS wisdom often does prevent
What lazy folly thinks inevitable:
Big, swelling clouds are by the wind blown o'er,
And threatening clouds may dwindle to a shower.

OLD PLAY.

REASON.

THOU shalt love the Lord thy God with all thy heart, and with all thy soul, and with all thy mind, and with all thy strength. MARK, xii, 30.

Trust in the Lord with all thy heart; and lean not to thine own understanding. PROVERBS, iii, 5.

Canst thou, by searching, find out God? Canst thou find out the Almighty unto perfection? JOB, xi, 7.

THOUGH Reason cannot through Faith's mysteries see,
It sees that there, and such they be;
Though it, like Moses, by a sad command
Must not come into th' Holy Land,
Yet thither it infallibly does guide,
And from afar 'tis all descried. COWLEY.

WITH scanty line shall Reason dare to mete
Th' immeasurable depths of Providence?
On the swol'n bladders of opinion borne,
She floats awhile, then, floundering, sinks absorbed
Within that boundless sea she strove to grasp.
Shall man, here stationed to revere that God
Who called him into being from the dust,
His moral scheme implead, and, impious, cite
Th' Almighty Legislator to the bar
Of erring intellect? GEORGE BALLY.

REASON the root; fair faith is but the flower;
The fading flower shall die, but reason lives
Immortal, as her Father in the skies. YOUNG

THROUGH Reason's wounds alone. thy faith can die.
YOUNG.

REASON progressive, instinct is complete;
Swift instinct leaps; slow reason feebly climbs.
Brutes soon their zenith reach; their little all
Flows in at once; in ages they no more
Could know, or do, or covet, or enjoy.
Were man to live coeval with the sun,
The patriarch pupil would be learning still;
Yet, dying, leave his lesson half unlearned.

YOUNG.

DIM as the borrowed beams of moon and stars
To lonely, weary, wandering travellers,
Is Reason to the soul; and as on high
Those rolling fires discover but the sky,
Not light us here; so Reason's glimmering ray
Was lent, not to assure our doubtful way,
But guide us upward to a better day.
And as those nightly tapers disappear,
When day's bright lord ascends our hemisphere;
So pale grows Reason, at Religion's sight;
So dies, and so dissolves, in supernatural light.

DRYDEN.

'TIS Reason our great Master holds so dear;
'Tis Reason's injured rights His wrath resents;
'Tis Reason's voice obeyed, His glories crown;
To give lost Reason life, He poured His own.

YOUNG.

WITH short plummets Heaven's deep well we sound,
That vast abyss where human wit is drowned.
In our small skiff we must not launch too far;
We here but coasters, not discoverers are.

DRYDEN.

REDEMPTION.

With the Lord there is mercy, and with Him is plenteous redemption PSALM cxxx, 7.

But of Him are ye in Christ Jesus, who, of God, is made unto us wisdom, and righteousness, and sanctification, and redemption:

That, according as it is written, He that glorieth, let him glory in the Lord. I. CORINTHIANS, i, 30, 31.

Neither by the blood of goats and calves, but by His own blood, He entered in once into the holy place, having obtained eternal redemption for us. HEBREWS, ix, 12.

Redemption! O, thou beauteous mystic plan!
Thou salutary source of life to man!
What tongue can speak thy comprehensive grace?
What thought thy depths unfathomable trace?
When lost in sin our ruined nature lay,
When awful justice claimed her righteous pay,
See the mild Saviour bend His pitying eye,
And stop the lightning just prepared to fly!

BOYSE.

Onward as we trace
God's oracles, Redemption is the point
To which they all converge. SAMUEL HAYES.

Half mankind maintain a churlish strife
With Him, the Donor of eternal life,
Because the deed, by which His love confirms
The largess He bestows, prescribes the terms.
Compliance with His will your lot ensures,
Accept it only, and the boon is yours.
And sure it is as kind to smile and give,
As with a frown to say, Do this, and live.

COWPER.

WHEN creatures had no real light
Inherent in them, Thou didst make the sun
Impart a lustre, and allow them bright;
And in this, show what Christ hath done.
GEORGE HERBERT.

BE every knee
To Christ in homage bent! Be every heart
In adoration, and in fervent prayer,
To Him poured forth! From His all-gracious birth,
The day-spring from on high descends: grim death,
Stripped of his boasted empire, prostrate falls:
The cerements of the dank, victorious grave
Are burst asunder: th' adamantine gates
Of Paradise unbarred: man's forfeit race
From the deep gulf of Erebus redeemed,
To life, to immortality arise. SAMUEL HAYES.

THE grand Redemption of degenerate man
Is not a single, independent act,
But one great system; that, perchance, involved
In the one only greater, God's high law
Pervading and supporting every part
Of the stupendous universe: to thee,
Dark are the system's limits; nay, the whole
To thee unknown, save some minuter spots,
Displayed to show the parts thou hast to act
In the alarming scene. JOHN HEY.

REDEMPTION! 't was creation more sublime;
Redemption! 't was the labour of the skies;
Far more than labour, it was death in Heaven:
A truth so strange! 't were bold to think it true,
If not far bolder still, to disbelieve. YOUNG.

O, HOW unlike the cumbrous works of man,
Heaven's easy, artless, unencumbered plan!
No meretricious graces to beguile,
No clustering ornaments to clog the pile;
From ostentation, as from weakness free,
It stands, like the cerulean arch we see,
Majestic in its own simplicity.
Inscribed above the portal, from afar
Conspicuous as the brightness of a star,
Legible only by the light they give,
Stand the soul-quickening words: Believe and live!

COWPER.

WITH outstretched arms,
Stern justice and soft-smiling love embrace,
Supporting, in full majesty, thy throne,
When seemed its majesty to need support,
Or that, or man, inevitably lost:
What, but the fathomless of love divine
Could labour such expedient from despair,
And rescue both? Both rescue? Both exalt!
O, how are both exalted by the deed!
The wondrous deed! or shall I call it more?
A wonder in Omnipotence itself!
A mystery no less to gods than men. YOUNG.

WHAT Adam had, and forfeited for all,
Christ keepeth now, who cannot fail or fall.

GEORGE HERBERT.

(*See also* ATONEMENT, CROSS, CRUCIFIXION.)

REFLECTION—MEMORY.

THAT which hath been, is now; and that which is to be, hath already been; and God requireth that which is past. ECCLESIASTES, iii, 15.

Ask now of the days that are past. DEUTERONOMY, iv, 32.

O Lord, Thou hast searched me and known me.

Thou knowest my down-sitting and mine up-rising; Thou understandest my thoughts afar off. PSALM cxxxix, 1. 2.

'TIS greatly wise to talk with our past hours,
And ask them what report they bore to Heaven,
And how they might have borne more welcome news.
Their answers form what men experience call;
If wisdom's friend, her best; if not, worst foe.

YOUNG.

THINK'ST thou to be concealed, thou little thought,
That in the curtained chamber of the soul
Dost wrap thyself so close, and dream to do
A secret work? Look to the hues that roll
O'er the changed brow—the moving lips behold—
Linking thee unto speech—the feet that run
Upon thy errands, and the deeds that stamp
Thy lineage plain before the noon-day sun;
Look to the pen that writes thy history down
In those tremendous books that ne'er unclose
Until the day of doom, and blush to see
How vain thy trust in darkness to repose,
Where all things tend to judgment. So beware,
O, erring human heart! what thought thou lodgest there

MRS. SIGOURNEY.

A SOUL without reflection, like a pile
Without inhabitant, to ruin runs. YOUNG.

LOOK at this skeleton of a once green leaf:
Time and the elements conspired its fall;
The worm hath eaten out the tenderer parts,
And left this curious anatomy
Distinct of structure — made so by decay.
So, at this moment, lies my life before me
In all its intricacies, all its errors. HENRY TAYLOR.

COMPANION none is like
Unto the mind alone,
For many have been harmed by speech,—
Through thinking, few, or none.
Fear oftentimes restraineth words,
But makes not thoughts to cease;
And he speaks best, that hath the skill
When for to hold his peace.

Our wealth leaves us at death,
Our kinsmen at the grave,
But virtues of the mind unto
The heavens with us we have;
Wherefore, for virtue's sake,
I can be well content
The sweetest time of all my life
To deem in thinking spent. LORD VAUX.

TIME, as he courses onwards, still unrolls
The volume of concealment. In the future,
As in the optician's glassy cylinder,
The undistinguishable blots and colours
Of the dim past collect and shape themselves,
Upstarting in their own completed image
To scare, or to reward. COLERIDGE.

THINK that is just; 't is not enough to do,
Unless thy very thoughts are upright too.
THOMAS RANDOLPH.

HAIL, Memory, hail! in thy exhaustless mine,
From age to age, unnumbered treasures shine!
Thought, and her shadowy brood, thy call obey,
And place and time are subject to thy sway!
Thy pleasures most we feel, when most alone;
The only pleasures we can call our own.
Lighter than air, Hope's summer visions die,
If but a fleeting cloud obscure the sky;
If but a beam of sober Reason play,
Lo, Fancy's fairy frost-work melts away!
But can the wiles of Art, the grasp of Power,
Snatch the rich relics of a well-spent hour?
These, when the trembling spirit wings her flight,
Pour round her path a stream of living light;
And gild those pure and perfect realms of rest,
Where Virtue triumphs, and her sons are blest!

ROGERS.

THE soul's life, mystic Memory, more sublime
  Than that which stores from wisdom's boundless sea—
She sleeps not 'neath the rapid wing of time,
  But garners for a long eternity. ANONYMOUS.

REGENERATION—RENEWAL.

NOT by works of righteousness which we have done, but according to His mercy He saved us, by the washing of regeneration, and renewing of the Holy Ghost. TITUS, iii, 5.

Verily, verily, I say unto thee, except a man be born again, he cannot see the kingdom of God. JOHN, iii, 3.

THERE are blest inhabitants of earth,
Partakers of a new ethereal birth,—
Their hopes, desires, and purposes estranged
From things terrestrial, and divinely changed;
Their very language of a kind that speaks
The soul's sure interest in the good she seeks.

COWPER

THE consciousness of faith, of sins forgiven,
Of wrath appeased, of heavy guilt thrown off,
Sheds on my breast its long-forgotten peace,
And, shining steadfast as the noon-day sun,
Lights me along the path that duty marks.

MRS. HALL.

WHEN man is born anew,
And being's perfect bliss is given,
Lo, a new Eden starts to view,
While angel-harps rejoice in Heaven—
'T is wondrous all, divinely bright,
And the new creature walks in light.

THOMAS GRINFIELD.

When all the breast is pure, each warm desire
Sublimed by holy Love's ethereal fire,
On winged words our breathing thoughts may rise,
And soar to Heaven, a grateful sacrifice.

James Scott.

(*See also* Heart—New Heart.)

THE REIGN OF CHRIST.

Beloved, now are we the sons of God, and it doth not yet appear what we shall be but we know that when He shall appear, we shall be like Him, for we shall see Him as He is. I. John, iii, 2.

Thy throne, O God, is for ever and ever: the sceptre of Thy kingdom is a right sceptre. Psalm xlv, 6.

He shall reign over the house of Jacob for ever, and of His kingdom there shall be no end. Luke, i, 33.

The wolf also shall dwell with the lamb, and the leopard shall lie down with the kid; and the calf, and the young lion, and the fatling together, and a little child shall lead them. Isaiah, xi, 6.

For the Lord shall comfort Zion: He will comfort all her waste places; and He will make her wilderness like Eden, and her desert like the garden of the Lord; joy and gladness shall be found therein, thanksgiving, and the voice of melody. Isaiah, li, 3.

And He shall judge among the nations, and rebuke many people: and they shall beat their swords into ploughshares, and their spears into pruning-hooks: nation shall not lift up sword against nation, neither shall they learn war any more. Isaiah, ii, 4.

Fair Sun of righteousness! in beauty rise,
And clear the mists that cloud the mental skies
To Judah's remnant, now a scattered train,
O great Messiah! show thy promised reign;
O'er earth, as wide Thy saving warmth diffuse,
As spreads the ambient air, or falling dews;
And haste the time when, vanquished by Thy power,
Death shall expire, and sin defile no more!

Samuel Boyse.

ALL hail!—The age of crime and suffering ends;
The reign of righteousness from Heaven descends;
Vengeance for ever sheathes the afflicting sword;
Death is destroyed, and Paradise restored;
Man, rising from the ruins of his fall,
Is one with God, and God is All in all.

JAMES MONTGOMERY.

THEN shall, gorgeous as a gem,
Shine thy mount, Jerusalem;
Then shall in the desert rise
Fruits of more than Paradise;
Earth by angel feet be trod,
One great garden of her God;
Till are dried the martyr's tears
Through a glorious thousand years.
Now, in hope of Him, we trust
Earth to earth, and dust to dust.

CROLY:

THE Lord shall comfort Zion,
  Her places waste restore,
And, of her silent wilderness,
  Make Eden bloom once more;
His garden she shall then become,
  And worthy of His choice,
Gladness and thanks in all her smiles,
  And music in her voice.

W. G. SIMMS.

NO more shall nation against nation rise,
Nor ardent warriors meet, with hateful eyes,
Nor fields with gleaming steel be covered o'er,
The brazen trumpets kindle rage no more;
But useless lances into scythes shall bend,
And the broad falchion in a ploughshare end.

POPE.

No sigh, no murmur the wide world shall hear;
From every face He wipes off every tear. POPE.

RISE, crowned with light, imperial Salem, rise!
Exalt thy towering head, and lift thine eyes!
See a long race thy spacious courts adorn;
See future sons, and daughters yet unborn,
In crowding ranks, on every side arise,
Discarding life, impatient for the skies!
See barbarous nations at thy gates attend,
Walk in thy light, and in thy temple bend.

POPE.

EARTH'S utmost bounds confess the awful sway,
The mountains worship, and the isles obey;
Nor sun nor moon they need, nor day nor night;
God is their Temple, and the Lamb their light.

BP. HEBER.

HARK! White-robed crowds their deep hosannas raise,
And the hoarse flood repeats the sound of praise;
Ten thousand harps attune the mystic song,
Ten thousand thousand saints the strain prolong;—
"Worthy the Lamb, omnipotent to save,
Who died, who lives, triumphant o'er the grave!"

BP. HEBER.

TIME, which, despotic o'er sublunar things,
Blasts the frail pageantry of mortal pride,
Which will in everlasting ruins whelm
The world's capacious orb, will only tend
To raise the glories of Messiah's reign,
To add new lustre to the realms of light.

SAMUEL HAYES.

THE lambs with wolves shall graze the verdant mead,
And boys in flowery bands the tiger lead.
The steer and lion in one crib shall meet,
And harmless serpents lick the pilgrim's feet.
The smiling infant in his hand shall take
The crested basilisk and speckled snake,
Pleased, the green lustre of the scales survey,
And with their forky tongues shall innocently play.

POPE.

THE seas shall waste, the skies in smoke decay,
Rocks fall to dust, and mountains melt away;
But, fixed, His word, His saving power remains;
Thy realm for ever lasts, thy own Messiah reigns.

POPE.

(*See also* ADVENT.)

RELIGION—PIETY.

GODLINESS is profitable unto all things, having promise of the life that now is, and of that which is to come. I. TIMOTHY, iv, 8.

Pure religion, and undefiled before God and the Father, is this, To visit the fatherless and widows in their affliction, and to keep himself unspotted from the world. JAMES, i, 27.

Seek ye first the kingdom of God and His righteousness, and all these things shall be added unto you. MATTHEW, vi, 33.

I am the vine, ye are the branches: he that abideth in me, and I in him, the same bringeth forth much fruit: for without me ye can do nothing. JOHN, xv, 5.

RELIGION pure,
Unchanged in spirit, though its forms and codes
Wear myriad modes,
Contains all creeds within its mighty span—
The love of God, displayed in love of man.

HORACE SMITH.

AND when Religion moves upon the face
Of the remote and multitudinous seas,
Be hers again the peaceful mien that charmed
Judea's midnight winds in secret prayer,
And walked, a spirit of prevailing love,
Upon the star-lit waves of Galilee.

A ALEXANDER.

THIS Religion, which dilates our thoughts
Of God Supreme to an infinity
Of awful greatness, yet connects us with Him,
As children, loved and cherished;—
Adoring awe, with tenderness united.

JOANNA BAILLIE.

BUT true religion, sprung from God above,
Is like her fountain—full of charity:
Embracing all things with a tender love.
Full of good-will and meek expectancy;
Full of true justice and sure verity,
In heart and voice: free, large, even infinite;
Not wedged in strait particularity,
But grasping all in her vast, active sprite—
Bright lamp of God, that men would joy in thy pure light!

HENRY MORE.

ARE virtue, then, and piety the same?
No; piety is more; 't is virtue's source;
Mother of every worth, as that of joy.

YOUNG.

SEEMING devotion doth but gild the knave
That 's neither faithful, honest, just, nor brave;
But where Religion doth with Virtue join,
It makes a hero like an angel shine.

WALLER.

Religion's all. Descending from the skies
To wretched man, the goddess, in her left,
Holds out this world, and in her right, the next.
Young

Religion! Providence! an after state!
Here is firm footing; here is solid rock!
This can support us; all is sea besides;
Sinks under us, bestows, and then devours.
His hand the good man fastens on the skies,
And bids earth roll, nor feels her idle whirl.
Young.

(*See also* Christianity.)

REMORSE—DESPAIR.

Godly sorrow worketh repentance to salvation, not to be repented of; but the sorrow of the world worketh death. II. Corinthians, vii, 10.

But ye have set at nought all my counsel, and would none of my reproof:
I also will laugh at your calamity, and mock when your fear cometh. Proverbs i, 25, 26.

How like gall and wormwood to the taste
The cup that we have longed to drain may prove!
Lydia Jane Pierson.

Who bears no trace of passion's evil force?
Who shuns thy sting, O, terrible Remorse?—
Who does not cast
On the thronged pages of his memory's book,
At times, a sad, and half-reluctant look,
Regretful of the Past? J. G. Whittier.

JUST Heaven instructs us, with an awful voice,
That Conscience rules us e'en against our choice,
Our inward monitress, to guide or warn,
If listened to; but if repelled with scorn,
At length, as dire Remorse, she re-appears,
Works in our guilty hopes and selfish fears!
Still bids, Remember! and still cries, Too late!
And while she scares us, goads us to our fate.

COLERIDGE.

HIS eye no more looked onward; but its gaze
Rests where Remorse a life misspent surveys;
What costly treasures strew that waste behind;
What whirlwinds daunt the soul that sows the wind!
By the dark shape of what he *is*, serene
Stands the bright ghost of what he might have been:
Here the vast lost, and there the worthless gain —
Vice scorned, yet woo'd, and Virtue loved in vain!

SIR E. B. LYTTON.

TRY what repentance can: what can it not?
Yet what can it, when one cannot repent?
O, wretched state! O, bosom black as death!
O, limed soul, that struggling to be free,
Art more engaged! SHAKSPEARE.

HOW awful is that hour, when conscience stings
  The hoary wretch, who on his death-bed hears,
Deep in his soul, the thundering voice that rings,
  In one dark, damning moment, crimes of years,
And, screaming like a vulture in his ears,
  Tells, one by one, his thoughts and deeds of shame;
How wild the fury of his soul careers!
  His swart eye flashes with intensest flame,
  And like the torture's rack the wrestling of his frame.

PERCIVAL.

My words fly up, my thoughts remain below;
Words without thoughts never to Heaven go.

SHAKSPEARE.

Pray can I not,
Though inclination be as sharp as will;
My stronger guilt defeats my strong intent;
And, like a man to double business bound,
I stand in pause where I should first begin,
And both neglect.

SHAKSPEARE.

My conscience hath a thousand several tongues,
And every tongue brings in a several tale,
And every tale condemns me for a villain.

SHAKSPEARE.

Some deluded minds,
Harrowed by penal terrors, in the gulf
Of black despair are whelmed. No ray of hope
Dispels the involving gloom; a Deity,
With all the thunder of dread vengeance round Him,
Is ever present to their tortured thoughts.

SAMUEL HAYES.

Calm, unruffled Joy,
With dove-like wing, infolds the virtuous breast,
While, armed with harpy talon, keen Remorse
Hovers o'er guilt, and poisons every sweet.

GEORGE BALLY.

To vengeance horrible aroused,
And clad in tenfold fierceness, shalt thou stand
Beside the atheist's bed; by his who oft,
With wit profane, and poignant blasphemy,
And specious show of argument, hath scoffed
Each awful truth, and ridiculed his God.

WILLIAM GIBSON.

THE past lives o'er again,
In its effects, and to the guilty spirit
The ever-frowning present is its image. COLERIDGE.

BUT conscience, in some awful, silent hour,
When captivating lusts have lost their power,
Perhaps when sickness, or some fearful dream
Reminds him of religion, hated theme!
Starts from the down on which she lately slept,
And tells of laws despised, at least not kept;
Shows with a pointing finger, but no noise,
A pale procession of past sinful joys;
All witnesses of blessings foully scorned,
And life abused; and, not to be suborned,
Mark these, she says, these, summoned from afar,
Begin their march to meet thee at the bar,
There find a Judge inexorably just,
And perish there, as all presumption must.
COWPER.

WHEN troubled conscience reads accusing scrolls,
Which witnessed are even by the breast's own blood,
O, what a terror wounds remorseful souls,
Who poison find what seemed a pleasing food.
STIRLING.

BUT dreadful is their doom whom doubt has driven
To censure fate, and pious hope forego:
Like yonder blasted boughs, by lightning riven,
Perfection, beauty, life, they never know,
But frown on all that pass, a monument of woe.
BEATTIE.

(*See also* CONTRITION, REPENTANCE.)

REPENTANCE—CONFESSION—CONVERSION.

REPENT ye, for the kingdom of Heaven is at hand. MATTHEW, iii, 2.

If we confess our sins, He is faithful and just to forgive us our sins, and to cleanse us from all unrighteousness. I. JOHN, i, 9.

When the wicked man turneth away from his wickedness that he hath committed, and doeth that which is lawful and right, he shall save his soul alive. EZEKIEL, xviii, 27.

Bring forth, therefore, fruits meet for repentance. MATTHEW, iii, 8.

And the times of this ignorance God winked at, but now commandeth all men every where to repent. ACTS, xvii, 30.

The Lord is not slack concerning His promise, as some men count slackness: but is long suffering to usward, not willing that any should perish, but that all should come to repentance. II. PETER, iii, 9.

Break off thy sins by righteousness, and thine iniquities by showing mercy to the poor. DANIEL, iv, 27.

'TIS not to cry God mercy, or to sit
And droop, or to confess that thou hast failed:
'Tis to bewail the sins thou didst commit;
And not commit those sins thou hast bewailed.
He that bewails, and not forsakes them too,
Confesses rather what he means to do. QUARLES.

REPENTANCE clothes in grass and flowers
The grave in which the past is laid.
JOHN STERLING.

HE who seeks Repentance for the past,
Should woo the angel virtue in the future.
SIR E. B. LYTTON.

NOT all the pride of empire
E'er gave such bless'd sensations as one hour
Of penitence, though painful. HENRY BROOKE

Repent, return, and live;
He who no penitent disdains,
New heavens, new earth can give.
Simple obedience shall restore
Green fields and sunny skies;
And hearkening to His voice, bring more
Than Eden to their eyes. Bernard Barton

O Lord, my God, I wandered have
As one that runs astray,
And have in thought, and word, and deed,
In idleness and play,
Offended sore Thy Majesty
In heaping sin to sin,
And yet Thy mercy hath me spared,
So gracious hast Thou been!
O Lord, my faults I now confess,
And sorry am therefor;
But not so much as fain I would:
O Lord, what wilt Thou more?
It is Thy grace must bring that spirit
For which I humbly pray,
And that this night Thou me defend,
As Thou hast done this day.
And grant when these mine eyes and tongue
Shall fail, through Nature's might,
That then the powers of my poor soul
May praise Thee, day and night!

Wm. Hunnis.

What sadder scene can angels view
Than self-deceiving tears,
Poured idly over some dark page
Of earlier life, though pride or rage
The record of to-day engage,
A woe for future years? Keble.

O BLEST Repentance, in thy weeping eye
Swim the pure beams of embryo-ecstacy.
And Faith, and Hope, and Love, and Joy, prepare
To still thy heart, and wipe thy bitter tear!
To thee alone the privilege is given,
By earthly woe, to kindle joy in Heaven,
For God Himself descends to soothe the heart
That weeps o'er sin, and struggles to depart;
And deeper transport swells the bliss above,
As seraphs sing the triumphs of His love.

J. K. MITCHELL.

HE that lacks time to mourn, lacks time to mend.
Eternity mourns that. 'T is an ill cure
For life's worst ills to have no time to feel them.

HENRY TAYLOR.

CONFESS yourself to Heaven;
Repent what's past; avoid what is to come;
And do not spread the compost on the weeds
To make them ranker. SHAKSPEARE.

O, turn, and be thou turned! The selfish tear,
In bitter thoughts of low-born care begun,
Let it flow on, but flow refined and clear,
The turbid waters brightening as they run.

Let it flow on, till all thine earthly heart
In penitential drops have ebbed away;
Then, fearless, turn where Heaven hath set thy part,
Nor shudder at the eye that saw thee stray.

O, lost and found! All gentle souls below
Their dearest welcome shall prepare, and prove
Such joy o'er thee as raptured seraphs know,
Who learn their lesson at the Throne of Love.

KEBLE.

No wounds like those a wounded spirit feels,
No cure for such, till God, who makes them, heals.
And thou, sad sufferer under nameless ill,
That yields not to the touch of human skill,
Improve the kind occasion, understand
A Father's frown, and kiss His chastening hand.

COWPER.

MUCH have we sinnéd to our shame,
 But spare us who our sins confess;
And for the glory of Thy name,
 To our sick souls afford redress.

DRUMMOND.

HEAVEN may forgive a crime to penitence,
For Heaven can judge if penitence be true.

DRYDEN.

As the fond sheep that idly strays,
With wanton play, through devious ways,
Which never hits the road of home,
O'er wilds of danger learns to roam,
Till, wearied out with idle fear,
And passing there, and turning here,
He will, for rest, to covert run,
And meet the wolf he strove to shun:
Thus wretched I, through wanton will,
Ran blind and headlong on in ill.
'Twas thus from sin to sin I flew,
And thus I might have perished too;
But mercy dropped the likeness here,
And showed and saved me from my fear,
While o'er the darkness of my mind
The sacred Spirit purely shined,
And marked and brightened all the way
Which leads to everlasting day;
And broke the thickening clouds of sin,
And fixed the light of love within.

PARNELL.

MORE shall thy penitent sighs
His endless mercy please,
Than their importune suits, which dream
That words God's wrath appease;
For heart contrite of faith
Is gladsome recompense,
And prayer fruit of faith whereby
God doth with sin dispense. SURREY.

(*See also* CONTRITION.)

REPUTATION—CHARACTER—FAME.

LET another man praise thee, and not thine own mouth; a stranger, and not thine own lips. PROVERBS, xxvii, 2.

They that forsake the law, praise the wicked; but such as keep the law contend with them. PROVERBS, xxviii, 4.

Woe unto you when all men shall speak well of you! for so did their fathers to the false prophets. LUKE, vi, 26.

Moreover, he must have a good report of them that are without; lest he fall into reproach and the snare of the devil. I. TIMOTHY, iii, 7.

Let not then your good be evil spoken of. ROMANS, xiv, 16.

The memory of the just is blessed, but the name of the wicked shall rot. PROVERBS, x, 7.

THE worthiness of praise distains his worth,
If that the praised himself bring the praise forth:
But what the repining enemy commends,
That breath fame follows; that praise sole, pure, transcends
SHAKSPEARE.

Too much honour—
O, 'tis a burden, 'tis a burden
Too heavy for a man that hopes for Heaven.
SHAKSPEARE.

Nor absolutely vain is human praise,
Where human is supported by divine. Young.

Who court applause, oblige the world in this;
They gratify man's passion to refuse. Young.

Honour's a fine, imaginary notion,
That draws on raw and inexperienced men
To real mischiefs, while they hunt a shadow.
Addison.

Do not neglect the candour of thy name;
Thou should'st not stain thy clothes, much less thy fame:
Fine houses men will build, repair, and trim,
And keep them neat without, and fair within:
But little they regard, if by foul ways
They blot their names, and slubber o'er their days:
Such men in life are odious, and shall be
In death a scandal to posterity.
I'll tread a righteous path; a good report
Makes men live long, although their life is short.
Watkins.

Fame is the shade of immortality,
And in itself a shadow. Soon as caught,
Condemned, it sinks to nothing in the grasp.
Young.

Who worship fame commit idolatry;
Make men their god, fortune and time their worth;
Form, but reform not, mere hypocrisy;
By shadows, only shadows bringing forth;
Which must, as blossoms, fade ere true fruit springs;
Like voice and echo joined, yet diverse things.
Lord Brooke.

THIRST of applause calls public judgment in
To poise our own, to keep an even scale,
And give endangered virtue fairer play. YOUNG

IF no basis bear my rising name
But the fallen ruins of another's fame;
Then teach me, Heaven! to scorn the guilty bays;
Drive from my breast that wretched lust of praise:
Unblemished let me live, or die unknown;
O, grant me honest fame, or grant me none.

POPE.

THE man we celebrate must find a tomb,
And we that worship him, ignoble graves.
Nothing is proof against the general curse
Of vanity, that seizes all below. COWPER.

WHY then doth flesh, a bubble-glass of breath,
  Hunt after honour and advancement vain,
And rear a trophy for devouring death,
  With so great labour and long-lasting pain,
  As if his days for ever should remain?
Sith all that in this world is great or gay,
Doth, as a vapour, vanish and decay. SPENSER.

FAME, if not double-faced, is double-mouthed,
And with contrary blast proclaims most deeds:
On both his wings, one black, the other white,
Bears greatest names in his wild airy flight.

MILTON.

REST—SLEEP.

THERE remaineth therefore a rest to the people of God. HEBREWS, iv, 9.

In returning and rest shall ye be saved; in quietness and confidence shall be your strength. ISAIAH, XXX, 15.

Come unto me all ye that labour, and are heavy laden, and I will give you rest. MATTHEW, xi, 28.

He giveth His beloved sleep. PSALM cxxvii, 2.

I will both lay me down in peace and sleep, for Thou, Lord, only makest me dwell in safety. PSALM iv, 8.

OF all the thoughts of God that are
Borne inward unto souls afar,
Along the Psalmist's music deep;
Now tell me if that any is,
For gift or grace, surpassing this—
"He giveth His beloved sleep." MISS BARRETT.

'TIS loving and serving the Greatest and Best,
'T is onward, unswerving, and this is true rest.
ANONYMOUS.

GOOD night!
Slumber till the morning light!
Slumber till the dawn of day
Brings its troubles with its ray!
Sleep without or fear or fright!
Our Father wakes! Good night!
Good night! KORNER.

MAKE then, while yet ye may, your God your friend,
And learn, with equal ease, to live or die.
WILLIAM MASON.

How blessed was that sleep
The sinless Saviour knew!
In vain the storm-winds blew,
Till He awoke to others' woes,
And hushed the billows to repose.

How beautiful is sleep!
The sleep that Christians know:
Ye mourners! cease your woe,
While soft upon his Saviour's breast,
The Righteous sinks to endless rest.

MRS. M'CARTER.

AND of my bed each sundry part
In shadows doth resemble
The sundry shapes of death, whose dart
Shall make my flesh to tremble:
My bed itself is like the grave,
My sheets the winding-sheet,
My clothes, the mould which I must have
To cover me most meet.

GEORGE GASCOIGNE.

NOT in this weary world of ours
Can perfect rest be found;
Thorns mingle with its fairest flowers
Even on cultured ground;
Earth's pilgrim still his loins must gird
To seek a lot more blest;
And this must be his onward word—
"In Heaven alone is rest."

BERNARD BARTON.

RESURRECTION.

I AM the resurrection and the life: he that believeth in me, though he were dead, yet shall he live; and whosoever liveth and believeth in me, shall never die. JOHN, xi, 25, 26.

He hath appointed a day in which He will judge the world in righteousness, by that Man whom He hath ordained; whereof He hath given assurance unto all men, in that He hath raised Him from the dead. ACTS, xvii, 31.

Now is Christ risen from the dead, and become the first-fruits of them that slept. I. CORINTHIANS, xv, 20.

So also is the resurrection of the dead. It is sown in corruption, it is raised in incorruption:

It is sown in dishonour; it is raised in glory: it is sown in weakness; it is raised in power:

It is sown a natural body; it is raised a spiritual body. I. CORINTHIANS, xv, 42—44.

The hour is coming in the which all that are in the graves shall hear His voice, and shall come forth; they that have done good unto the resurrection of life, and they that have done evil unto the resurrection of damnation. JOHN, v, 28, 29.

THESE ashes too, the little dust
Our Father's care shall keep,
Till the last angel rise and break
The long and dreary sleep.
Then Love's soft dew on every eye
Shall shed its mildest rays;
And the long-silent dust shall burst
With shouts of endless praise. KIRKE WHITE.

So, when the tomb's dull silence finds an end,
The blessed dead to endless youth shall rise;
And hear th' archangel's thrilling summons blend
Its tone with anthems from the upper skies.
WILLIS G. CLARK.

AN angel's arm can't snatch me from the grave!
Legions of angels can't confine me there. YOUNG

THIS dust shall live again, I said,
  Though 'tis but pauper flesh;
These bleaching bones the word of God
  Shall clothe with life afresh.

THOMAS MCKELLAR.

YET life again shall heave the mouldering breast,
And a new impulse stir the depths below—
A deathless spring shall o'er these ashes bloom,
And win th' immortal tenant from the tomb.

A. ALEXANDER.

FORGOTTEN generations live again,
Assume the bodily shapes they owned of old,
Beyond the flood:—the righteous of their times
Embrace and weep, they weep the tears of joy.
The sainted mother wakes, and in her lap
Clasps her dear babe, the partner of her grave,
And heritor, with her, of Heaven,—a flower
Washed by the blood of Jesus from the stain
Of native guilt, even in its early bud.

KIRKE WHITE.

THE trumpet! the trumpet! the dead have all heard:
Lo, the depths of the stone-covered chancel are stirr'd:
From the sea, from the land, from the South and the
    North,
The vast generations of man are come forth.

H. H. MILMAN.

BUT has not Jesus passed the tomb,
  To break its bars away?
And, darting through its fearful gloom
  The beams of endless day,
Does He not, from the other side,
Bid none to fear, since He has died?

HANNAH F. GOULD.

WHAT though my body run to dust
Faith cleaves unto it, counting every grain,
With an exact and most particular trust,
Reserving all for flesh again.

GEORGE HERBERT.

MAJESTICAL He rose: trembled the earth;
The ponderous gate of stone was rolled away;
The keepers fell, the angels, awe-struck, sunk
Into invisibility, while forth
The Saviour of the world walked, and stood
Before the sepulchre, and viewed the clouds,
Empurpled glorious by the rising sun. GRAHAM.

MAN but dives in death;
Dives from the sun, in fairer day to rise;
The grave his subterranean road to bliss. YOUNG.

JESUS is risen! triumphal anthems sing!
Thus from dead winter mounts the sprightly spring;
Thus does the sun from night's black shades return,
And thus the single bird wings from the Arabian urn
Jesus is risen! He shall the world restore!
Awake, ye dead! dull sinners, sleep no more!

WESLEY.

CHRIST hath arisen! Oh! not one cherished head
Hath 'midst the flowery sods been pillowed here
Without a hope, (howe'er the heart hath bled
In its vain yearnings o'er the unconscious bier,)
A hope upspringing clear
From those majestic tidings of the morn
Which lit the living way to all of woman born.

MRS. HEMANS.

Lo! Jesus' power the sleep of death hath broken,
  And wiped the tear from sorrow's drooping eye!
Look up, ye mourners, hear what He hath spoken—
  "He that believes on me shall never die."
Through faith and love your spirits shall be kept,
Hope brighter grew on earth, when "Jesus wept."

MRS. ST. LEON LOUD

HARK! through Heaven's wide reverberating vault
The clanging trumpet sounds the awakening peal.
Obedient tombs expand their marble jaws,
And every sad repository hears
The quickening voice, and renders back its trust
To light and life; each particle dispersed
Crowds to a heap, and builds the identic man.
Changed are the living, and alive the dead.
Lo! cited myriads fill the extended plain,
And, trembling, to the Grand Tribunal press.

GEORGE BALLY.

AND through the vale of death we pass to life.
But what is there in death to blast our hopes?
Behold the universal works of nature,
Where life still springs from death. To us the sun
Dies ev'ry night, and ev'ry morn revives:
The flow'rs, which winter's icy hand destroyed,
Lift their fair heads, and live again in spring.
Mark with what hopes, upon the furrowed plain,
The careful plowman casts the pregnant grain;
There hid, as in a grave, awhile it lies,
Till the revolving season bids it rise;
Till nature's genial pow'rs command a birth,
And, potent, call it from the teeming earth;
Then large increase the bury'd treasures yield,
And with full harvest crown the plenteous field.

NICHOLAS ROWE

Ye vainly wise! ye blind presumptuous! now,
Confounded in the dust, adore that power
And wisdom oft arraigned: see now the cause
Why unassuming worth in secret lived,
And died neglected: why the good man's share
In life was gall and bitterness of soul:
Why the lone widow and her orphans pined
In starving solitude, while luxury,
In palaces, lay straining her low thoughts
To form unreal wants. THOMSON.

(*See also* JUDGMENT.)

RETRIBUTION—PUNISHMENT.

RULERS are not a terror to good works, but to the evil. Wilt thou then not be afraid of the power? do that which is good, and thou shalt have praise of the same:

For he is the minister of God to thee for good. But if thou do that which is evil, be afraid; for he beareth not the sword of God in vain: for he is the minister of God, a revenger to execute wrath on him that doeth evil. ROMANS, xiii, 3, 4.

UNPUNISHED 'scape for heinous crime some one,
But unavenged in mind or body, none.
MIRROR FOR MAGISTRATES.

IF either vice or virtue we abandon,
We either are rewarded as we serve,
Or else are plagued, as our deeds deserve.
MIRROR FOR MAGISTRATES.

How just soever
Our reasons are to remedy our wrongs,
We're yet to leave them to their will and power,
Who to that purpose have authority. MASSINGER.

YE princes all, and rulers every one,
  In punishment beware of hatred's ire.
Before you scourge, take heed; look well thereon:
  In wrath's ill will, if malice kindle fire,
  Your hearts will burn in such a hot desire,
That, in those flames, the smoke shall dim your sight,
Ye shall forget to join your justice right.

You should not judge till things be well discerned;
  Your charge is still to maintain upright laws:
In conscience' rules ye should be thoroughly learned—
  Where clemency bids wrath and rashness pause;
  And further saith, strike not without a cause:
And when ye smite, do it for justice' sake;
Then in good part each man your scourge will take.

THOMAS CHURCHYARD.

(*See also* JUSTICE.)

REVELATION.

THE gospel and the preaching of Jesus Christ, according to the revelation of the mystery, which was kept secret since the world began, but now is made manifest. ROMANS, xvi, 25, 26.

The wrath of God is revealed from Heaven against all ungodliness and unrighteousness of men, who hold the truth in unrighteousness:

Because that which may be known of God is manifest in them; for God hath showed it unto them. ROMANS, i, 18, 19.

God, who at sundry times and in divers manners spake in time past unto the fathers by the prophets,

Hath in these last days spoken unto us by His Son. HEBREWS, i, 1, 2.

'TIS Revelation satisfies all doubts,
Explains all mysteries, except her own;
And so illuminates the path of life,
That fools discover it, and stray no more. COWPER.

SAD error this, to take
The light of Nature, rather than the light
Of Revelation for a guide. As well
Prefer the borrowed light of earth's pale moon
To the effulgence of the noon-day sun.

DAVID BATES.

O VAIN Philosophy! thou wandering light
Which hast so oft misled our steps, attend!
And, prostrate at this heavenly shrine, lament
Thy blindness, and forego thy pride; here cast
Thy trophies down, undeck thyself of all
Thy borrowed plumes, and own the fountain whence
Thy hoary sons received the living fire,
Which animates the glowing page they penned!

WILLIAM HODSON.

COLD and obscure, in vain the king and sage
Gave law and learning to the darkened age.
There was no present faith, no future hope,
Earth bounded then the earth-drawn horoscope;
Till to the East there rose the promised star—
Till rose the Sun of Righteousness afar—
Till on a world redeemed the Saviour shone,
Earth for His footstool,—Heaven for His throne.

MISS LANDON.

REVEALED religion first informed thy sight,
And Reason saw not till Faith sprung to light.
Hence all thy natural worship takes the source:
'T is Revelation, what thou think'st discourse,
Else how comest thou to see these truths so clear,
Which so obscure to heathens did appear?

DRYDEN.

Thy throne is darkness in the abyss of light,
A blaze of glory that forbids the sight;
O, teach me to believe Thee thus concealed,
And search no farther than Thyself revealed.

Dryden.

(*See also* Bible, Gospel.)

REVENGE—FORGIVENESS.

The discretion of a man deferreth his anger, and it is his glory to pass over a transgression. Proverbs, xix, 11.

Wherefore, my beloved brethren, let every man be swift to hear, slow to speak, slow to wrath:

For the wrath of man worketh not the righteousness of God. James, i, 19, 20.

Dearly beloved, avenge not yourselves, but rather give place unto wrath: for it is written, Vengeance is mine, I will repay, saith the Lord. Romans, xii, 19.

Let all bitterness, and wrath, and anger, and clamour, and evil-speaking, be put away from you, with all malice:

And be ye kind to one another, tender-hearted, forgiving one another; even as God, for Christ's sake, hath forgiven you. Ephesians, iv, 31, 32.

Why should man,
For a poor hasty syllable or two,
And vented only in forgetful fury,
Chain all the hopes and riches of his soul
To the revenge of that? Die lost for ever!
For he that makes his last peace with his Maker
In anger, anger is his peace eternally:
He must expect the same return again
Whose venture is deceitful. Rowley.

For this to Tyranny belongs,
To forget service, but remember wrongs.

Denham.

I NEVER thought an angry person valiant:
Virtue is never aided by a vice. BEN JONSON.

How rash, how inconsiderate is rage!
How wretched, O, how fatal is our error,
When to revenge precipitate we run!
Revenge, that still with double force recoils
Back on itself, and is its own revenge.
While to the short-lived, momentary joy,
Succeeds a train of woes — an age of torment.
FROWDE.

THESE, by their bloody marks in combat dyed,
Through anger, the disease of beasts untamed;
Whose wrath is anger, but in men 'tis pride;
Yet theirs is cruelty, ours, courage named.
SIR WILLIAM DAVENANT.

THEN for revenge, by great souls was it ever
Contemned, though offered; entertained by none
But cowards, base and abject spirits; strangers
To moral honesty, and never yet
Acquainted with religion. MASSINGER.

A WRONG avenged is doubly perpetrated;
Two sinners stand, where lately stood but one.
THOMAS MCKELLAR.

SPEAK not of vengeance! 'tis the right of God.
"Vengeance is His." Who shall usurp the bolt
And launch it for Omnipotence? shall man
Assume the right of judgment, or prescribe
How far the line of mercy shall extend,
Or punishment shall stretch its iron rod?
In thine own cause to judge, who gave thee right,
Presumptuous man! C. P. LAYARD.

MAN'S disposition is for to requite
An injury before a benefit:
Thanksgiving is a burden and a pain;
Revenge is pleasing to us, as our gain. HERRICK.

So prone to error is our mortal frame,
Time could not stop without a trace of horror,
If wary nature on the human heart,
Amid its wild variety of passions,
Had not impressed a soft and yielding sense,
That when offences give resentment birth,
The kindly dews of penitence may raise
The seeds of mutual mercy and forgiveness.

GLOVER.

THE fairest action of our human life
  Is, scorning to revenge an injury;
For who forgives without a further strife,
  His adversary's heart doth to him tie:
And 'tis a firmer conquest, truly said,
To win the heart, than overthrow the head.

LADY CAREW.

MARK well the terms
On which our final absolution rests.
Forgiveness such as that which here on earth
To others we impart, the righteous Judge
Will unto us accord at the dread day
Of universal judgment. SAMUEL HAYES.

To conquer hate,
And in its place to cherish love unfeigned,
Forgiveness and forgetfulness of wrongs,
No precepts but the perfect law of Christ,
No teacher but the blessed Son of God,
Could e'er instruct mankind. C. P. LAYARD

Yes, yes; let a man, when his enemy weeps,
  Be quick to receive him a friend;
For thus on his head in kindness he heaps
  Hot coals to refine and amend;
And hearts that are Christian more eagerly yearn,
  As a nurse on her innocent pet;
Over-leaps that, once bitter, to penitence turn,
  And whisper, "Forgive and forget."

TUPPER.

RIVERS—LIVING WATERS.

He shall be like a tree planted by the rivers of water, that bringeth forth his fruit in his season his leaf also shall not wither, and whatsoever he doeth shall prosper. PSALM i, 3.

Whosoever drinketh of the water that I shall give him, shall never thirst; but the water that I shall give him shall be in him a well of water springing up into everlasting life. JOHN, iv, 14.

There is a river, the streams whereof shall make glad the city of God, the holy place of the tabernacles of the Most High. PSALM xlvi, 4.

And he showed me a pure river of the water of life, clear as crystal, proceeding out of the throne of God and of the Lamb.

In the midst of the street of it, and on either side of the river, was there the tree of life, which bare twelve manner of fruits, and yielded her fruit every month: and the leaves of the tree were for the healing of nations. REVELATIONS, xxii, 1, 2.

Bountiful rivers! not upon the earth
Is record traced of God's exuberant grace
So deeply graven, as the channels worn
By ever-flowing streams.

THOMAS WARD.

River! river! headlong river!
  Down you dash unto the sea;
Sea, that line hath never sounded;
Sea, that voyage hath never rounded,
  Like unto eternity!

MRS. SOUTHEY

AND see the rivers, how they run
Through woods and meads, in shade and sun:
Sometimes swift, sometimes slow,
Wave succeeding wave, they go
A various journey to the deep,
Like human life to endless sleep. DYER.

AROUND Thy throne, in peaceful streams,
O God! celestial pleasure glides;
The brightened wave Thine image beams,
Untinged by sorrow's darkened tides.

That stream my fainting spirit cheers
When sultry suns pour down their heat;
And when I cross the vale of tears,
It makes the cup of sorrow sweet.
JOHN ALEXANDER.

THOU, who, when wandering Israel, parched and dying,
Unto the prophet cried in sore distress,
Heard, and in mercy to their plaint, replying,
Bade the flood gush amid the wilderness—
Hear me! To Thee my soul in suppliance turneth,
Like the lorn pilgrim on the sands accursed;
For life's sweet waters, God! my spirit yearneth—
Give me to drink! I perish here, of thirst!
MRS. M. E. HEWITT.

THE SABBATH.

REMEMBER the Sabbath day to keep it holy. EXODUS, xx, 10.

The Sabbath was made for man, not man for the Sabbath.

Therefore the Son of man is Lord also of the Sabbath day. MARK, ii, 27, 28.

Thus saith the Lord, Keep ye judgment, and do justice: for my salvation is near to come, and my righteousness to be revealed.

Blessed is the man that doeth this, and the son of man that layeth hold on it; that keepeth the Sabbath from polluting it, and keepeth his hand from doing any evil. ISAIAH, lvi, 1, 2.

And upon the first day of the week, when the disciples came together to break bread, Paul preached unto them. ACTS, xx, 7.

Upon the first day of the week let every one of you lay by him in store, as God hath prospered him. I. CORINTHIANS, xvi, 2.

I had gone with the multitude, I went with them to the house of God, with the voice of joy and praise, with a multitude that kept holyday. PSALM xlii, 4.

Enter into His gates with thanksgiving, and into His courts with praise. PSALM c, 4.

HE who ordained the Sabbath, loves the poor.
O. W. HOLMES.

SEE, through the streets that slumbered in repose,
The living current of devotion flows;
Its varying forms, in one harmonious band,—
Age leading childhood by its dimpled hand,
Want in the robe whose faded edges fall
To tell of rags beneath the Tartan shawl,
And wealth, in silks that, fluttering to appear,
Lift the deep borders of the proud Cashmere.
O. W. HOLMES.

THE rich man's day — he feels his poverty,
His need of grace bestowed without a price:—
The poor man's day — he learns his high degree —
That he is noblest who has least of vice.
THOMAS MCKELLAR.

THIS transitory scene
Of murmuring stillness, busily serene;
This solemn pause, the breathing space of man,
The halt of toil's exhausted caravan,
Comes sweet with music to thy wearied ear;
Rise, with its anthems, to a holier sphere!

O. W. HOLMES.

THE day that God has bless'd
Comes tranquilly on with its welcome rest.
It speaks of creation's early bloom;
It speaks of the Prince who burst the tomb.
Then summon the spirit's exalted powers,
And devote to Heaven the hallowed hours.

HENRY WARE, JR.

THE solemn tolling of the Sabbath bell
Hath something in it holier than of earth;
And when loud anthems to Jehovah swell,
The spirit longeth for a heavenly birth;
And, catching impulse from the good man's prayer,
The heart is softened to contrition there.

ISAAC F. SHEPARD.

THE All-beneficent
Cares for man's better nature, and has given
This Sabbath-rest to lead his thoughts to Heaven.
Myriads of thanks for this divinest gift,
For this perpetually recurring day—
Wherein both rich and poor—bond—free—can lift
Their hopes above this fading world, and pray.

E. J. EAMES.

THE cheerful Sabbath bells, wherever heard,
Strike pleasant on the sense, most like the voice
Of one who from the far-off hills proclaims
Tidings of good to Zion.

CHARLES LAMB

Wakeners of prayer in man — his resting bowers
  As on he journeys in the narrow way,
Where, Eden-like, Jehovah's walking hours
  Are waited for, as in the cool of day.
Days fixed by God for intercourse with dust,
  To raise our thoughts and purify our powers;
Periods appointed to renew our trust—
  A gleam of glory after six days' showers.

Bernard Barton.

With silent awe I hail the sacred morn,
  Which slowly wakes while all the fields are still;
A soothing calm on every breeze is borne,
  A graver murmur gurgles from the rill,
  And echo answers softer from the hill,
And softer sings the linnet from the thorn,
  The skylark warbles in a tone less shrill:
Hail, light serene! Hail, sacred Sabbath morn!
The rooks float by in silent, airy drove;
  The sun a placid, yellow lustre shows;
The gales, that lately sighed along the grove,
  Have hushed their downy wings in dead repose;
The hovering rack of clouds forgets to move:
  So smiled the day, when the first morn arose!

Dr. Leyden.

The Sabbath bell,
That over wood, and wild, and mountain-dell
Wanders so far, chasing all thoughts unholy
With sounds most musical, most melancholy.

Samuel Rogers.

Bright shadows of true rest! some shoots of bliss;
Heaven once a week;
The next world's gladness pre-possessed in this.

Henry Vaughan.

Thou art a day of mirth,—
And where the week-days trail on ground,
Thy flight is higher, as thy birth:
O, let me take thee at the bound,
Leaping with thee from seven to seven,
Till that we both, being tossed from earth,
Fly, hand in hand, to Heaven.

George Herbert.

Amidst the earthiness of life,
Vexation, vanity, and strife,—
Sabbath! how sweet thy holy calm
Comes o'er the soul, like healing balm;
Comes, like the dew to fainting flowers,
Renewing their enfeebled powers.

Thomas Grinfield.

Yes! blessed Sabbath morn, thy light
Is affluent in pure delight
To those who love thy rest;
Beyond thy sun, a heavenly ray
Adds moral lustre to the day,
And shines into the breast.

J. K. Mitchell.

The morning stars
Together sang, and all the sons of God
Shouted for joy! Loud was the peal; so loud
As would have quite o'erwhelmed human sense;
But to the earth it came a gentle strain,
Like softest fall breathed from Æolian lute,
When, 'mid the chords, the evening gale expires.
"Day of the Lord! creation's hallowed close!
Day of the Lord!" (prophetical they sang)
"Benignant mitigation of that doom
Which must, ere long, consign the fallen race,
Dwellers in yonder star, to pain and woe."

James Grahame.

YET every day in seven, at least,
  One bright republic shall be known;—
Man's world awhile hath surely ceased,
  When God proclaims His own!
Six days may rank divide the poor,
  O Dives! from thy banquet-hall—
The seventh, the Father opes the door,
  And holds His feast for all!

SIR E. B. LYTTON.

Too soon our earthly Sabbaths end!
Cares of a work-day will return,
And faint our hearts, and fitful, burn:
O, think, my soul, beyond compare
Think what a Sabbath must be there;
Where all is holy bliss, that knows
Nor imperfection, nor a close.

THOMAS GRINFIELD.

ON the seventh day reposing, lo! the great Creator stood,
Saw the glorious work accomplished,—saw, and felt that it was good;
Heaven, earth, man, and beast have being, day and night their courses run,—
First creation,—infant manhood,—earliest Sabbath,—it is done.

On the seventh day reposing, Jesus filled His sainted tomb,
From His spirit's toil retreating, while He broke man's fatal doom;
'T was a new creation bursting, brighter than the primal one,—
'T is fulfilment,—reconcilement; 't is redemption,—it is done.

DA COSTA.

When through the peaceful parish swells
The music of the Sabbath bells,
Duly tread the sacred road
Which leads you to the house of God;
The blessing of the Lamb is there,
For "God is in the midst of her."

Bishop Mant

The day that God calls His, make not thine own
By sports or play, though 'tis a custom grown;
God's day of mercy whoso doth profane,
God's day of judgment doth for him remain.

Anonymous. 1600.

SAFETY—SALVATION.

He that walketh uprightly, walketh surely. Proverbs, x, 9.

The name of the city from that day shall be, The Lord is there. Ezekiel, xlviii, 35

The steps of a good man are ordered by the Lord; and he delighteth in His way. Though he fall, he shall not be utterly cast down; for the Lord upholdeth him with His hand. Psalm xxxvii, 23, 24.

Receiving the end of your faith, even the salvation of your souls. I. Peter, i, 9.

As birds their infant brood protect,
  And spread their wings to shelter them,
Thus saith the Lord to His elect,—
  So will I guard Jerusalem.
Let earth repent, and hell despair,
  This city has a sure defence;
Her name is called "The Lord is there,"
  And who has power to drive Him thence?

Cowper.

Too happy men were, if they understood
There is no safety but in doing good. Fountain.

ABROAD, at home, in weal, in woe,
That service which to Heaven you owe,
That bounden service duly pay,
And God shall be your strength alway.

BP. MANT.

A CHEERFUL confidence I feel,
  My well-placed hopes with joy I see;
My bosom glows with heavenly zeal
  To worship Him who died for me.
As man, He pities my complaint;
  His power and truth are all divine;
He will not fail, He cannot faint,
  Salvation's sure, and must be mine.

COWPER.

FROM the sword at noon-day wasting,
  From the noisome pestilence,
In the depth of midnight blasting,
  God shall be thy sure defence:
Fear not thou the deadly quiver,
  When a thousand feel the blow;
Mercy shall thy soul deliver,
  Though ten thousand be laid low.

MONTGOMERY.

KNOW well, my soul, God's hand controls
  Whate'er thou fearest;
Round Him, in calmest music, rolls
  Whate'er thou hearest.

WHAT to thee is shadow, to Him is day,
  And the end He knoweth;
And not on a blind and aimless way
  The spirit goeth.

J. G. WHITTIER.

A FEW forsake the throng: with lifted eyes,
Ask wealth of Heaven, and gain a real prize—
Truth, wisdom, grace, and peace like that above,
Sealed with His signet whom they serve and love.
COWPER.

(*See also* HEAVEN, REGENERATION—TRUST IN GOD.)

THE SAVIOUR.

A MAN shall be as a hiding-place from the wind, and as a covert from the tempest as rivers of water in a dry place, as the shadow of a great rock in a weary land. ISAIAH, xxxii, 2.

And in that day there shall be a root of Jesse, which shall stand for an ensign of the people; to it shall the Gentiles seek: and his rest shall be glorious. ISAIAH, xi, 10.

In this was manifested the love of God toward us, because that God sent His only begotten Son into the world, that we might live through Him.

Herein is love, not that we loved God, but that He loved us, and sent His Son to be the propitiation for our sins. I. JOHN, iv, 9, 10.

And we have seen, and do testify, that the Father sent the Son to be the Saviour of the world. I. JOHN, iv, 14.

Neither is there salvation in any other: for there is no other name under Heaven, given among men, whereby we might be saved. ACTS, iv, 12.

Wherefore He is able also to save them to the uttermost that come unto God, by Him, seeing He ever liveth to make intercession for them. HEBREWS, vii, 25.

HIM who bore
Our form, our woes;—that man might evermore,
In succouring woe-worn man, the God, made Man, adore!
SIR E. B. LYTTON.

AMID our waste, be He a living spring;
Amid our lawless wars, a peaceful king;
In our dark night, be He a dawning star;
In woe a friend, to aid us come from far.
JOHN STERLING.

Zeigler. Sartain.

Trust in God.

To me, O Lord, be Thou "The Way,"
  To me be Thou "The Truth;"
To me, my Saviour, be "The Life,"
  Thou Guardian of my youth!

So shall that Way be my delight,
  That Truth shall make me free;
That Life shall raise me from the dead,
  And then I'll live to Thee! LEIGH RICHMOND

LIKE us a man, He trode on earthly soil,
He bore each pang, and strove in weary toil;
He spake with human words, with pity sighed;
Like us He mourned, and feared, and wept, and died.

Yet all Thy fulness, Father, dwelt in Him,
In whom no shadow made the glory dim;
Such strength, O God! from Him to us derive,
And make, by life from Him, our death alive.

JOHN STERLING.

HIS love at once, and dread, instructs our thought,—
As man He suffered, and as God He taught.

WALLER.

REJECTED, scorned,
Despised, a man of sorrow and distress,
To all the ills which poverty's chill cold,
Or power of tyrant malice could inflict,
Exposed a victim, through life's wretched vale
Our blest Redeemer passed. SAMUEL HAYES.

O SAVIOUR God! O Lamb once slain!
At thought of Thee, Thy love, Thy flowing blood,
All thoughts decay; all things remembered fade;
All hopes return; all actions done by men
Or angels disappear, absorbed and lost POLLOK.

Christ, the Lamb, in radiance sits enthroned,
The lively Image of His Father's grace.
O Flower of love! O glorious Morning Star!
O Sun of righteousness, whose healing wings
Brought life, and peace, and mercy from afar!
From Thee, the light, thou beaming Fountain, springs,
That guides poor mortals in their weary way,
Through black affliction's night, to pleasure's endless day
James Scott

Of all creation first,
Begotten Son, divine Similitude,
In whose conspicuous countenance, without cloud
Made visible, the Almighty Father shines,
Whom else no creature can behold: on Thee
Impressed, the effulgence of His glory bides;
Transfused in Thee His ample spirit rests.
The Heaven of heavens, and all the powers therein
By Thee created. Milton.

And when insulted justice claimed
A victim for His shrine,
This faithful Friend, unsought, unblamed,
Laid down His life for mine.
The tortures I deserved, He bore,
And died upon the tree—
O, let my prostrate soul adore
The Friend that died for me! Thomas Ward.

His was a life of miracles, and might,
And charity, and love. Smart.

O, how easy
Is His ungalling yoke, and all His burdens
'T is ecstacy to bear. Smart.

He is a path, if any be misled;
He is a robe, if any naked be;
If any chance to hunger, He is bread;
If any be a bondman, He is free;
If any be but weak, how strong is He!
  To dead men life He is, to sick men health;
  To blind men sight, and to the needy, wealth—
  A pleasure without loss, a treasure without stealth.

GILES FLETCHER.

Centred in Christ, who fires the soul within,
The flesh shall know no pain, the soul no sin:
E'en in the terrors of expiring breath
We bless the friendly stroke, and live—in death.

ANONYMOUS.

A Saviour's light shall break,
A ray from Jacob's star the darkness streak:
To Him the fairest scenes their lustre owe;
His covenant brightens the celestial bow;
His vast benevolence profusely spreads
The yellow harvests, and the verdant meads.

JOHN DUICK.

He will redeem our deadly, drooping state;
He will bring home the sheep that go astray;
He will help those that hope in Him alway;
He will appease our discord and debate;
He will soon save, though we repent us late.
He will be ours, if we continue His;
He will bring bale to joy and perfect bliss;
He will redeem the flock of His elect
    From all that is,
    Or was, amiss,
Since Abraham's heirs did first His laws reject.

GEORGE GASCOIGNE.

O, WHO shall paint Him?—Let the sweetest tone
That ever trembled on the harps of Heaven,
Be discord; let the chanting seraphim,
Whose anthem is eternity, be dumb;
For praise and wonder, adoration, all
Melt into muteness ere they soar to Thee,
Thou sole Perfection! Theme of countless worlds.

ROBERT MONTGOMERY.

HE from thick films shall purge the visual ray,
And on the sightless eye-balls pour the day:
'T is He the obstructed paths of sound shall clear,
And bid new music charm the unfolding ear:
The dumb shall sing, the lame his crutch forego,
And leap, exulting, like the bounding roe.

POPE.

AND like the grateful showers that glad the fields,
And bid the valleys bloom in purer green,
So shall His presence bid mankind rejoice,
So shall His smile make glad the utmost lands.
And Saba's kings shall greet Him with a gift,
And Tarshish, and the isles, shall own their Lord,
And Ethiopia lift to Heaven her hands:
So shall all earth adore Him. ARTHUR C. COXE

THOU art the Way, the Truth, the Life—
And hearts that, with presumption rife,
Would seek through other means to gain
Light, Truth, and Life, but toil in vain:
Thy Hand alone controls our way,
Thy Truth bids darkness turn to day;
And they Eternal Life have gained
Whose names are written on Thy Hand.

S. D. PATTERSON.

WHEN, blind with sin, my Father's will
  I reckless disobeyed,
One pitying Friend bore with me still,
  And, interceding, prayed. THOMAS WARD.

(*See also* ATONEMENT.)

SCIENCE—PHILOSOPHY.

CANST thou bind the sweet influences of Pleiades, or loose the bands of Orion? JOB, xxxviii, 31.

Hast thou entered into the springs of the sea, or hast thou walked in the search of the depth? JOB, xxxviii, 16.

Who hath directed the spirit of the Lord, or, being His counsellor, hath taught Him?

With whom took He counsel, and who instructed Him, and taught Him in the path of judgment, and taught Him knowledge, and showed to Him the way of understanding? ISAIAH, xl, 13, 14.

Beware lest any man spoil you through philosophy and vain deceit, after the tradition of men, after the rudiments of the world, and not after Christ. COLOSSIANS, ii, 8.

O, Timothy, keep that which is committed to thy trust, avoiding profane and vain babblings, and oppositions of science, falsely so called:

Which some professing, have erred concerning the faith. I. TIMOTHY, vi, 20, 21.

UNNUMBERED systems rise and fall,
And every learned age brings new deceits;
Whilst towering pride still lifts her ready hand
To crush the fond delusion of the day,
And instant rear a stronger in its place.
CHARLES JENNER.

HOW sightless soars philosophy, whene'er
She quits the beaten track which nature points,
And Reason, yet with prejudice untinged;
When, impious, she assumes creative power,
And builds a world without an architect!
GEORGE BALLY.

THE philosophic tower, from whence you boast
To look all nature through, and pity man
Bewildered in the mazy vale below,
Shook with each slight interrogation, nods:
And when the storm of argument assaults,
The treacherous basis sinks, and down it falls.

GEORGE BALLY.

WE that acquaint ourselves with every zone,
  And pass both tropics, and behold both poles;
When we come home are to ourselves unknown,
  And unacquainted still with our own souls.

SIR JOHN DAVIES.

THROUGH knowledge we behold the world's creation:
  How in his cradle first he fostered was;
And judge of nature's cunning operation,
  How things she formed of a formless mass:
By knowledge we do learn ourselves to know;
And what to man, and what to God we owe.

SPENSER.

KNOWLEDGE is not happiness, and science
But an exchange of ignorance for that
Which is another kind of ignorance. BYRON.

  IN sciences to seem profound,
  We dive so deep we find no ground;
And the more knowledge we procure,
The more it doth our minds allure,
  Of mysteries the depth to sound;
  Thus our desires we never bound;
Which by degrees thus drawn on still,
  The memory may not endure;
But like the tubs which Danaus' daughters fill,
  Doth drink no oftener than constrained to spill.

EARL OF STERLINE

LEARNING and arts are theories, not practics:
To understand is all they study to;
Men strive to *know* too much, too little *do*.

MIDDLETON

THE lamp of revelation only shows
What human wisdom cannot but oppose,—
That man, in nature's richest mantle clad,
And graced with all philosophy can add,
Though fair without, and luminous within,
Is still the progeny and heir of sin.
Thus taught, down falls the plumage of his pride,
He feels the need of an unerring guide,
And knows that, falling, he shall rise no more,
Unless the power that bade him stand, restore.
This is indeed philosophy: this known,
Makes wisdom worthy of the name, his own;
And, without this, whatever he discuss,—
Whether the space betwixt the stars and us
Whether he measure earth, compute the sea,
Weigh sunbeams, carve a fly, or spit a flea,—
The solemn trifler, with his boasted skill,
Toils much, and is a solemn trifler still;
Blind was he born, and his misguided eyes
Grown dim in trifling studies, blind he dies.

COWPER

WHEN knowledge, at her Father's dread command,
Resigned to Israel's king her golden key,
O, to have joined the frequent auditors
In wonder and delight, that whilom heard
Great Solomon descanting on the brutes;
O, how sublimely glorious to apply
To God's own honour, and good-will to man,
That wisdom he alone, of men, possessed
In plenitude so rich, and cope so rare.

SMART.

LEARNING itself, received into a mind
By nature weak, or viciously inclined,
Serves but to lead philosophers astray,
Where children would with ease discern the way.
COWPER.

BEHOLD
Where yon pellucid, populous hive presents
A yet uncopied model to the world!
There Machiavel, in the reflecting glass,
May read himself a fool. The chemist there
May, with astonishment invidious, view
His toils out-done by each plebeian bee,
Who, at the royal mandate, on the wing,
From various herbs, and from discordant flowers,
A perfect harmony of sweets compounds. SMART.

SURVEY the magnet's sympathetic love,
That woos the yielding needle; contemplate
Th' attractive amber's power, invisible
Ev'n to the mental eye; or when the blow
Sent from th' electric sphere assaults thy frame,
Show me the hand that dealt it!—Baffled here
By His Omnipotence, Philosophy
Slowly her thoughts inadequate revolves,
And stands with all His circling wonders round her,
Like heavy Saturn, in th' ethereal space
Begirt with an inexplicable ring. SMART.

WHILE the laborious crowds
Ply the tough oar, Philosophy directs
The ruling helm; or like the liberal breath
Of potent Heaven, invisible, the sail
Swells out and bears th' inferior world along.
THOMSON.

WITH thee, serene Philosophy, with thee
And thy bright garland, let me crown my song!
Effusive source of evidence and truth!
A lustre shedding o'er the ennobled mind
Stronger than summer noon; and pure as that
Whose mild vibrations soothe the parted soul,
New to the dawning of celestial day.
Hence through her nourished powers, enlarged by thee,
She springs aloft, with elevated pride,
Above the tangling mass of low desires
That bind the fluttering crowd; and, angel-winged,
The heights of science and of virtue gains,
Where all is calm and clear; with nature round,
Or in the starry regions, or the abyss,
To reason and to fancy's eye displayed:
The first up-tracing from the dreary void,
The chain of causes and effects to Him,
The world-producing Essence, who alone
Possesses being; while the last receives
The whole magnificence of Heaven and earth,
And every beauty, delicate or bold,
Obvious or more remote, with livelier sense,
Diffusive painted on the rapid mind. THOMSON.

THE SEA.

THEY that go down to the sea in ships, that do business in great waters,

These see the works of the Lord, and His wonders in the deep.

For He commandeth and raiseth the stormy wind, which lifteth the waves thereof.

They mount up to the heavens, they go down again to the depths; their soul is melted because of trouble.

They reel to and fro, and stagger like a drunken man, and are at their wits' end.

Then they cry unto the Lord in their trouble, and He bringeth them out of their distresses.

He maketh the storm a calm, so that the waves thereof are still.

Then are they glad because they are quiet; so He bringeth them unto their desired haven. PSALM cvii, 23—30.

Hitherto shalt thou come, but no farther: and here shall thy proud waves be stayed. JOB, xxxviii, 11.

And the sea gave up the dead which were in it. REVELATION, xx, 13.

FOR often the dauntless mariner knows
That he must sink to the land beneath,
Where the diamond on trees of coral grows,
In the emerald halls of Death, of Death.

Onward we sweep through smooth and storm:
We are voyagers all in shine or gloom;
And the dreamer who skulks by his chimney walls,
Drifts in his sleep to Doom, to Doom.

JOHN STERLING.

SEA!—of Almightiness itself the immense
And glorious mirror!—how thy azure face
Renews the heavens in their magnificence!
What awful grandeur rounds thy heavy space:
Thy surge two worlds eternal-warring sweeps,
And God's throne rests on thy majestic deeps.

CHENEDOLLE.

How humbling to one, with a heart and a soul,
To look on thy greatness, and list to its roll;
To think how that heart in cold ashes shall be,
While the voice of Eternity rises from thee!

But when thy deep surges no longer shall roll,
And the firmament's length is drawn back like a scroll,
Then — then shall the spirit that sighs by thee now,
Be more mighty, more lasting, more chainless than thou!

JOHN A. SHEA.

O, IT gladdeneth much my very soul
  The smallest ship to see;
For I know, where'er a sail is spread,
  God speaketh audibly.

MARY HOWITT.

How oft the ruddy cheek will pale
  To leave the earth behind!
How oft the glowing heart will quail
  Before the tempest wind!
We fear the billows' dash, but why?
  There's One to guard and save;
There's One whose wide and watchful eye
  Sleeps not above the wave.

ELIZA COOK.

THOU, Thou alone, with whom, enthroned on high,
Sits co-essential wisdom, bad'st subside
The valleys, and the mountains, from amidst
Th' o'erwhelming moisture, heave their brow sublime.
The liquid troops, obedient to Thy voice,
Fled to the appointed station. Thou a bound
Hast set, they cannot pass; nor ever spread
Their flowing mantle o'er th' invested earth:
Thou to the sea sayest,—Hitherto advance,
And here thy proud licentious waves be stayed.

GEORGE BALLY.

SEE how, beneath the moonbeam's smile,
  Yon little billow heaves its breast,
And foams and sparkles for awhile,—
  Then, murmuring, subsides to rest.
Thus man, the sport of bliss and care,
  Rises on time's eventful sea;
And, having swelled a moment there,
  Thus melts into Eternity! THOMAS MOORE.

MYSTERIOUS deep, farewell!
I turn from thy companionship, but lo,
Thy voice doth follow me. 'Mid lonely bower,
Or twilight dream, or wakeful couch, I hear
That solemn and reverberated hymn
From thy deep organ, which doth speak God's praise
In thunder, night and day. Still by my side,
Even as a dim-seen spirit, deign to walk,
Prompter of holy thought, and type of HIM,
Sleepless, immutable, omnipotent.

MRS. SIGOURNEY.

To thee the love of woman hath gone down;
  Dark flow thy tides o'er manhood's noble head,
O'er youth's bright looks, and beauty's flowery crown!
  Yet must thou hear a voice — Restore the dead!
Earth shall reclaim her precious things from thee:—
    Restore the dead, thou sea! MRS. HEMANS.

THE prayer is said,
And the last rite man pays to man is paid;
The plashing water marks his resting-place,
And folds him round, in one long, cold embrace;
Bright bubbles for a moment sparkle o'er,
Then break, to be, like him, beheld no more;
Down, countless fathoms down, he sinks to sleep,
With all the nameless shapes that haunt the deep.

CHARLES SPRAGUE.

GOD of the dark and heavy deep!
  The waves lie sleeping on the sands,
Till the fierce trumpet of the storm
  Hath summoned up their slumbering bands;
Then the white sails are dashed like foam,
  Or hurry, trembling, o'er the seas,
Till, calmed by Thee, the sinking gale
  Serenely breathes,—Depart in peace.

W. B. O. PEABODY.

DEEP calleth unto deep. And what are we,
That hear the question of that voice sublime?
O, what are all the notes that ever rung
From war's vain trumpet, by thy thundering side!
Yea, what is all the riot man can make
In his short life, to thy unceasing roar!
And yet, bold babbler, what art thou to Him
Who drowned a world, and heaped the waters far
Above its loftiest mountains?—a light wave,
That breaks, and whispers of its Maker's might.

J. G. C. BRAINARD.

THE SEASONS.

And God said, Let there be lights in the firmament of the heaven, to divide the day from the night; and let them be for signs, and for seasons, and for days, and for years. Genesis, i, 14.

While the earth remaineth, seed-time and harvest, and cold and heat, and summer and winter, and day and night, shall not cease. Genesis, viii, 22.

He changeth the times and the seasons. Daniel, ii, 21.

He giveth snow like wool: He scattereth the hoar-frost like ashes.

He casteth forth His ice like morsels: who can stand before His cold?

He sendeth out His word, and melteth them: He causeth His wind to blow, and the waters flow. Psalm cxlvii, 16—18.

The earth, which drinketh in the rain which cometh oft upon it, and bringeth forth fruits meet for them by whom it is dressed, receiveth blessing from God. Hebrews vi, 7.

These, as they change, Almighty Father, these
Are but the varied God. The rolling year
Is full of Thee. Forth in the pleasing Spring
Thy beauty walks, Thy tenderness and love.
Wide flush the fields; the softening air is balm;
Echo the mountains round; the forest smiles;
And every sense, and every heart is joy.
Then comes Thy glory in the Summer months,
With light and heat refulgent. Then Thy sun
Shoots full perfection through the swelling year;
And oft Thy voice in dreadful thunder speaks;
And oft at dawn, deep noon, or falling eve,
By brooks and groves, in hollow whispering gales.
Thy bounty shines in Autumn unconfined,
And spreads a common feast for all that live.
In Winter awful Thou! with clouds and storms
Around Thee thrown, tempest o'er tempest rolled,
Majestic darkness! on the whirlwind's wing,
Riding sublime, Thou bid'st the world adore,
And humblest nature with Thy northern blast.

Thomson.

What prodigies can power divine perform
More grand than it produces year by year,
And all in sight of inattentive man?
Familiar with the effect, we slight the cause,
And in the constancy of nature's course,
The regular return of genial months,
See nought to wonder at. Cowper.

When Spring unlocks the flowers to paint the laughing soil,
When Summer's balmy showers refresh the mower's toil,
When Winter binds in frosty chains the fallow and the flood,
In God the earth rejoiceth still, and owns his Maker good.

The flowers of Spring may wither—the hope of Summer fade—
The Autumn droop in Winter—the birds forsake the shade—
The wind be lulled—the sun and moon forget their old decree—
But we in nature's latest hour, O Lord! will cling to Thee! Bp. Heber.

Sow thy seed, and reap in gladness!
  Man himself is all a seed;
Hope and hardship, joy and sadness,
  Slow the plant to ripeness lead.

John Sterling.

See! full of hope, thou trustest to the earth
  The golden seed, and waitest till the Spring
Summons the buried to a happier birth;
  But, in Time's furrow duly scattering,
Think'st thou how deeds, by wisdom sown, may be
  Silently ripen'd for eternity? Schiller.

When youthful Spring around us breathes,
  Thy spirit warms her fragrant sigh;
And every flower that Summer wreathes,
  Is born beneath Thy kindling eye;
Where'er we turn Thy glories shine,
And all things fair and bright are thine.

Thomas Moore.

There seems a voice in every gale,
  A tongue in every opening flower,
Which tells, O God, the wondrous tale
  Of Thy indulgence, love, and power:
The birds, that rise on quivering wing,
  Appear to hymn their Maker's praise,
And all the mingling sounds of Spring
  To Thee a general anthem raise. Mrs. Opie.

"Life has no second youth," yet all may keep
A Spring-time of the feelings; and although
Years may come round me with their blighting chill,
And stern realities my spirit fill,
I'll guard these simple tastes, and ever bless
That God who planted in my inmost heart
A sympathy for things that can impart,
Unto the humblest lot, a loftiness. Mary E. Lee.

Thick in yon stream of light, a thousand ways,
Upward and downward, thwarting and convolved,
The quivering nations sport; till, tempest-winged,
Fierce Winter sweeps them from the face of day:
Even so luxurious men, unheeding, pass
An idle Summer-life in fortune's shine,
A season's glitter! Thus they flutter on
From toy to toy, from vanity to vice;
Till, blown away by death, oblivion comes
Behind, and strikes them from the Book of life!

Thomson.

O, THUS hath life its eventide
  Of sorrow, loneliness, and grief;
And thus, divested of its pride,
  It withers like the yellow leaf:—
O, such is life's Autumnal bower
  When plundered of its Summer bloom;
And such is life's Autumnal hour
  Which heralds man unto the tomb.

JAMES G. BROOKS.

WHETHER in youth, like early fruit,
Or in the sere and solemn suit
Of our autumnal age, like wheat
Ripened, and for the reaper fit,
Thou cut us off, O God, may we
Gathered unto Thy garner be! H. H. WELD.

THE Angel comes! he comes to reap
  The harvest of the Lord!
O'er all the earth, with fatal sweep,
  Wide waves his flamy sword.

And who are they, in sheaves, to bide
  The fire of vengeance, bound?
The tares, whose rank, luxuriant pride
  Choked the fair crop around.

And who are they, reserved in store
  God's treasure-house to fill?
The wheat, a hundred fold that bore
  Amid surrounding ill. H. H. MILMAN.

THE wind breathes low, the withering leaf
  Scarce whispers from the tree;
So gently flows the parting breath
  When good men cease to be.

W. B. O. PEABODY.

The leaves around me falling
  Are preaching of decay;
The hollow winds are calling,—
  "Come, pilgrim, come away:"
The day in night declining
  Says, I must, too, decline;
The year, its bloom resigning,
  Its lot foreshadows mine.   British Magazine.

Come thou to life's feast
With dove-eyed meekness, and bland charity,
And thou shalt find even Winter's rugged blasts
The minstrel teacher of thy well-tuned soul,
And when the last drop of its cup is drained—
Arising with a song of praise — go up
To the eternal banquet.   Mrs. Sigourney.

Whether men sow or reap the fields,
Her admonitions nature yields;
That not by bread alone we live,
Or what a hand of flesh can give;
That every day should leave some part
Free for a Sabbath of the heart;
So shall the seventh be truly blest,
From morn to eve, with hallowed rest.
Wordsworth.

'T is past! no more the Summer blooms!
  Ascending in the rear,
Behold, congenial Autumn comes,
  The Sabbath of the year!
What time thy holy whispers breathe,
The pensive evening shade beneath,
  And twilight consecrates the floods;
While nature strips her garment gay,
And wears the verdure of decay,
  O, let me wander through the sounding woods!
Logan.

TRUTH bids me look on men as Autumn leaves;
And all they bleed for, as the Summer's dust,
Driven by the whirlwind. YOUNG

I DEEM thee not unlovely, though thou com'st
With a stern visage. To the tuneful bird,
The blushing floweret, the rejoicing stream,
Thy discipline is harsh. But unto man,
Methinks, thou hast a kindlier ministry.
Thy lengthened eve is full of fireside joys,
And deathless linking of warm heart to heart,
So that the hoarse storm passes by unheard.
Earth robed in white, a peaceful Sabbath holds,
And keepeth silence at her Maker's feet:
She ceaseth from the harrowing of the plough,
And from the harvest-shouting. MRS. SIGOURNEY.

'TIS done! Dread Winter spreads his latest glooms,
And reigns tremendous o'er the conquered year.
How dead the vegetable kingdom lies!
How dumb the tuneful! Horror wide extends
His desolate domain. Behold, fond man!
See here thy pictured life; pass some few years,
Thy flowering Spring, thy Summer's ardent strength,
Thy sober Autumn, fading into age,
And pale, concluding Winter comes at last,
And shuts the scene. Ah! whither now are fled
Those dreams of greatness? Those unsolid hopes
Of happiness? Those longings after fame?
Those restless cares? Those busy, bustling days?
Those gay-spent festive nights? Those veering thoughts,
Lost between good and ill, that shared thy life?
All now are vanished! Virtue sole survives,
Immortal, never-failing friend of man,
His guide to happiness on high. THOMSON.

SECTS—CONTROVERSY.

Him that is weak in the faith receive ye, but not to doubtful disputations. Romans xiv, 1.

Now this I say, that every one of you saith, I am of Paul; and I of Apollos; and of Cephas; and I of Christ.

Is Christ divided? was Paul crucified for you? or were ye baptized in the name of Paul? 1 Corinthians, i, 12, 13.

With zeal we watch,
And weigh the doctrine, while the spirit 'scapes;
And in the carving of our cummin-seeds,
Our metaphysical hair-splittings, fail
To note the orbit of that star of love
Which never sets. Mrs. Sigourney.

Each differing sect whose base
Is on the same pure word, doth strictly scan
Its neighbour's superstructure,—point and arch,—
Buttress and turret,—till the hymn of praise,
That from each temple should go up to God,
Sinks in the critic's tone. Mrs. Sigourney.

True piety, without cessation tost
By theories, the practic part is lost;
And like a ball bandied 'twixt pride and wit,
Rather than yield, both sides the prize will quit:
Then while his foe the gladiator spoils,
The atheist, looking on, enjoys the spoils.

Denham.

Commentators each dark passage shun,
And hold their farthing candles to the sun.

Young.

WERE love, in these the world's last doting years,
As frequent as the want of it appears,
The churches warmed, they would no longer hold
Such frozen figures, stiff as they are cold;
Relenting forms would lose their power, or cease,
And e'en the dipped and sprinkled live in peace;
Each heart would quit its prison in the breast,
And flow in free communion with the rest.

COWPER.

SPIRITUAL, choleric critics, which in all
Religions find faults, and forgive no fall,
Have, through this zeal, virtue but in their gall.

DANIEL.

DIVINITY, wrested by some factious blood,
Draws blood, swells battles, and o'erthrows all good.

JOHN WEBSTER.

SOMETIMES the father differs from the son
As doth the Gospel from the Alcoran,
Or Loyola from Calvin; which two brands
In strange combustion hurl fair Europe's lands.

HOWEL.

SOME faiths are like those mills that cannot grind
Their corn, unless they work against the wind.

QUARLES.

WE toil
To controvert, to argue, to defend,
Camping against imaginary foes,
And visioned heresies. Even brethren deem
A name of doctrine, or a form of words,
A dense partition-wall,—though Christ hath said,
"See that ye love each other." MRS. SIGOURNEY.

Some raw divines no sooner are espoused
To their first wives, and in the temple housed,
But straight the peace is broke: they now begin
To appoint the field to fight the battles in:
Schoolmen must war with schoolmen, text with text;
The first 's the Chaldee's paraphrase; the next
The Septuagint; opinion thwarts opinion;
The Papist holds then the first, the last the Arminian;
And then the councils must be called to advise,
What this of Lateran says, and that of Nice;
And here the point must be anew disputed,
Arius is false, and Bellarmine 's confuted:
Thus, with the sharp artillery of their wit,
They shoot at random, careless where they hit:
The slightly-studied Fathers must be prayed,
Although on small acquaintance, into aid;
Whose glorious varnish must impose a gloss
Upon their paint, whose gold must gild their dross.
Now Martin Luther must be purged, by them,
From all his errors, like a school-boy's theme:
Free-will 's disputed, consubstantiation,
And the deep ocean of predestination;
Where, daring venture oft too far into 't,
They, Pharaoh like, are drowned both horse and foot.

Francis Quarles.

SELF-DENIAL—FASTING.

He that is slow to anger, is better than the mighty; and he that ruleth his spirit than he that taketh a city. PROVERBS, xvi, 32.

If any man will come after me, let him deny himself, and take up his cross, and follow me. MATTHEW, xvi, 24.

And they that are Christ's have crucified the flesh, with the affections and lusts. GALATIANS, v, 24.

Moreover, when ye fast, be not, as the hypocrites, of a sad countenance: for they disfigure their faces, that they may appear unto men to fast. MATTHEW, vi, 16.

In good or ill, leave casuists on the shelf—
He never errs who sacrifices self.

SIR E. B. LYTTON.

Humility o'er self victorious,
Of earth's triumphs the most glorious. WM. PETER.

Brave conquerors!—for so you are,
That war against your own affections,
And the huge army of the world's desires.

SHAKSPEARE.

Keep thou Zion-ward thy face,
Ask in faith, the aid of grace,
Use the strength which grace shall give,
Die to self, in Christ to live. BERNARD BARTON.

When thou a fast would'st keep,
Make not its homage cheap,
By publishing its signs to every eye:
But let it be between
Thyself and the Unseen,
So shall it gain acceptance from on high.

BERNARD BARTON.

Who would the title of true worth were his,
Must vanquish vice, and no base thoughts conceive:
The bravest trophy ever man obtained,
Is that which o'er himself, himself hath gained.
Earl of Sterline.

Who fights
With passions and o'ercomes, he is endued
With the best virtue,—passive fortitude.
Massinger.

Rarely shall that path be trod,
Which without horror leads to death's abode.
Some few, by temperance taught, approaching slow,
To distant fate by easy journeys go;
Gently they lay them down, as evening sheep
On their own woolly fleeces softly sleep. Dryden.

SELFISHNESS—SELF-LOVE.

This know also, that in the last days perilous times shall come, for men shall be lovers of their own selves, covetous, boasters, proud. II. Timothy, iii, 1, 2.

Let no man seek his own, but every man another's wealth. I. Corinthians, x, 24.

Therefore, all things whatsoever ye would that men should do to you, do ye even so to them: for this is the law and the prophets. Matthew, vii, 12.

For what is vice? Self-love in a mistake;
A poor blind merchant, buying toys too dear.
And virtue what? 'T is self-love in her wits,
Quite skilful in the market of delight.
Self-love's good sense is love of that dread Power,
From whom herself, and all she can enjoy.
Other self-love is but disguised self-hate,
More mortal than the malice of our foes. Young.

Self-love never yet could look on truth,
But with bleared beams; sleek flattery and she
Are twin-born sisters, and so mix their eyes,
As, if you sever one, the other dies. Ben Jonson.

Who live but for themselves are but for show;
And stand like barren trees, where good might grow.
Richard Brome.

SELF-KNOWLEDGE.

Stand in awe, and sin not: commune with your own heart upon your bed, and be still. Psalm iv, 4.

Ponder the path of thy feet, and let all thy ways be established. Proverbs, iv, 25.

The spirit of man is the candle of the Lord, searching all the inward parts of the belly. Proverbs, xx, 27.

Self-knowledge, truly learned, of course implies
The rich possession of a nobler prize;
For self to self, and God to man revealed
(Two themes to nature's eyes for ever sealed,)
Are taught by rays that fly with equal pace
From the same centre of enlightening grace.
Cowper.

Man's science is the culture of his heart;
And not to lose his plummet in the depths
Of nature, or the more profound of God. Young.

Man's life, sir, being
So short, and then the way that leads unto
The knowledge of ourselves so long and tedious,
Each minute should be precious.
Beaumont and Fletcher.

To spread the page of Scripture, and compare
Our conduct with the laws engraven there;
To measure all that passes in the breast,
Faithfully, fairly by that sacred test;
To dive into the sacred deeps within,
To spare no passion, and no favourite sin,
And search the themes, important above all,
Ourselves, and our recovery from our fall.

COWPER.

SELF-MURDER.

THEN said his wife unto him, Dost thou still retain thine integrity? Curse God, and die.

But he said unto her, Thou speakest as one of the foolish women speaketh. What. shall we receive good at the hand of God, and shall we not receive evil? In all this did not Job sin with his lips. JOB, ii, 9, 10.

My times are in Thy hand. PSALM xxxi, 15.

Thou shalt not kill. EXODUS, xx, 13.

DREADFUL attempt!
Just reeking from self-slaughter, in a rage
To rush into the presence of our Judge!
As if we challenged Him to do His worst,
And mattered not His wrath.

BLAIR.

VAIN man! 'tis Heaven's prerogative
To take, what first it deigned to give—
Thy tributary breath:
In awful expectation placed,
Await thy doom, nor, impious, haste
To pluck from God's right hand, His instruments of death.

THOMAS WHARTON.

THOUGH life seem one uncomfortable void,
Guilt at thy heels, before thy face despair;
Yet, gay this scene, and light this load of woe,
Compared with thy hereafter. BP. PORTEUS.

SELF-RIGHTEOUSNESS.

EVERY one that exalteth himself shall be abased, and he that humbleth himself shall be exalted. LUKE, xviii, 14.

For they, being ignorant of God's righteousness, and going about to establish their own righteousness, have not submitted themselves to the righteousness of God. ROMANS x, 3.

But we are all as an unclean thing, and all our righteousnesses are as filthy rags.

We do not present our supplications before Thee for our righteousnesses, but for Thy great mercies. DANIEL, ix, 18,

O, SHALL God tolerate the meanest prayer
That humbly seeks His high supernal throne,
And man — presumptuous Pharisee — declare
His fellow's voice less welcome than his own?
MRS. NORTON.

WHAT is all righteousness that men devise?
What, but a sordid bargain for the skies?
But Christ as soon would abdicate His own,
As stoop from Heaven to sell the proud a throne.
COWPER.

SERVICE—OBEDIENCE.

LET every soul be subject unto the higher powers. For there is no power but of God; the powers that be are ordained of God.

Whosoever, therefore, resisteth the power, resisteth the ordinance of God: and they that resist shall receive to themselves damnation. ROMANS, xiii, 1, 2.

Render, therefore, unto Cæsar the things which be Cæsar's, and unto God the things which be God's. LUKE, xx, 25.

HAD I but served my God with half the zeal
I served my king, He would not, in mine age,
Have left me naked to mine enemies.

SHAKSPEARE.

EXPECT not more from servants than is just;
Reward them well, if they observe their trust,
Nor them with cruelty, or pride invade;
Since God and nature them our brothers made.

DENHAM.

THE good needs fear no law,
It is his safety, and the bad man's awe.

MASSINGER.

FOR government, though high, and low and lower
Put into parts, doth keep in one consent
Congruing in a full and natural close
Like music.
Therefore Heaven doth divide
The state of man in divers functions,
Setting endeavour in continual motion;
To which is fixed as an aim, or butt,
Obedience. SHAKSPEARE.

We must learn to obey;
True virtue still directs the noble way. ROWLEY.

SICKNESS—PESTILENCE.

THOU shalt not be afraid for the terror by night, nor for the arrow that flieth by day: Nor for the pestilence that walketh in darkness: nor for the destruction that wasteth at noon-day. PSALM xci, 5, 6.

Let us fall now into the hand of the Lord; for His mercies are great; and let me not fall into the hand of man. II. SAMUEL, xxiv, 14.

The prayer of faith shall raise the sick, and the Lord shall raise him up. JAMES, v, 15.

BUT chiefly, Thou,
Whom soft-eyed pity once led down from Heaven
To bleed for man, to teach him how to live,
And O, still harder lesson, how to die;
Disdain not Thou to smooth the restless bed
Of sickness and of pain. BP. PORTEUS.

DELAY not, sinner, till the hour of pain
To seek repentance: pain is absolute,
Exacting all the body and the brain,
Humanity's stern king, from head to foot:
How canst thou pray, when fevered arrows shoot
Through this torn targe, while every bone doth ache,
And the scared mind raves up and down her cell,
Restless, and begging rest, for mercy's sake?
Add not to death the bitter fears of hell;
Take pity on thy future self, poor man,
While yet in strength thy timely wisdom can;
Wrestle to-day with sin; and spare that strife
Of meeting all its terrors in the van,
Just at the ebbing agony of life. TUPPER.

THE daily lessening of our life shows, by
A little dying, how outright to die.
SIR WILLIAM DAVENANT.

Is not His deed, whatever thing is done
  In Heaven and earth? Did not He all create
To die again! All ends that was begun;
  Their times in His eternal book of fate
  Are written sure, and have their certain date.
Who, then, can strive with strong necessity,
  That holds the world in his still changing state,
Or shun the death ordained by destiny?
When hour of death is come, let none ask whence, nor
    why. SPENSER.

THE life of all his blood
Is touched corruptibly; and his pure brain,
Which some suppose the soul's frail dwelling-house,
Doth, by the idle comments that it makes,
Foretel the ending of mortality. SHAKSPEARE.

IT is an easy thing for him who has
No pain, to talk of patience. TOURNEUR.

AT dead of night,
In sullen silence, stalks forth pestilence:
Contagion, close behind, taints all her steps
With poisonous dew; no smiting hand is seen,
No sound is heard, but soon her secret path
Is marked with desolation; heaps on heaps
Promiscuous drop. No friend, no refuge near;
All, all is false and treacherous around;
All that they touch, or taste, or breathe, is Death.
BP. PORTEUS.

THE fountains of the deep their barriers break;
Above, below, the rival torrents pour,
And drown Creation; or in floods of fire
Descends a living cataract, and consumes
An impious race. BP. PORTEUS.

SIGHT—EYES.

The light of the body is the eye: if, therefore, thine eye be single, thy whole body shall be full of light.

But if thine eye be evil, thy whole body shall be full of darkness. If, therefore, the light that is in thee be darkness, how great is that darkness! Matthew, vi, 22, 23.

He that formed the eye, shall He not see? Psalm xciv, 9.

First the two eyes, that have the seeing power,
Stand as one watchman, spy, or sentinel,
Being placed aloft within the head's high tower;
And though both see, yet both but one thing tell.

These mirrors take into their little space
The forms of moon, and sun, and every star,
Of every body, and of every place,
Which with the wide world's arms embraced are:

Yet their best objects, and their noblest use,
Hereafter, in another world, will be;
When God in them shall heavenly light infuse,
That face to face they may their Maker see.

Here are they guides, which do the body lead,
Which else would stumble in eternal night;
Here in this world they do most knowledge read,
And are the casements which admit most light.

Sir John Davies.

The difference is as great between
The optics seeing, as the object seen.
All manners take a tincture from our own,
Or some, discoloured, through our passions shown.

Pope.

Blest eyes, which see the things we see!
And yet this tree of life hath proved
To many a soul a poison-tree,
Beheld and not beloved.

So like an Angel's is our bliss,
(O, thought to comfort and appal)
It needs must bring, if used amiss,
An Angel's hopeless fall. Keble.

SILENCE—SOLITUDE.

The Lord is in His holy temple; let all the earth keep silence before Him. Habakkuk, ii, 20.

Be silent, O all flesh, before the Lord. Zechariah, ii, 13.

When thou prayest, enter into thy closet. Matthew, vi, 6.

And when He had sent the multitudes away, He went up into a mountain apart, to pray; and when the evening was come, He was there alone. Matthew, xiv, 23.

Mine eyes prevent the night-watches that I might meditate in Thy word. Psalm cxix, 148.

Even a fool, when he holdeth his lips, is counted wise: and he that shutteth his lips, is esteemed a man of understanding. Proverbs, xvii, 28.

Silence! coeval with eternity;
Thou wert, ere nature's self began to be;
'T was one vast nothing all, and all slept fast in thee.
Pope.

There is an awful stillness in this place,
A Presence that forbids to break the spell,
Till the heart pours its agony in tears.
Rufus Dawes.

The silence, often, of pure innocence,
Persuades when speaking fails. Shakspeare.

IN silence mend what ills deform thy mind;
But all thy good impart to all thy kind.
JOHN STERLING.

TRUE prayer is not the noisy sound
That clamorous lips repeat,
But the deep silence of a soul
That clasps Jehovah's feet. MRS. SIGOURNEY

O SACRED solitude, divine retreat!
Choice of the prudent, envy of the great!
By the pure stream, or in the waving shade,
We court fair wisdom, that celestial maid;
The genuine offspring of her loved embrace,
Unknown on earth, are innocence and peace.
YOUNG.

No, 'tis not here that solitude is known.
Through the wide world, he only is alone
Who lives not for another. ROGERS.

FOR oh! those transient gleams of Heaven,
To calmer, purer spirits given,
Children of hallowed peace, are known
In solitude and shade alone! MRS. HEMANS.

NOT always he
Hath holiest heart, whose worship is most loud,
And that is purest prayer, where one alone is bowed.
GEO. H. COLTON.

O, LOST to virtue, lost to manly thought,
Lost to the noble sallies of the soul!
Who think it solitude to be alone.
Communion sweet! Communion large and high!
Our reason, guardian angel, and our God! YOUNG.

'Tis the felt presence of the Deity.
Few are the faults we flatter, when alone.
Vice sinks in her allurements, is ungilt,
And looks, like other objects, black by night.

YOUNG.

If thus our Lord Himself withdrew,
  Stealing at times away,
E'en from the loved, the chosen few,
  In solitude to pray;
How should His followers, frail and weak,
Such seasons of retirement seek!

BERNARD BARTON.

Place me on some desert shore
Foot of man ne'er wandered o'er;
Lock me in a lonely cell
Beneath some prison citadel;
Still, here or there, within I find
My quiet kingdom of the mind;
Nay, 'mid the tempest fierce and dark,
Float me in peril's frailest barque,
My quenchless soul could sit and think,
And smile at danger's dizziest brink;
And wherefore? God, my God is still
King of kings in good and ill;
And where He dwelleth — every where —
Safety supreme and peace are there;
And where He reigneth — all around —
Wisdom, and love, and power are found
And, reconciled to Him and bliss,
"My mind to me a kingdom is."

TUPPER

What awful joy! what mental liberty!

YOUNG

THE world excluded, every passion hushed,
And opened a calm intercourse with Heaven,
Here the soul sits in council; ponders past,
Predestines future action; sees, not feels,
Tumultuous life, and reasons with the storm;
All her lies answers, and thinks down her chains.

YOUNG.

HOW wise a short retreat to steal,
The vanity of life to feel,
And from its cares to fly:
To act one calm, domestic scene,
Earth's bustle and the grave between,
Retire, and learn to die! HANNAH MORE.

WISDOM'S self
Oft seeks so sweet, retired solitude;
Where, with her best nurse — contemplation —
She plumes her feathers, and lets go her wings,
That in the various bustle of resort
Were all too muffled, and sometimes impaired.

MILTON.

SIN—SHAME.

UNTO them that are defiled and unbelieving is nothing pure; but even their mind and conscience is defiled. TITUS, i, 15.

Shame shall be the promotion of fools. PROVERBS, iii, 35.

Raging waves of the sea, foaming out their own shame. JUDE, 13.

Let not sin, therefore, reign in your mortal bodies, that ye should obey it in the lusts thereof. ROMANS, vi, 12.

The wages of sin is death. ROMANS, vi, 23.

THE guilt being great, the fear doth still exceed,
And extreme fear can neither fight nor fly,
But, coward-like, with trembling terror die.

SHAKSPEARE.

CAN that be good, of which the outward signs
Are the thief's posture, and the coward's tread?

EPES SARGENT.

WHAT havoc hast thou made, foul monster, Sin!
Greatest and first of ills! The fruitful parent
Of woes of all dimensions! But for thee,
Sorrow had never been!

BLAIR.

GUILT is the source of sorrow; 'tis the fiend—
The avenging fiend—that follows us behind
With whips and stings: the blest know none of this;
But rest in everlasting peace of mind,
And find the height of all their heaven is goodness.

ROWE.

WHO loves to sin, in hell his portion's given;
Who dies to sin shall, after, live in heaven.

FRANCIS QUARLES.

THE other shape,
If shape it might be called that shape had none
Distinguishable in member, joint, or limb;
Or substance might be called that shadow seemed,
For each seemed either; black it stood as night,
Fierce as ten furies, terrible as hell,
And shook a dreadful dart; what seemed his head,
The likeness of a kingly crown had on.
Satan was now at hand; and from his seat
The monster, moving onward, came as fast
With horrid strides, hell trembled as he strode.

MILTON.

'TIS fearful building upon any sin:
One mischief entered, brings another in;
The second pulls a third, the third draws more,
And they for all the rest set ope the door:
Till custom take away the judging sense,
That to offend we think it no offence.

WILLIAM SMITH. (1615.)

O, THE dangerous siege
Sin lays about us! And the tyranny
He exercises, when he hath expunged:
Like to the horror of a winter's thunder,
Mixed with a gushing storm, that suffers nothing
To stir abroad on earth but their own rages,
Is sin, when it hath gathered head above us:
No roof, no shelter will secure us so,
But he will drown our cheeks in fear or woe.

CHAPMAN.

I NE'ER heard yet,
That any of these bolder vices wanted
Less impudence to gainsay what they did,
Than to perform it first. SHAKSPEARE.

WHAT if the sinner's magazines are stored
With the rich spoils that Ophir's mines afford?
What if he spends his happy days and nights
In softest joys, and undisturbed delights?
Where is his hope at last, when God shall wrest
His trembling soul from his reluctant breast?
SIR RICHARD BLACKMORE

THAT sin does ten times aggravate itself,
That is committed in an holy place;
An evil deed done by authority,
Is sin and subornation; deck an ape
In tissue, and the beauty of the robe
Adds but the greater scorn unto the beast;
The poison shows worst in a golden cup;
Dark night seems darker by the lightning's flash;
Lilies that fester smell far worse than weeds;
And every glory that inclines to sin,
The shame is treble by the opposite.
OLD PLAY. (1597.)

WHEN men's intents are wicked, their guilt haunts them
But when they're just, they're armed, and nothing daunts
them. MIDDLETON.

THE man that blushes is not quite a brute.
YOUNG.

FOR he that but conceives a crime in thought,
Contracts the danger of an actual fault;
Then what must he expect, that still proceeds
To finish sin, and work up thoughts in deeds?
DRYDEN

WISDOM and goodness to the vile seem vile,
Filths savour but themselves. SHAKSPEARE

WHEN at first from virtue's path we stray,
How shrinks the feeble heart with sad dismay!
More bold at length, by powerful habit led,
Careless and sered, the dreary wilds we tread;
Behold the gaping gulph of sin with scorn,
And plunging deep, to endless death are borne.

JAMES SCOTT

FAULTS in the life breed errors in the brain,
And these reciprocally those again.
The mind and conduct mutually imprint
And stamp their image in each other's mint.

COWPER.

O, HOW unsufferable is the weight
Of sin! how miserable is their state,
The silence of whose secret sin conceals
The smart, till justice to revenge appeals!

FRANCIS QUARLES.

OUR sins, like to our shadows,
When our day is in its glory, scarce appeared:
Towards our evening, how great and monstrous!

SUCKLING.

To threats the stubborn sinner oft is hard,
Wrapped in his crimes, against the storm prepared;
But when the milder beams of mercy play,
He melts, and throws his cumbrous cloak away.

DRYDEN.

O, MORE than sottish
For creatures of a day, in gamesome mood,
To frolic on eternity's dread brink
Unapprehensive; when, for aught we know,
The very next swol'n surge shall sweep us in

BLAIR.

YE who for the living lost
  That agony in secret bear,
Who shall with soothing words accost
  The strength of your despair?
Grief for your sake is scorn for them
Whom ye lament, and all condemn;
And o'er the world of spirits lies
A gloom from which ye turn your eyes.

WM. C. BRYANT

COUNT all the advantage prosperous vice attains,
'T is but what virtue flies from, and disdains.

POPE.

CROWS are fair with crows;
Custom in sin gives sin a lovely dye;
Blackness in Moors is no deformity. DEKKER.

HOW guilt, once harboured in the conscious breast,
Intimidates the brave, degrades the great!

DR. JOHNSON.

THOU mayest from law, but not from scorn escape;
The pointed finger, cold, averted eye,
Insulted virtue's hiss, thou canst not fly.

CHARLES SPRAGUE.

SIN, like a bee, unto thy hive may bring
A little honey, but expect the sting. WATKYNS.

(*See also* THE FALL, FRAILTY, TEMPTATION.)

SINAI—THE LAW.

THE law was our schoolmaster to bring us unto Christ, that we might be justified by faith. GALATIANS, iii, 24.

For Christ is the end of the law for righteousness to every one that believeth. ROMANS, x, 4.

The law is holy; and the commandment holy, and just, and good. ROMANS, vii, 12.

THOSE laws which from Mount Sinai
Jehovah, clothed with terrors, while thick clouds
And darkness wrapt him round, pronounced, in sounds
Which chilled the hearts of those we heard, and froze
Their very blood. Beneath His awful feet
Earth trembled, and the lofty mountain shook;
Hoarse thunder growled, and livid lightnings flashed,
While sounds of horror and distress amid
The howling wilderness were heard.

WILLIAM HODSON.

FROM Sinai's top Jehovah gave the law,
Life for obedience, death for every flaw.
When the great Sovereign would His will express,
He gives a perfect rule, what can He less?
And guards it with a sanction as severe
As vengeance can inflict, or sinners fear:
Else His own glorious rights He would disclaim,
And man might safely trifle with His name.
He bids him glow with unremitting love
To all on earth, and to Himself above
Condemns the injurious deed, the slanderous tongue,
The thought that meditates a brother's wrong;
Brings not alone the more conspicuous part—
His conduct—to the test, but tries his heart.

COWPER.

THE mountain rocked round Sinai's trembling sides;
In gloomy spires the dreadful smoke arose;
Angelic trumpets pierced the ethereal vault;
Wide-echoing thunder rent the conscious air;
Fierce lightning shot its terrors through the sky;
All nature spake, and with convulsive shock
Gave awful proof of the descending God.

SAMUEL HAYES.

GOD from the Mount of Sinai, whose grey top
Shall tremble, He descending, will Himself,
In thunder, lightning, and loud tempest's sound,
Ordain them laws; part such as appertain
To civil justice, part religious rites
Of sacrifice, informing them by types
And shadows, of that destined Seed to bruise
The serpent, by what means He shall achieve
Mankind's deliverance. But the voice of God
To mortal ear is dreadful! They beseech
That Moses might repeat to them His will,
And terror cease. He grants what they besought,
Instructed that to God is no access
Without Mediator, whose high office now
Moses in figure bears, to introduce
One greater, of whose day he shall foretell.

MILTON.

SLANDER—FALSEHOOD—SOPHISTRY.

Thou shalt not bear false witness against thy neighbour. Exodus, xx, 16.

Lying lips are abomination to the Lord. Proverbs, xii, 22.

Woe unto them that call evil good, and good evil; that put darkness for light, and light for darkness; that put bitter for sweet, and sweet for bitter. Isaiah, v, 20.

No, 'tis slander,
Whose edge is sharper than the sword; whose tongue
Out-venoms all the worms of Nile; whose breath
Rides on the posting wind, and doth belie
All corners of the world; kings, queens, and states,
Maids, matrons, nay, the secrets of the grave,
The viperous slander enters. Shakspeare.

The hint malevolent, the look oblique,
The obvious satire, or implied dislike,
The sneer equivocal, the harsh reply,
And all the cruel language of the eye;
The artful injury, whose venomed dart
Scarce wounds the hearing, while it stabs the heart;
The guarded phrase, whose meaning kills.
Hannah More.

Sin ever must
Be tortured with the rack of his own frame;
For he that holds no faith, shall find no trust,
But, sowing wrong, is sure to reap the same.
Daniel.

Lying's a certain mark of cowardice:
And when the tongue forgets its honesty,
The heart and hand may drop their functions too,
And nothing worthy be resolved or done.
Thomas Southern.

Woe unto those that countenance a sin,
Siding with vice that it may credit win,
By their unhallowed vote; that do benight
The truth with error, putting dark for light,
And light for dark; that call an evil good,
And would by vice have virtue understood.

Bishop King.

Sophistry cleaves close to and protects
Sin's rotten trunk, concealing its defects:
Mortals, whose pleasures are their only care,
First wish to be imposed on, and then are;
And lest the fulsome artifice should fail,
Themselves will hide its coarseness with a veil.
Not more industrious are the just and true
To give to virtue what is virtue's due—
The praise of wisdom, comeliness, and worth,
And call her charms to public notice forth—
Than vice's mean and disingenuous race
To hide the shocking features of her face.
Her form with dress and lotion they repair;
Then kiss their idol, and pronounce her fair.

Cowper.

(*See also* Tongue.)

SOLOMON.

And God said to Solomon, Because this was in thy heart, and thou hast not asked riches, wealth, or honour, nor the life of thine enemies, neither yet hast asked long life; but hast asked wisdom and knowledge for thyself that thou mayest judge my people, over whom I have made thee king:

Wisdom and knowledge is granted unto thee; and I will give thee riches, and wealth, and honour, such as none of the kings have had that have been before thee, neither shall there any after thee have the like. II. Chronicles, i, 11, 12.

'T was thee
The Almighty chose among the sons of men,
To dedicate a temple to His name,
Where He, whose awful presence fills the vast
Immensity of space, who makes the clouds
His chariot, rides sublime the whirlwind's wing,
And guides the raging storm, would deign to dwell,
And make His presence known. The exalted task
Thy wisdom worthily performed.

William Hodson.

In wealth, in power, tranquillity, and fame,
His mightier son, high-favoured Solomon,
Serene in strength, and dreadful without war,
Reigns jubilant: in knowledge peerless he,
With proverb, meditation, holy song,
Exalts the soul; while o'er his laws preside
Truth uncorrupt, integrity severe,
By keen discernment led. With lustrous train
See Sheba's queen, to prove his wisdom come,
And kings from every realm, admiring, hear
His varied eloquence; admiring, view
Magnificence and regal state profuse
Beyond compare.

Charles Hoyle.

But who is he, deep musing? In his mind
He seems to weigh, in reason's scales, mankind;
Fixed contemplation holds his steady eyes—
I know the sage, the wisest of the wise,
Blest with all man could wish, or prince obtain,
Yet his great heart pronounced those blessings vain.

Bp. Lowth.

A righteous sceptre in Jerusalem
Reigned over Israel; and the arts of peace
In higher honour placed King David's son,
Than all the father's fierce and weary wars.
Plenty and comfort blessed the labouring poor,
And splendour graced the noble and the wise:
Silver was nothing counted; massive gold
Adorned the temple and the royal board,
And richly-laden ships, from distant shores,
Swelled the king's tribute and the people's wealth.
Worthier than gold, than jewels far more rare,
Was the king's wisdom; all the people bowed
Before the mighty mind of Solomon,
For God was with him.

H. H. Weld.

THE SOUL.

And the Lord God formed man of the dust of the ground, and breathed into his nostrils the breath of life, and man became a living soul. Genesis, ii, 7.

For what is a man profited, if he shall gain the whole world, and lose his own soul? Or what shall a man give in exchange for his soul? Matthew, xvi, 16.

Though life, since finite, has no ill excuse
For being but in finite objects learned,
Yet sure the soul was made for little use,
Unless it be in infinites concerned.

Sir William Davenant.

But Thou which didst man's soul of nothing make,
And when to nothing it was fallen again,
To make it new, the form of man didst take,
And, God with God, becam'st a man with men:
Thou that hast fashioned twice this soul of ours,
So that she is by double title thine;
Thou only know'st her nature and her powers,
Her subtile form Thou only canst define.

Sir John Davies.

For from the birth
Of mortal man, the sovereign Maker said,
That not in humble, nor in brief delight,
Not in the fading echoes of renown,
Power's purple robe, nor pleasure's flowery lap,
The Soul should find enjoyment: but from these
Turning, disdainful, to an equal good,
Through all the ascent of things enlarge her view,
Till every bound at length should disappear,
And infinite perfection close the scene. Akenside

DEARLY pays the soul
For lodging ill; too dearly rents her day. YOUNG.

FAR beneath
A soul immortal, is a mortal joy. YOUNG.

THE soul on earth is an immortal guest,
Condemned to starve at an unreal feast:
A spark, which upward tends by nature's force;
A stream, diverted from its parent source;
A drop, dissevered from the boundless sea;
A moment, parted from eternity;
A pilgrim, panting for the rest to come;
An exile, anxious for his native home.
HANNAH MORE.

THAT mysterious thing,
Which hath no limit from the walls of sense,—
No chill from hoary time,—with pale decay
No fellowship,—but shall stand forth unchanged,
Unscorched amid the resurrection fires,
To bear its boundless lot of good or ill.
MRS. SIGOURNEY.

THE Soul!—the Soul!—with its eye of fire,
Thus, thus shall it soar when its foes expire;
It shall spread its wings o'er the ills that pained,
The evils that shadowed, the sins that stained;
It shall dwell where no rushing cloud hath sway,
And the pageants of earth shall have melted away.
MRS. SIGOURNEY.

THE soul of man (let man in homage bow
Who names his soul) a native of the skies!
High-born and free, her freedom should maintain,
Unsold, unmortgaged for earth's little bribes.
YOUNG.

Poor soul, the centre of my sinful earth,
Fooled by those rebel powers that thee array,
Why dost thou pine within, and suffer dearth,
Painting thy outward walls so costly gay?
Why so large cost, having so short a lease,
Dost thou upon thy fading mansion spend?
Shall worms, inheritors of this excess,
Eat up thy charge? Is this thy body's end?
Then, soul, live thou upon thy servant's loss,
And let that pine to aggravate thy store;
Buy terms divine in selling hours of dross;
Within be fed, without be rich no more;
So shalt thou feed on death, that feeds on men;
And, death once dead, there's no more dying then.

SHAKSPEARE.

(*See also* IMMORTALITY.)

SUPERSTITION—BIGOTRY.

Now the Spirit speaketh expressly that in the latter times some shall depart from the faith, giving heed to seducing spirits and doctrines of devils;

Speaking lies in hypocrisy; having their conscience seared with a hot iron;

Forbidding to marry, and commanding to abstain from meats which God hath created to be received with thanksgiving, of them which believe and know the truth. ROMANS, IV, 1–3.

FELL Superstition leads
Her horrid train, engendered in the womb
Of her own mad imaginings — remorse,
And dark distrust, and phrenzied hate, and fear,
Blackening the liquid air, the bright-eyed earth,
The trust-inspiring stars.

A. ALEXANDER.

CEREMONY leads her bigots forth,
Prepared to fight for shadows of no worth;
While truths on which eternal things depend,
Find not, or hardly find, a single friend;
As soldiers watch the signal of command,
They learn to bow, to kneel, to sit, to stand;
Happy to fill religion's vacant place
With hollow form, and gesture, and grimace.

COWPER.

VISIONS and inspirations some expect
Their course here to direct.
Like senseless chemists, their own wealth destroy,
Imaginary gold to enjoy.
So stars appear to drop to us from the sky,
And gild the passage as they fly;
But when they fall, and meet the opposing ground,
What but a sordid slime is found? COWLEY.

CAN wars and jars, and fierce contention,
Swol'n hatred, and consuming envy, spring
From piety? No; 't is opinion
That makes the riven Heaven with trumpets ring,
And thundering engine murderous balls outsling,
And send men's groaning ghosts to lower shade
Of horrid hell. This the wide world doth bring
To devastation — makes mankind to fade:
Such direful things doth false religion persuade.

HENRY MORE.

MOCK not flesh and blood
With solemn reverence. SHAKSPEARE.

HEART-CHILLING Superstition! thou can'st glaze
Even pity's eye with her own frozen tear.

COLERIDGE.

But hence, far hence be ostentatious pomp,
And superstition's tinsel. What avails
The splendid temple, decorated shrine?
What all the pageantry of laboured art?
Can God's pervading eye, like the frail sense
Of mortals, be deluded by the guise
Of outward beauty? SAMUEL HAYES

(*See also* MARTYRDOM.)

SYCOPHANCY—CUSTOM—FASHION

THOU shalt not follow a multitude to do evil. EXODUS, xxiii, 2.
Be not conformed to this world. ROMANS, xii, 2.
Meddle not with him that flattereth with his lips. PROVERBS, xx, 19.
A man that flattereth his neighbour, spreadeth a net for his feet. PROVERBS, xxix, 5.
A wise man feareth, and departeth from evil. PROVERBS, xiv, 16.

CUSTOM does often reason over-rule,
And only serves for reason to the fool.
ROCHESTER

PRACTISED their master's notions to embrace,
Repeat his maxims, and reflect his face;
With every wild absurdity comply,
And view each object with another's eye;
To shake with laughter ere the jest they hear,
To pour, at will, the counterfeited tear;
And as their patron hints the cold or heat,
To shake in dog-days, in December sweat:
How, when competitors like these contend,
Can surly virtue hope to find a friend?
DR. JOHNSON.

AH, spare your idol! Think him human still;
Charms he may have, but he has frailties too!
COWPER.

AS love of pleasure into pain betrays,
So most grow infamous through love of praise.
But whence for praise can such an ardour rise,
When those who bring that incense we despise?
For such the vanity of great and small,
Contempt goes round, and all men laugh at all.
POPE.

WHAT custom wills, in all things should we do 't,
The dust on antique time would lie unswept,
And mountainous error be too highly heaped
For truth to over-peer. SHAKSPEARE.

HE does me double wrong
That wounds me with the flatteries of his tongue.
SHAKSPEARE.

PARENT of wicked, bane of honest deeds,
Pernicious flattery! thy malignant seeds
In an ill hour, and by a fatal hand,
Sadly diffused o'er virtue's gleby land,
With rising pride amidst the corn appear,
And choke the hopes and harvest of the year.
PRIOR.

NOR custom, nor example, nor vast numbers
Of such as do offend, make less the sin.
For each particular crime, a strict account
Will be exacted; and that comfort which
The damned pretend fellows in misery,
Takes nothing from their torments. MASSINGER.

HABITS are soon assumed, but when we strive
To strip them off, 't is being flayed alive!

COWPER.

AWAY with custom! 't is the plea of fools
Where crimes enormous, that debase the man,
Rise in their own defence; the long-drawn roll
Where the ascent and fall of states or men
Stand variously pourtrayed, what is it else
Than a sad series of collective guilt,
Whence custom for each wantonness of ill
May draw the shameful precedent? C. P. LAYARD.

SYMPATHY—COURTESY—KINDNESS.

FINALLY, be all of one mind, having compassion one of another; love as brethren, be pitiful, be courteous. I. PETER, iii, 8.

Jesus wept. JOHN, xi, 35.

To him that is afflicted, pity should be showed from his friend. JOB, vi, 14.

Shouldest not thou have had compassion on thy fellow-servant, even as I had pity on thee? MATTHEW, xviii, 33.

NO radiant pearl which crested fortune wears,
No gem that, sparkling, hangs from beauty's ears,
Not the bright stars which night's blue arch adorn,
Nor rising sun that gilds the vernal morn,
Shine with such lustre as the tear that breaks
For others' woe, down virtue's lovely cheeks.

————————.

SPEAK gently!——'t is a little thing
Dropped in the heart's deep well;
The good, the joy that it may bring,
Eternity shall tell. DAVID BATES.

Our fellow-sufferer yet retains
A fellow-feeling of our pains;
And still remembers, in the skies,
His tears, and agonies, and cries.

In every pang that rends the heart,
The Man of Sorrows had a part;
He sympathizes in our grief,
And to the sufferer sends relief. John Logan.

The Son of God, in doing good,
  Was fain to look to Heaven, and sigh;
And shall the heirs of sinful blood
  Seek joy unmixed in charity?
God will not let love's work impart
Full solace, lest it steal the heart;
Be thou content in tears to sow,
Blessing, like Jesus, in thy woe. Keble.

Where bright imagination reigns,
The fine-wrought spirit feels acuter pains;
Where glow exalted sense and taste refined,
There keener anguish rankles in the mind;
There, feeling is diffused in every part,
Thrills in each nerve, and lives in all the heart;
And those whose generous souls each tear would keep
From others' hearts, are born themselves to weep.
Hannah More.

And tears once filled His eye
  Beside a mortal's grave,
Who left His throne on high
  The lost to seek and save.
And fresh, from age to age,
  Their memory shall be kept,
While man shall bless the page
  Which tells that Jesus wept! Bernard Barton.

Sweet sensibility! thou keen delight!
Unprompted moral! sudden sense of right!
Perception exquisite! fair virtue's seed!
Thou quick precursor of the liberal deed!
Thou hasty conscience! reason's blushing morn!
Instinctive kindness, ere reflection's born!
Prompt sense of equity! to thee belongs
The swift redress of unexamined wrong!
Eager to serve, the cause perhaps untried,
But always apt to choose the suffering side!

Hannah More.

Hast thou no human friend
To whom in hours like these to turn,
When thine o'erburdened soul will yearn
Its bitterness to end?
O, still despair not — there is One
To whom sad hearts have often gone —
Though rich the gifts for which they pray,
None ever came unblest away:
Then, though all earthly ties be riven,
Smile, for thou hast a Friend in Heaven.

Miss M. H. Rand.

His sweetest mind,
'Tween mildness tempered and low courtesy,
Could leave as soon to be, as not be kind:
Churlish despite ne'er looked from his calm eye,
Much less commanded in his gentle heart.
To baser men fair looks he would impart;
Nor could he cloak ill thoughts in complimental art.

Phineas Fletcher.

TEMPTATION.

LEAD us not into temptation. MATTHEW, vi, 13.

Watch and pray, that ye enter not into temptation: for the spirit indeed is willing but the flesh is weak. MATTHEW, xxvi, 41.

There hath no temptation taken you but such as is common to man: but God is faithful, who will not suffer you to be tempted above that ye are able; but will, with the temptation, also make a way to escape, that ye may be able to bear it. I. CORINTHIANS, x, 13.

Brethren, if a man be overtaken in a fault, ye which are spiritual, restore such an one in the spirit of meekness; considering thyself, lest thou also be tempted. GALATIANS, vi, 1.

PERHAPS thou dost but try me—yet take heed!
There's naught so monstrous but the mind of man,
In some condition, may be brought to approve:
Theft, sacrilege, treason, and parricide,
When flattering opportunity enticed,
And desperation drove, have been committed
By those who once would start to hear them named.
LILLO.

No mortal footing treads so firm in virtue
As always to abide the slippery path,
Nor deviate with the bias. HENRY BROOKE.

VIRTUE'S no virtue whiles it lives secure;
When difficulty waits on't, then 'tis pure.
JOHN QUARLES.

THEY that fear the adder's sting will not come
Near her hissing. GEORGE CHAPMAN.

HOW oft the sight of means to do ill deeds,
Makes ill deeds done! SHAKSPEARE.

Ay me! how many perils do enfold
The righteous man, to make him daily fall!
Were not that heavenly grace doth him uphold,
And stedfast truth acquit him out of all.

SPENSER.

Thus the fond heart, by some dear passion swayed,
Frail and corrupt, is soon to sin betrayed;
Vice by degrees a firm possession gains,
And o'er the willing soul despotic reigns;
Dreadful no more the withered hag appears,
Pursued by doubts, and harrowed up by fears:
Tricked out in lavish ornaments, she smiles,
A dangerous Circe fraught with chainful wiles.

JAMES SCOTT.

O, trembling, learn
That Peter, too, was chosen by his Lord,
Admonished, and forewarned, and resolute,
And sworn to persevere in righteousness;
Yet in the hour of trial, Peter fell.
Into temptation lead us not, O God!
But with Thy hand deliver us from ill!

COCKBURN.

A slight, a single glance,
And shot at random, often has brought home
A sudden fever to the throbbing heart
Of envy, rancour, or impure desire.
We see, we hear with peril; safety dwells
Remote from multitude. YOUNG.

Oftentimes, to win us to our harm,
The instruments of darkness tell us truths;
Win us with honest trifles, to betray us
In deepest consequence. SHAKSPEARE.

BETWEEN the acting of a fearful thing
And the first motion, all the interim is
Like a phantasma, or a hideous dream:
The genius and the mortal instruments
Are then in council; and the state of man,
Like to a little kingdom, suffers then
The nature of an insurrection. SHAKSPEARE.

HIS unexhausted mine the sordid vice
Avarice shows, and virtue is his price.
Here various motives his ambition raise—
Power, pomp, and splendour, and the thirst of praise.
There beauty woos him with expanded arms;
E'en Bacchanalian madness has its charms.
Nor these alone, whose pleasures less refined
Might well alarm the most unguarded mind,
Seek to supplant his inexperienced youth,
Or lead him devious from the path of truth;
Hourly allurements on his passions press,
Safe in themselves, but dangerous in excess.

COWPER.

THANKFULNESS—GRATITUDE.

LIGHT is sown for the righteous, and gladness for the upright in heart. PSALM xcvii, 11.

A merry heart maketh a cheerful countenance. PROVERBS, xv, 13.

By Him therefore let us offer the sacrifice of praise to God continually, that is, the fruit of our lips, giving thanks to His name. HEBREWS, xiii, 15.

Giving thanks always for all things to God and the Father, in the name of our Lord Jesus Christ. EPHESIANS, v, 20.

LOVE rules the universal heart of man
Through all its range of age, rank, place, and mood;
But thou, since first in Heaven her reign began,
Her holiest offspring art, O Gratitude!
Man's hard, stern heart grows soft, with thee imbued,
And sweeter swells the fount of woman's love:—
O, let thy forms in dwellings wide and rude,
Nor doubt, nor scorn, in polished bosoms move:
Since, wheresoe'er thou be, thou comest from above!

GEO. H. COLTON.

AND, as the grateful peasant cried,
To whom earth's goods thou hadst denied,
Blessing his God, through every ill,
The light of day was left him still;
So I give thanks, whate'er befall,
Thou still hast left what gladdens all.

THOMAS WARD.

NOT thankful when it pleaseth *me*;
As if Thy blessings had spare days:
But such a heart whose pulse may be
Thy praise.

GEORGE HERBERT.

THE cherub Gratitude — behold her eyes!
With love and gladness weepingly they shed
Ecstatic smiles; the incense that her hands
Uprear, is sweeter than the breath of May,
Caught from the nectarine's blossom, and her voice
Is more than voice can tell; to Him she sings,
To Him who feeds, who clothes, and who adorns,
Who made, and who preserves, whatever dwells
In air, in steadfast earth, or fickle sea. SMART.

HE whose days in wilful woe are worn,
The grace of his Creator doth despise,
That will not use His gifts, for thankless niggardise.
SPENSER.

A BLESSING given to those will not disburse
Some thanks, is little better than a curse.
Great Giver of all blessings, Thou that art
The Lord of gifts, give me a grateful heart;
O, give me that, or keep Thy favours from me!
I wish no blessings with a vengeance to me.
FRANCIS QUARLES.

WHILE this immortal spark of heavenly flame
Distends my breast, and animates my frame,
To Thee my ardent praises shall be borne
On the first breeze that wakes the blushing morn;
The latest star shall hear the pleasing sound,
And nature in full choir shall join around.
When full of Thee, my soul excursive flies
Through earth, air, ocean, or Thy regal skies;
From world to world new wonders still I find,
And all the Godhead flashes on my mind.
When, winged with whirlwinds, vice shall take its flight
To the deep bosom of eternal night,
To Thee my soul shall endless praises pay:
Join, men and angels! join the exalted lay.
BLACKLOCK

TIME.

SEE, then, that ye walk circumspectly, not as fools, but as wise,
Redeeming the time, because the days are evil. EPHESIANS, v, 15, 16.

A thousand years, in Thy sight, are but as yesterday when it is past, and as a watch in the night. PSALM xc, 4.

Man that is born of a woman is of few days, and full of trouble. JOB, xiv, 1.

A MOMENT is a mighty thing
Beyond the soul's imagining;
For in it, though we trace it not,
How much there crowds of varied lot;
How much of life, life cannot see
Darts onward to eternity! ROBERT MONTGOMERY.

ALL hail, thou viewless one! whose lonely wings
Sweep o'er the earth, unwearied and sublime!
Mysterious agent of the King of kings,
Whom conquerors obey, and man calls Time!
Compared with thee, even centuries in their might,
Seem but like atoms in the sun's broad ray;
Thou sweep'st them on, in thy majestic flight,
Scattering them from thy plumes, like drops of spray
Cast from the ocean, in its scornful play.
MRS. AMELIA B. WELBY.

IT is ten o'clock:
Thus may we see how the world wags;
'T is but an hour ago since it was nine;
And after an hour more, 't will be eleven;
And so from hour to hour we ripe and ripe,
And so from hour to hour we rot and rot,
And thereby hangs a tale. SHAKSPEARE.

Consider every hour
Of life, each moment, as an interval
On which eternal happiness depends.

Samuei Hayes.

Time's glory is to calm contending kings,
To unmask falsehood, and bring truth to light;
To stamp the seal of time on aged things,
To wake the morn, and sentinel the night,
To wrong the wronger, till he render right.

Shakspeare.

Be silent and still, for his end draweth near,
And watch with a quivering breath;
No mortal eye beheld his birth,
But all shall behold his death,
For the nations from every land and clime
Shall gather to gaze on the close of Time.

The Moon shall look down with a tearful eye,
And the Sun shall withhold his fire,
And the hoary Earth, all parched and dry,
Shall flame for his funeral pyre,
When the Angel, that standeth on earth and shore,
Proclaimeth that "Time shall be no more!"

Edward Pollok.

O Time! the fatal wreck of mortal things,
That draws oblivion's curtain over kings,
Their sumptuous monuments, men know them not,
Their names, without a record, are forgot,
Their parts, their ports, their pomp's all laid i' the dust,
Nor wit, nor gold, nor buildings, 'scape Time's rust;
But he whose name is 'graved in the white stone,
Shall last and shine when all of these are gone.

Mrs. Anne Bradstreet.

Heir of eternal life, reflect, O man,
What to thyself thou owest, whose endless doom
Hangs on this squandered moment, or the next.
George Bally.

Time destroyed,
Is suicide where more than blood is spilt. Young.

Throw years away!
Throw empires, and be blameless. Moments seize
Heavens on their wing: a moment we may wish,
When worlds want wealth to buy. Young.

Now! It is gone.—Our brief hours travel post,
Each with its thought or deed, its Why or How:
But know each parting hour gives up a ghost,
To dwell within thee—an eternal Now!
Coleridge.

Before my breath, like blazing flax,
Man and his marvels pass away;
And changing empires wane and wax,
Are founded, flourish, and decay.

Redeem mine hours—the space is brief—
While in my glass the sand grains shiver,
And measureless thy joy or grief,
When Time and thee shall part, for ever!
Sir Walter Scott.

O Time! than gold more sacred; more a load
Than lead to fools, and fools reputed wise.
What moment granted man without account?
What years are squandered, wisdom's debt unpaid!
Our wealth in days all due to that discharge.
Young.

TOIL—LABOUR.

IN the sweat of thy face shalt thou eat bread, till thou return unto the ground
GENESIS, iii, 19.

IN labourers' ballads oft more piety
God finds, than in Te Deums' melody.

DR. DONNE.

CHEERED with the view, man went to till the ground
From whence he rose; sentenced indeed to toil,
As to a punishment, yet (even in wrath
So merciful is Heaven) this toil became
The solace of his woes, the sweet employ
Of many a live-long hour, and surest guard
Against disease and death.

BP. PORTEUS.

(*See also* WORKS.)

THE TONGUE.

If any man among you seem to be religious, and bridleth not his tongue, but deceiveth his own heart, that man's religion is vain. James, i, 26.

The tongue is a little member, and boasteth great things. Behold, how great a matter a little fire kindleth!

And the tongue is a fire, a world of iniquity: so is the tongue among our members, that it defileth the whole body, and setteth on fire the course of nature; and it is set on fire of hell. James, iii, 5, 6.

The tongue can no man tame; it is an unruly evil, full of deadly poison.

Therewith bless we God, even the Father; and therewith curse we men, which are made after the similitude of God.

Out of the same mouth proceedeth blessing and cursing. My brethren, these things ought not so to be. James, iii, 8—10.

The tongue of the wise useth knowledge aright, but the mouth of fools poureth out foolishness. Proverbs, xv, 2.

A wholesome tongue is a tree of life, but perverseness therein is a breach in the spirit. Proverbs, xv, 4.

The man
In whom this spirit entered, was undone.
His tongue was set on fire of hell, his heart
Was black as death, his legs were faint with haste
To propagate the lie his soul had framed.

Pollok.

Like a moral pestilence,
Before his breath the healthy shoots and blooms
Of social joy and happiness, decayed. Pollok.

Swear not; an oath is like a dangerous dart,
Which, shot, rebounds to strike the shooter's heart.

Thomas Randolph.

First think; and if thy thoughts approve thy will,
Then speak; and, after, that thou speakest fulfil.

Thomas Randolph.

O, ASK of Heaven to teach thy tongue
  A true, a reverent tone;
Full oft attuned to praise and prayer,
  And still to vice unknown!
And rather be it mute for aye,
  Than yield its music sweet
To malice, scorn, impurity,
  To slander or deceit! MRS. OSGOOD.

ILL deeds are doubled with an evil word.
SHAKSPEARE.

SACRED interpreter of human thought,
How few respect, or use thee as they ought!
But all shall give account of every wrong,
Who dare dishonour or defile the tongue;
Who prostitute it in the cause of vice,
Or sell their glory at the market price! COWPER

WHEN thou dost tell another's jest, therein
Omit the oaths which true wit cannot need:
Pick out of tales the mirth, but not the sin:
He pares his apple that would cleanly feed.
HERBERT.

DARE to be true; nothing can need a lie
A fault which needs it most, grows two thereby.
HERBERT.

REPROVE not, in their wrath, incensed men;
Good counsel comes clean out of season then:
But when his fury is appeased, and past,
He will conceive his fault, and mend at last.
When he is cool and calm, then utter it;
No man gives physic in the midst o' the fit.
RANDOLPH

MARK how the scorpion falsehood
Coils round in its own perplexity, and fixes
Its sting in its own head. COLERIDGE.

(*See also* SLANDERS, *&c.*)

TREACHERY—SUSPICION.

YEA, mine own familiar friend, in whom I trusted, which did eat of my bread, hath lifted up his heel against me. PSALM xli, 9.

Surely in vain the net is spread in the sight of any bird. PROVERBS, i, 17.

Faithful are the wounds of a friend, but the kisses of an enemy are deceitful. PROVERBS, xxvi, 6.

Deceit is in the heart of them that imagine evil. PROVERBS, xii, 20.

FOR pleasures, vanities, and hates,
The compact we renew,
And Judas rises in our hearts—
We sell our Saviour too.
How, for some moments' vain delights,
We will embitter years,
And in our youth lay up for age
Only remorse and tears. MISS LANDON.

A HOLY name, and words of natural duty,
Are blasted by a thankless traitor's utterance.
COLERIDGE.

So Judas kissed his Master,
And cried, All hail!—when as he meant—all harm.
SHAKSPEARE.

THOUGH those that are betrayed
Do feel the treason sharply, yet the traitor
Stands in worse case of woe. SHAKSPEARE.

FILIAL ingratitude!
Is it not as this mouth should tear this hand,
For lifting food to 't? SHAKSPEARE.

WHOSE own hard dealing teaches them suspect
The thoughts of others. SHAKSPEARE.

NOT war alone, (though still the growing earth
Has known the thunders of his iron car,)
But all the false humanities which lurk
Beneath the forms of peace; the smile that stabs,
The law that is a snare, the treacherous gifts
Of Commerce, joying in her fair deceits,
By turns supply the enginery of ill.
A. ALEXANDER.

O, THERE are moments of our lives, when such
As will not help to lift us, strike us down!
When the green bough just bends so near our clutch,
When the light rope so easily was thrown,
That they are murderers that beheld us drown.
Well spoke the poet-heart so tried by woe,
That there are hours when left, despairing, lone,
"Each idle on-looker appears a foe,"
For hate can scarce do worse than no compassion show.
MRS. NORTON.

WHEN man from bliss, through disobedience, fell,
Within his mind degenerate was born
The fiend Suspicion, child of conscious guilt
And trembling fear; she taught him to perceive,
As if reflected back, in other minds
The numerous ills he nourished in his own,
And with the jaundiced eye of jealousy
To scan another's deeds. LAYARD.

TRUST IN GOD—DIVINE PROTECTION.

THEREFORE take no thought, saying, What shall we eat? or, What shall we drink or, Wherewithal shall we be clothed?

(For after all these things do the Gentiles seek:) for your heavenly Father knoweth that ye have need of all these things. MATTHEW, vi, 31, 32.

God is our refuge and strength, a very present help in trouble. PSALM xlvi, 1.

I know whom I have believed, and am persuaded that He is able to keep that which I have committed to Him against that day. II. TIMOTHY, i, 12.

I SHOULD on God alone so much depend,
That I should need nor wealth nor other friend.

GEORGE WITHER.

LORD, mail my heart with faith, and be my shield,
And if a world confront me, I'll not yield.

FRANCIS QUARLES.

IN Thee, dear Lord, my pensive soul respires,
Thou art the fulness of my choice desires;
Thou art that sacred Spring, whose waters burst
In streams to him that seeks with holy thirst.

FRANCIS QUARLES.

AND though sometimes Thou seem'st Thy face to hide
As one that had withdrawn his love from me,
'Tis that my faith may to the full be tried,
And that I may thereby the better see
How weak I am, when not upheld by Thee!

THOMAS ELLWOOD.

GOD shall be my hope,
My stay, my guide, and lantern to my feet.

SHAKSPEARE.

THE Christian's trust — the Christian's trust —
    Nurtured by promises;
Pure through corruption's moth and rust;
Firm amid nature's graves and dust,
    And all life's severed ties.

From "CAPRICES."

HE that doth the ravens feed,
Yea, providently caters for the sparrow,
Be comfort to my age!

SHAKSPEARE.

ON God for all events depend;
You cannot want when God's your friend.
Weigh well your part, and do your best;
Leave to your Maker all the rest.
The hand which formed thee in the womb,
Guides from the cradle to the tomb.

COTTON.

SOME in chariots, some in horses,
  We in God Jehovah, trust;
And, while He our sure resource is,
  They are fallen in the dust:
Save, Jehovah, save and hear us,
  King of glory, King of might;
When we call, be ever near us,—
  Ever for Thy servants fight.

TUPPER.

BUT Thou art true, incarnate Lord!
  Who didst vouchsafe for man to die;
Thy smile is sure, Thy plighted word
  No change can falsify.

I bent before Thy gracious throne,
  And asked for peace with suppliant knee;
And peace was given — nor peace alone,
  But faith, and hope, and ecstacy!

WORDSWORTH

TRUTH—INSPIRATION.

When He, the Spirit of truth, is come, He will guide you unto all truth. John, xvi, 13.

Buy the truth, and sell it not: also wisdom, and instruction, and understanding. Proverbs, xxiii, 23.

Jesus saith unto him, I am the Way, and the Truth, and the Life: no man cometh unto the Father, but by me. John, xiv, 6.

It is the Spirit that beareth witness, because the Spirit is Truth. I. John, v, 6.

The seat of truth is in our secret hearts,
Not in the tongue, which falsehood oft imparts.

Brandon.

Truth is in each flower,
As well as in the solemnest things of God.
Truth is the voice of Nature and of Time—
Truth is the startling monitor within us—
Nought is without it, it comes from the stars,
The golden sun, and every breeze that blows—
Truth, it is God! and God is every where!

William Thompson Bacon.

Truth, crush'd to earth, shall rise again;
The eternal years of God are hers:
But Error, wounded, writhes with pain,
And dies among his worshippers.

Wm. C. Bryant.

Defend the truth; for that who will not die,
A coward is, and gives himself the lie.

Thomas Randolph.

Truth, in her pure simplicity, wants art
To put a feigned blush on. John Ford.

ALL truth is precious, if not all divine,
And what dilates the powers must needs refine.

COWPER.

IMMORTAL Truth! by inspiration taught,
Thou spurn'st the servile chains of human art;
In native majesty arrayed, thou shed'st
Thy radiant beams through all this vale below,
Thy piercing voice resounds through distant climes,
By all distinguished, and by all adored.

CHARLES JENNER.

MARBLE and recording brass decay,
And, like the 'graver's memory, pass away;
The works of man inherit, as is just,
Their author's frailty, and return to dust;
But truth divine for ever stands secure,
Its head is guarded, at its base is sure;
Fixed in the rolling flood of endless years,
The pillar of the eternal plan appears;
The raving storm and dashing wave defies,
Built by that Architect who built the skies.

COWPER.

BUT what is Truth? 'T was Pilate's question, put
To Truth itself, that deigned him no reply.
And wherefore? Will not God impart His light
To them that ask it? Freely,—'tis His joy,
His glory, and His nature, to impart.
But to the proud, uncandid, insincere,
Or negligent enquirer, not a spark. COWPER.

UNBELIEF—DOUBTS.

UNTO the pure, all things are pure; but unto them that are defiled and unbelieving is nothing pure; but even their mind and conscience is defiled. TITUS, i, 15.

Take heed, brethren, lest there be in any of you an evil heart of unbelief, in departing from the Living God. HEBREWS, iii, 12.

For what if some did not believe? Shall then unbelief make the faith of God without effect? ROMANS, iii, 3.

And he that doubteth is damned if he eat, because he eateth not of faith: for whatsoever is not of faith is sin. ROMANS, xiv, 23.

He that believeth on Him is not condemned: but he that believeth not is condemned already, because he hath not believed in the name of the only-begotten Son of God. JOHN, iii, 18.

THE voluptuaries who ne'er forget
One pleasure lost, lose Heaven without regret;
Regret would rouse them, and give birth to prayer;
Prayer would add faith, and faith would fix them there.

COWPER.

HEAVEN on such terms!—they cry with proud disdain,—
Incredible, impossible, and vain!—
Rebel, because 'tis easy to obey;
And scorn, for its own sake, the gracious way.

COWPER.

OUR doubts are traitors,
And make us lose the good we oft might win,
By fearing to attempt. SHAKSPEARE.

OUR infidels are Satan's hypocrites;
Pretend the worst, and at the bottom fail.
When visited by thought (thought will intrude,)
Like him they serve, they tremble, and believe.

YOUNG.

If man sleeps on, untaught by what he sees,
Can he prove infidel to what he feels? YOUNG.

For all thy rankling doubts so sore,
  Love thou thy Saviour still;
Him for thy Lord and God adore,
  And ever do His will.
Though vexing doubts may seem to last,
Let not thy soul be quite o'ercast;
Soon will He show thee all His wounds, and say,
Long have I known thy name—know thou my face alway

KEBLE.

Nice philosophy
May tolerate unlikely arguments,
But Heaven admits no jests! Wits that presumed
On wit too much, by striving how to prove
There was no God with foolish grounds of art,
Discovered first the nearest way to hell,
And filled the world with devilish atheism.
Such questions, youth, are fond; far better 'tis
To bless the sun, than reason why it shines;
Yet he thou talk'st of is above the sun.

JOHN FORD.

Thou canst accomplish all things, Lord of might!
And every thought is naked to Thy sight.
But O, Thy ways are wonderful, and lie
Beyond the deepest reach of mortal eye.
Oft have I heard of Thine Almighty power,
But never saw Thee till this dreadful hour.
O'erwhelmed with shame, the Lord of life I see,
Abhor myself, and give my soul to Thee.
Nor shall my weakness tempt Thine anger more:
Man was not made to *question*, but *adore*.

YOUNG.

PARTS push us on to pride, and pride to shame;
Pert infidelity is wit's cockade
To grace the brazen brow that braves the skies.

YOUNG.

SCEPTIC! no more the dazzling beams withstand,
Bright emanations of a sapient God;
But, taught by nature, nature's Lord adore:
From known effects of order and design,
Rise to the self-existent Cause Supreme:
The depths of wisdom, far as human ken
Can penetrate, explore; and here attain
A foretaste of that knowledge, which, perhaps,
With angels poring o'er the text abstruse,
And in ecstatic admiration lost,
Will, in eternity's unceasing round,
The intuition of thy soul absorb.

GEORGE BALLY.

(*See also* ATHEISM.)

VANITY—FOPPISHNESS.

Is not the life more than meat, and the body than raiment? MATTHEW, vi, 25.

Whose adorning, let it not be that outward adorning of plaiting the hair, and of wearing of gold, or of putting on of apparel;

But let it be the hidden man of the heart, in that which is not corruptible, even the ornament of a meek and quiet spirit, which is in the sight of God of great price. I. PETER, iii, 3, 4.

WITH eager feeding, food doth choke the feeder:
Light vanity, insatiate cormorant,
Consuming means, soon preys upon itself.

SHAKSPEARE.

WHAT!—will a man play tricks, will he indulge
A silly fond conceit of his fair form,
And just proportion, fashionable mien,
And pretty face, in presence of his God?

COWPER.

A HEAVENLY mind
May be indifferent to her house of clay,
And slight the hovel, as beneath her care;
But how a body so fantastic, trim,
And quaint in its deportment and attire,
Can lodge a heavenly mind, demands a doubt.

COWPER.

HE that is of reason's skill bereft,
And wants the staff of wisdom him to stay,
Is like a ship in midst of tempest left,
Withouten helm or pilot her to sway;
Full sad and dreadful is that ship's event:
So is the man that wants intendiment. SPENSER.

'T IS an old maxim in the schools,
That vanity 's the food of fools.
SWIFT.

THE joy that vain amusement gives,
O, sad conclusion that it brings,
The honey of a crowded hive
Defended by a thousand stings.
'T is thus the world rewards the fools
That live upon her treacherous smiles;
She leads them, blindfold, by her rules,
And ruins all whom she beguiles.
COWPER.

How vain a thing
It is, for men to take a pride in that
Which was at first an emblem of their shame.
MAY.

NATURE may be vain-glorious, well as art:
We may as lowly before God appear,
Drest with a glorious pearl, as with a tear.
JOHN CLEVELAND.

(*See also* EARTH, PRIDE, SELF, *&c.*)

VIRTUE—THE VIRTUES.

THE fruit of the Spirit is love, joy, peace, long-suffering, gentleness, goodness, faith, Meekness, temperance: against such there is no law. GALATIANS, v, 22, 23.

Finally, brethren, whatsoever things are true, whatsoever things are honest, whatsoever things are just, whatsoever things are pure, whatsoever things are lovely, whatsoever things are of good report, if there be any virtue, and if there be any praise, think on these things. PHILIPPIANS, iv, 8.

Add to your faith, virtue. II. PETER, i, 5.

THERE heavenly knowledge shines in glittering pride,
And patience sits, with meek, submissive smile
Disarming stern oppression; justice there
Erects her rigid test of right and wrong;
And there, with God's own armour all begirt,
Stands fortitude, erect in Christian strength;
There temperance stands with ever-watchful eye,
To curb the passions with a steady rein;
And candour there her golden rule displays,
To act by others as thy heart must wish
They, in like circumstance, should act by thee;
But chiefly there, in ever-fixed seat,
Sits Heaven-born charity. * * *
With such bright guests the Christian mind is stored,
Pledges of truest knowledge, joy, and peace.

CHARLES JENNER.

EVERY vice to virtue is allied,
And thin partitions their weak bounds divide:
To the pale miser, bent with sordid pain,
And brooding, harpy-like, o'er ill-got gain,
His favourite vice the garb of virtue wears,
And, drest by passion, honest thrift appears.

JAMES SCOTT.

O Thou! by whose almighty nod the scale
Of empire rises, or alternate falls,
Send forth the saving Virtues round the land
In bright patrol: white peace and social love;
The tender-looking charity, intent
On gentle deeds, and shedding tears through smiles;
Undaunted truth, and dignity of mind;
Courage composed and keen; sound temperance,
Healthful in heart and look; clear chastity,
With blushes reddening as she moves along,
Disordered at the deep regard she draws;
Rough industry; activity untired,
With copious life informed, and all awake.

Thomson.

God weighs the heart, whom we can never move
By outward actions without inward love.

Watkyns.

Honour is
Virtue's allowed ascent; honour that clasps
All-perfect justice in her arms; that craves
No more respect than what she gives; that does
Nothing but what she'll suffer. Massinger.

WAR—GLORY

FROM whence come wars and fightings among you? Come they not hence, even of our lusts, which war in your members? JAMES, iv, 1.

Thus saith the Lord, Let not the wise man glory in his wisdom, neither let the mighty man glory in his might, let not the rich man glory in his riches:

But let him that glorieth glory in this, that he understandeth and knoweth me, that I am the Lord which exercise loving-kindness, judgment, and righteousness in the earth: for in these things I delight, saith the Lord. JEREMIAH, ix. 23, 24.

For they got not the land in possession by their own sword, neither did their own arm save them. PSALM xliv, 3.

He delighteth not in the strength of the horse: He taketh not pleasure in the legs of a man. PSALM xlvii, 10.

The Lord trieth the righteous; but the wicked, and him that doeth violence, His soul hateth PSALM xi, 5.

SUCH is war!
O heavens! when will the spiritual Sun arise,
And with His beams effulgent, drive away
The mists of error that so long have hung
Their dark, unnatural drapery o'er the mind,
That broods o'er human carnage! when will man
Turn from the path of Cain, and learn to see
A brother without hating? RUFUS DAWES.

A MOURNFUL scroll
Of mighty deeds, all blotted o'er with blood,
And blistered, in its proudest passages,
With woman's heart-wrung tears; while every leaf
Of deathless laurel which enrolled his name,
Was dripping with the hot and bitter drops,
By misery wrung, from hearts whence he had torn
The loving and beloved. LYDIA JANE PIERSON.

NOR absolutely vain is human praise,
Where human is supported by divine. YOUNG.

And when upon his casque the lurid light
That men call glory dwelt, he turned away,
Disgusted, from the foul phosphoric light
That feeds on death and torture, blood and tears,
And sighs from withering hearts.

Lydia Jane Pierson.

Alas, for human greatness! and alas,
For glory's splendour on a mortal brow!
The stateliest realms must down to ruin pass,
And mightiest monarchs to a mightier bow:
Alas! will death ne'er spare a gallant foe?

C. W. Everest

How like a fiend may man be made,
Plying the foul and monstrous trade
Whose harvest-field is human life,
Whose sickle is the reeking sword!
Quenching, with reckless hands in blood,
Sparks kindled by the breath of God;
Urging the deathless soul, unshriven
Of open guilt, or secret sin,
Before the bar of that pure Heaven,
The holy only, enter in!

J. G. Whittier.

One Cæsar lives — a thousand are forgot. Young.

The proud victor's plume,
The hero's trophied fame, the warrior's wreath
Of blood-dashed laurel — what will these avail
The spirit parting from material things?
One slender leaflet from the tree of peace,
Borne, dove-like, o'er the waste and warring earth,
Is better passport at the gate of Heaven.

Mrs. Sigourney.

O, SHAME to men! devil with devil damned
Firm concord holds, men only disagree
Of creatures rational, though under hope
Of heavenly grace, and God proclaiming peace,
Yet live in hatred, enmity, and strife
Among themselves, and levy cruel wars,
Wasting the earth, each other to destroy;
As if, (which might induce us to accord,)
Man had not hellish foes enough besides,
That day and night for his destruction wait.

MILTON

THERE, under a wide oak, disconsolate,
And drowned in tears, a mournful widow sate.
High in the boughs a murdered father hung;
Beneath, the children round the mother clung:
They cried for food, but 'twas without relief;
For all they had to live upon was grief.
A sorrow so intense, such deep despair,
No creature merely human long could bear.
First in her arms her weeping babes she took,
And with a groan did to her husband look;
Then leaned her head on theirs, and sighing, cried,
"Pity me, Saviour of the world!" and died.

POMFRET.

O WAR, thou son of hell,
Whom angry heavens do make their minister!

SHAKSPEARE.

WATCHFULNESS.

If therefore thou shalt not watch, I will come on thee as a thief, and thou shalt not know what hour I will come upon thee. REVELATIONS, iii, 3.

What I say unto you, I say unto all, watch. MARK, xiii, 37.

But the end of all things is at hand, therefore be ye sober, and watch unto prayer I. PETER, iv, 7.

Awake, thou that sleepest, and arise from the dead, and Christ shall give thee light EPHESIANS, v, 14.

O THOU, who in the garden's shade
Didst wake Thy weary ones again,
Who slumbered at that fearful hour,
Forgetful of Thy pain;

Bend o'er us now, as over them,
And set our sleep-bound spirits free;
Nor leave us slumbering in the watch
Our souls should keep with Thee!

J. G. WHITTIER.

So teach us, Lord, to count our days,
And eye their constant race,
To measure what we want in time,
By wisdom and by grace. CHRISTOPHER PITT.

WATCH, remember, seek, and strive,
Exert thy former pains;
Let thy timely care revive,
And strengthen what remains:
Cleanse thine heart, thy works amend,
Former times to mind recall;
Lest my sudden stroke descend,
And smite thee once for all. COWPER.

Up! 'tis no dreaming time! Awake! Awake!
For He who sits on the high Judge's seat,
Doth in His record mark each wasted hour,
Each idle word. Take heed thy shrinking soul
Find not their weight too heavy, when it stands
At that dread bar from whence is no appeal.
Lo, while ye trifle, the light sand steals on,
Leaving the hour-glass empty, and thy life
Glideth away; — stamp wisdom on its hours.

Mrs. Sigourney.

Lord! we sit and cry to Thee,
  Like the blind beside the way:
Make our darkened souls to see
  The glory of Thy perfect day!
Lord! rebuke our sullen night,
And give Thyself unto our sight! H. H. Milman.

Think not of rest; though dreams be sweet,
Start up, and ply your heavenward feet.
Is not God's oath upon your head,
Ne'er to sink back on slothful bed,
Never again your loins untie,
Nor let your torches waste and die,
Till, when the shadows thickest fall,
Ye hear your Master's midnight call? Keble.

AWAKE!

Thou who shalt wake when the creation sleeps;
When, like a taper, all these suns expire;
When Time, like him of Gaza in his wrath,
Plucking the pillars that support the world,
In Nature's ample ruins lies intombed;
And midnight, universal midnight reigns!

Young

GIRD thee, and do thy watching well,
Duty's Christian sentinel!
Sloth and slumber never had part
In the warrior's will, or the patriot's heart;
Soldier of God, on an enemy's shore,
Slumber and sloth thrall *thee* no more! TUPPER.

WIDOWHOOD.

A FATHER of the fatherless, and a Judge of the widows, is God in His holy habitation. PSALM, lxviii, 5.

Learn to do well; seek judgment, relieve the oppressed, judge the fatherless, plead for the widow. ISAIAH, i, 17.

The blessing of him that was ready to perish came upon me, and I caused the widow's heart to sing for joy. JOB, xxix, 13.

As bereavement bendeth o'er the brow
Buoyant so lately, cold and quiet now,
Unbidden memory through her tears can trace
Each cherished outline of that placid face;
And fond affection linger by the bed,
To fix the last expression of the dead.

From "CAPRICES.

MY wife! how fondly shall thy memory
Be shrined within the chamber of my heart!
Thy virtuous worth was only known to me,
And I can feel how hard it is to part.
Farewell, sweet spirit! thou shalt ever be
A star to guide me up to Heaven and thee.

J. L. CHESTER.

SEE, but glance briefly, sorrow-worn and pale,
Those sunken cheeks beneath the widow's veil;
Alone she wanders where with *him* she trod,
No arm to stay her, but she leans on God.

O. W. HOLMES.

WISDOM.

WISDOM is better than rubies, and all the things that may be desired are not to be compared with it. PROVERBS, viii, 11.

The Lord possessed me in the beginning of His way, before His works of old.

I was set up from everlasting, from the beginning, or ever the earth was. PROVERBS, viii, 22, 23.

The fear of the Lord is the beginning of wisdom : a good understanding have all they that do His commandments. PSALM, cxi, 10.

Wisdom is the principal thing; therefore get wisdom : and with all thy getting, get understanding. PROVERBS, iv, 7.

THE wise, I here observe,
Are wise towards God, in whose great service still,
More than in that of kings, themselves they serve.

SIR W. DAVENANT.

WHEN did wisdom covet length of days?
Or seek its bliss in pleasure, wealth, or praise?
No :—wisdom views with an indifferent eye
All finite things, as blessings born to die.

HANNAH MORE.

THUS wisdom's words discover
  Thy glory and Thy grace,
Thou everlasting Lover
  Of our unworthy race!
Thy gracious eye surveyed us
  Ere stars were seen above;
In wisdom Thou hast made us,
  And died for us in love.

COWPER.

Wisdom smiles, when humbled mortals weep.
When sorrow wounds the breast, as ploughs the glebe,
And hearts obdurate feel the softening shower,
Her seeds celestial then glad wisdom sows,
Her golden harvest triumphs in the soil. Young.

Wisdom is humble, said the voice of God.
'T is proud, the world replied. Wisdom, said God,
Forgives, forbears, and suffers, not for fear
Of man, but God. Wisdom revenges, said
The world; is quick and deadly of resentment,
Thrusts at the very shadow of affront,
And hastes, by death, to wipe its honour clean.
Wisdom, said God, loves enemies, entreats,
Solicits, begs for peace. Wisdom, replied
The world, hates enemies, will not ask peace,
Conditions spurns, and triumphs in their fall.
Wisdom mistrusts itself, and leans on Heaven,
Said God. It trusts and leans upon itself,
The world replied. Wisdom retires, said God,
And counts it bravery to bear reproach,
And shame, and lowly poverty, upright;
And weeps with all who have just cause to weep.
Wisdom, replied the world, struts forth to gaze,
Treads the broad stage of life with clamorous foot,
Attracts all praises, counts it bravery
Alone to wield the sword, and rush on death;
And never weeps, but for its own disgrace.
Wisdom, said God, is highest, when it stoops
Lowest before the Holy Throne; throws down
Its crown, abased; forgets itself, admires,
And breathes adoring praise. There wisdom stoops
Indeed, the world replied; there stoops, because
It must, but stoops with dignity; and thinks
And meditates, the while, of inward worth.

Pollok.

It is the way we go, the way of life;
  A drop of pleasure in a sea of pain,
A grain of peace amid a load of strife,
  With toil and grief, and grief and toil again:
Yea:—but for this; the firm and faithful breast,
  Bolder than lions, confident and strong,
That never doubts its birthright to be blest,
  And dreads no evil, while it does no wrong:
This, this is wisdom, manful and serene;
  Towards God, all penitence, and prayer, and trust;
But to the troubles of this shifting scene,
  Simply courageous, and sublimely just;
Be then, such wisdom thine, my heart within,—
There is no foe, nor woe, nor grief, but Sin.

Tupper.

WIT.

A man hath joy by the answer of his mouth: and a word spoken in due season, how good is it! Proverbs, xv, 23.

In the lips of him that hath understanding, wisdom is found. Proverbs, x, 13.

The words of a man's mouth are as deep waters, and the well-spring of wisdom as a flowing brook. Proverbs, xviii, 6.

That to great faithless wits can truth dispense
Till 't turn their witty scorns to reverence:
Make them confess their greatest error springs
From curious gazing on the least of things;
With reading smaller prints they spoil their sight,
Darken themselves, then rave for want of light:
Show them how full they are of subtle sin,
When faith's great cable they would nicely spin
To reason's slender threads; then, falsely bold,
When they have weakened it, cry, It will not hold!

Sir W. Davenant.

Is sparkling wit the world's exclusive right?
The fixed fee-simple of the vain and light?
Can hopes of Heaven, bright prospects of an hour,
That come to waft us out of sorrow's power,
Obscure or quench a faculty that finds
Its happiest soil in the serenest minds?
Religion curbs indeed its wanton play,
And brings the trifler under rigorous sway,
But gives it usefulness unknown before,
And, purifying, makes it shine the more.
A Christian's wit is inoffensive light,
A beam that aids, but never grieves the sight.

COWPER.

WOMAN.

WHO can find a virtuous woman? for her price is far above rubies. PROVERBS, xxxi, 10.

Nevertheless, neither is the man without the woman, neither the woman without the man in the Lord. I. CORINTHIANS, xi, 11.

And the Lord God said, It is not good that the man should be alone: I will make a help-meet for him. GENESIS, ii, 18.

So woman, born to dignify retreat,
Unknown to flourish, and unseen be great,
To give domestic life its sweetest charm,
With softness polish, and with virtue warm:
Fearful of fame, unwilling to be known,
Should seek but Heaven's applauses and her own;
Should dread no blame but that which crimes impart,
The censures of a self-condemning heart.

HANNAH MORE.

To be man's tender mate was woman born,—
And, in obeying nature, she best serves
The purposes of Heaven.

SCHILLER.

BUT never, in her varied sphere,
Is woman to the soul more dear
Than when the homely task she plies,
With cheerful duty in her eyes;
And, every lowly path well trod,
Looks meekly upward to her God.

CAROLINE GILMAN.

AND, lest a life without the genial aid
Of social intercourse, should barren prove
Of real joys, a partner God bestowed,
Whose milder converse, and endearing love,
Might cheer the lonely hour. SAMUEL HAYES.

HE is a parricide to his mother's name,
And with an impious hand murthers her fame,
That wrongs the praise of woman; that dares write
Libels on saints, or with foul ink requite
The milk they lent us. RANDOLPH.

WORKS.

So likewise, when ye shall have done all those things which are commanded you, say, We are unprofitable servants; we have done that which was our duty to do. LUKE, xvii, 10.

But be ye doers of the word, and not hearers only, deceiving your own selves. JAMES, i, 22.

But whoso looketh into the perfect law of liberty, and continueth therein, he being not a forgetful hearer, but a doer of the work, this man shall be blessed in his deed. JAMES, i, 25.

Let your light so shine before men, that they may see your good works, and glorify your Father which is in Heaven. MATTHEW, v, 13.

HEAVEN doth with us as we with torches do;
Not light them for themselves: for if our virtues
Did not go forth of us, 't were all alike
As if we had them not. SHAKSPEARE.

To pray, without devotion, is to prate;
And hearing is but half our exercise:
We ought not, therefore, to regard alone
How often, but how well, the work be done.
GEORGE WITHER.

More will I do:
Though all that I can do is nothing worth;
Since that my penitence comes after all,
Imploring pardon. SHAKSPEARE.

When deeds pull down, words can repair no faith.
CHAPMAN.

Droop not, though shame, sin, and anguish are round thee
Bravely fling off the cold chain that hath bound thee;
Look to yon pure Heaven smiling beyond thee!
Rest not content in thy darkness — a clod!
Work — for some good — be it ever so slowly;
Cherish some flower, be it ever so lowly;
Labour! all labour is noble and holy:
Let thy good deeds be thy prayer to thy God!
MRS. F. S. OSGOOD.

What crowns of recompense betide
The true in death, and strong in virtue here;
A heart emboldened for its heavenward march,
As by some mighty melody within!
The end eternity's triumphal arch,
And laurels which no toil of earth can win,
Untouched by blasting years, and all unstained by sin.
GRENVILLE MELLEN.

When our souls leave this dwelling,
The glory of one fair and virtuous action
Is above all the scutcheons on our tomb,
Or silken banners over us. SHIRLEY.

IF faith produce no works, I see
That faith is not a living tree.
Thus faith and works together grow,
No separate life they e'er can know:
They're soul and body, hand and heart,—
What God hath joined, let no man part.

HANNAH MORE.

WITH humble penitence
Work out your own salvation, from above
Suppliant conciliate that all-powerful aid—
That mercy which alone preserves, redeems.

SAMUEL HAYES.

WHEN I hungered, ye denied me meat;
When I was thirsty, ye refused the cup;
Against my misery ye shut the door.
When on the bed of sickness I was cast,
When in the bonds of tyranny I lay,
To the loud cries of sorrow ye were deaf,
From my distress ye turned away your eyes;
For that relief ye impiously denied
Your suffering brethren, ye refused to me.

C. P. LAYARD.

THOSE precious seeds
Of charity and love, which here on earth
Were sown in sorrow, shall produce their fruit,
An endless harvest of eternal joy. C. P. LAYARD.

FELLOW-WORKERS are we: hour by hour,
Human tools are shaping Heaven's great schemes,
Till we see no limit to man's power,
And reality outstrips old dreams.
Toil and struggle, therefore, work and weep,
In God's acre ye shall calmly sleep,
When the night cometh. MRS. EMBURY.

YOUTH.

REJOICE, O young man, in thy youth, and let thy heart cheer thee in the days of thy youth, and walk in the ways of thy heart, and in the sight of thine eyes; but know thou, that for all these things God will bring thee into judgment. ECCLESIASTES, xi, 9.

Remember now thy Creator in the days of thy youth, while the evil days come not, nor the years draw nigh when thou shalt say, I have no pleasure in them. ECCLESIASTES, xii, 1.

I love them that love me; and those that seek me early shall find me. PROVERBS, viii, 17.

Wherewithal shall a young man cleanse his way? By taking heed thereto, according to Thy word. PSALM, cxix, 9.

It is good for a man that he bear the yoke in his youth. LAMENTATIONS, iii, 27.

THRICE happy he whose downy age had been
Reclaimed by scourges from the prime of sin;
And, early seasoned with the taste of truth,
Remembers his Creator in his youth.

FRANCIS QUARLES.

PUT childish things away is in the warning;
And grant me, Lord, this with the Psalmist's prayer,—
Remember not the follies of my youth,
But in Thy goodness think upon me, Lord!

A. C. COXE.

LIVE that thy young and glowing breast
Can think of death without a sigh,
And be assured that life is best
Which finds us least afraid to die.

ELIZA COOK.

VIRTUE with peculiar charms appears,
Crowned with the garland of life's blooming years.

COWPER

Come, while the blossoms of thy years are brightest,
  Thou youthful wanderer in a flowery maze;
Come, while the restless heart is bounding lightest,
  And joy's pure sunbeams tremble in thy ways;
Come while sweet buds, like summer flowers unfolding,
  Waken rich feelings in the careless breast;
While yet thy hand the ephemeral wreath is holding,
  Come — and secure interminable rest!

Come, while the morning of thy life is glowing,
  Ere the dim phantoms thou art chasing die;
Ere the gay spell which earth is round thee throwing,
  Fades, like the crimson from a sunset sky;
Life hath but shadows, save a promise given,
  Which lights the future with a fadeless ray;
O, touch the sceptre! — win a hope in Heaven;
  Come, turn thy spirit from the world away!

WILLIS G. CLARK.

Youth lost in dissipation, — we deplore
Through life's sad remnant, what no sighs restore;
Our years, a fruitless loss without a prize,
Too many — yet too few to make us wise.

COWPER.

Grace is a plant, where'er it grows,
  Of pure and heavenly root;
But fairest in the youngest shows,
  And yields the sweetest fruit. COWPER.

Something of youth I in old age approve,
But more the marks of age in youth I love.
Who this observes, may in his body find
Decrepit age, but never in his mind

DENHAM.

"Heaven lies about us in our infancy!"
If so, we should not with indifference meet
Aught that recalls a memory so sweet
As one of bright and early days gone by!
For, could we but abide continually
As we were wont in hours so fair and fleet,
Like little children, guiltless of deceit,
This o'er the world were glorious mastery.

Bernard Barton.

ZEAL—FANATICISM.

Forasmuch as ye are are zealous of spiritual gifts, seek that ye may excel to the edifying of the church. I. Corinthians, xiv 12.

They have a zeal of God, but not according to knowledge. Romans, x, 2.

Our Saviour Christ gave Himself for us that He might redeem us from all iniquity and purify unto Himself a peculiar people, zealous of good works. Titus, ii, 14.

What! is fanatic frenzy scorned so much,
And dreaded more than a contagious touch?
I grant it dangerous, and approve your fear,
That fire is catching, if you draw too near;
But sage observers oft mistake the flame,
And give true piety that odious name. Cowper.

Fanaticism, soberly defined,
Is the false fire of an o'erheated mind;
It views the truth with a distorted eye,
And either warps, or lays it useless by;
'T is narrow, selfish, arrogant, and draws
Its sordid nourishment from man's applause;
And while, at heart, sin unrelinquished lies,
Presumes itself chief favourite of the skies.

Cowper.

To tremble, (as the creatures of an hour
Ought, at the view of an Almighty Power)
Before His presence, at whose awful throne
All tremble in all worlds except our own;
To supplicate His mercy, love His ways,
And prize them above pleasure, wealth, or praise;
Though common sense, allowed a casting voice,
And free from bias, must approve the choice;
Convicts a man fanatic in the extreme,
And wild as madness in the world's esteem.

COWPER.

FAR other flame the vain enthusiast feels
When, reason by delusive fancy led
In sad captivity, the thoughts confused
Rush on his mind in dark and doubtful sense,
His mind a chaos of blind zeal, that spurns
Th' unerring clue which mild discretion lends.
Perchance the clashing images strike out
Some ray of casual light; how soon
The weak and momentary glance is lost
Beneath a load of wild obscurity!
Much does he labour with some weighty thought
Of faith, of grace, of Heaven, perchance of hell,
But all in vain he draws the thread confused
To tedious length; the end eludes his search,
And leaves him wrapt in wild perplexity,
Recoiling still on the same beaten track.

CHARLES JENNER.

PEARLS

OF

SACRED POETRY.

BY

REV. H. HASTINGS WELD.

ILLUSTRATED.

PUBLISHED BY
ALLEN BROTHERS,
NEW YORK.

PEARLS

FROM THE

AMERICAN

FEMALE POETS.

BY

CAROLINE MAY.

ILLUSTRATED.

PUBLISHED BY
ALLEN BROTHERS,
NEW YORK.

www.ingramcontent.com/pod-product-compliance
Lightning Source LLC
LaVergne TN
LVHW020934110826
845150LV00004B/859
9781425552572